Microsoft®

E-Commerce
Strategies

Charles Trepper

PUBLISHED BY
Microsoft Press
A Division of Microsoft Corporation
One Microsoft Way
Redmond, Washington 98052-6399

Library of Congress Cataloging-in-Publication Data
Trepper, Charles H.
      E-Commerce Strategies / Charles H. Trepper.
            p. cm.
      Includes index.
      ISBN 0-7356-0723-0
      1. Electronic commerce--Planning. 2. Strategic planning.   3. Inernet
marketing--Planning.   4. Business enterprises--Computer networks--Planning. I. Title.

HF5548.32.T74   2000
658.8'4--dc21   99-059500

Printed and bound in the United States of America.

1 2 3 4 5 6 7 8 9   WCWC   5 4 3 2 1 0

Distributed in Canada by Penguin Books Canada Limited.

A CIP catalogue record for this book is available from the British Library.

Microsoft Press books are available through booksellers and distributors worldwide. For further information about international editions, contact your local Microsoft Corporation office or contact Microsoft Press International directly at fax (425) 936-7329. Visit our Web site at mspress.microsoft.com.

Active Directory, ActiveX, BackOffice, bCentral, FrontPage, Hotmail, JScript, LinkExchange, Microsoft, Microsoft Press, MoneyCentral, MSDN, MSN, NetMeeting, Outlook, PivotTable, Visual Basic, Visual C++, Visual FoxPro, Visual InterDev, Visual J++, Visual SourceSafe, Visual Studio, WebTV, WebTV Network, Windows, and Windows NT are either registered trademarks or trademarks of Microsoft Corporation in the United States and/or other countries. Other product and company names mentioned herein may be the trademarks of their respective owners.

The example companies, organizations, products, people, and events depicted herein are fictitious. No association with any real company, organization, product, person, or event is intended or should be inferred.

Acquisitions Editor: Juliana Aldous
Project Editor: Thom Votteler

This book is dedicated to everyone who helped me crunch through this tome,
including people, animals, and cartoon characters.

Contents at a Glance

Table of Contents

Acknowledgments

This book would never have been possible without the input and assistance from literally dozens of people, animals, and cartoon characters (some of those listed might fit into multiple categories!).

Thanks to the team at Microsoft Press, including Thom Votteler (decent Pokémon trainer), Juliana Aldous, Tracy Thomsic, Anne Hamilton, Jim Brown (who started this whole project). Thanks also to the production staff at ProImage: Jimmie Young, Susan Christophersen, Allen Wyatt, Peter Boit, Michael Risse, Charles Freeman, Ajay Murthy. "I must also express appreciation to Bill Gates, who laid the foundation for this book in his book *Business @ The Speed of Thought*. Special thanks to the Microsoft business partners and customers who are profiled in this book. They made electronic commerce real with examples of their successes.

Thanks also to the following: Purdue University's professor extraordinaire Kathryne Newton; University of Minnesota's Lester Wanninger; Attorney William Henney; Steve McConnell of Construx; Web guru William Wells; Jason Stell of iVillage.com; John Murrin and Jerry Klingner of Homesource; and the crew at Application Development Trends Magazine: Mike Bucken, Jack Vaughan, and Kim Hefner. Thanks also to the analyst groups, including Dale Kutnick and Aaron Zornes of Meta, Steve Diorio of IMT Strategies, Dwight Davis at Summit Strategies, Andrew Bartels of the Giga Group, Bruce Temkin at the Forrester Group, and the staffs at Ernst & Young and Jupiter Communications. From PwC, thanks to Larry Kanter, Bill Boni, and Doug Wilson. Thanks to Jake Levine and Matthew Benson of Bivings Woodell, Jill Spiegel of Goal Getters, and Emily Glassman of Amazon.com.

Special thanks to Pat Lindquist and Associates, the world's greatest public relations firm. As usual, my family provided the support that I always need when I take on these projects. And of course, thanks to Snoopy the rabbit and to the whole Pokémon gang.

Introduction

E-commerce is growing at an incredible pace. Many organizations and individuals are looking to the Web as the future, definitive source for information, goods, services, and communication. As the amount of business transacted over the Web grows, the value of goods, services, and information exchanged over the Internet seems to double or triple each year. Often organizations—small and large, nonprofit and for-profit, privately and publicly held—are being pushed to the Web by both customers and competitors. In some cases, traditional brick-and-mortar businesses are playing catch-up and entering the e-commerce arena late in the game. All indications are that e-commerce will continue to grow, so many organizations may find themselves either having to go online or go out of business.

WHAT IS E-COMMERCE?

In its purest form, e-commerce is simply any business transaction that takes place via digital processes over a network. E-commerce, however, is really much more than just exchanging products or services for money over the Internet. E-commerce is an enabling technology that allows businesses to increase the accuracy and efficiency of business transaction processing. E-commerce is also a way for organizations to exchange information with customers and vendors to the benefit of everyone involved. Eventually, e-commerce will likely replace the movement of paper within and between organizations, as well as between organizations and consumers.

E-Commerce and the Digital Nervous System

Digital nervous system technology can help organizations share their systems capabilities and the knowledge contained in those systems with business partners and customers. Sharing information up and down the supply chain allows organizations to more tightly integrate their systems with those of their business partners (see Chapter 1, "Go Online or Go Out of Business" Chapter 7, "E-Commerce Best Practices" and Chapter 8, "Brand Management Strategies").

E-commerce best practices often result in greatly reduced supply chain costs, fewer inventory outages, and higher-quality products made with less waste. By automating their supply chain, organizations increase the accuracy and efficiency of information and material flow from supplier to customer. Digital nervous system technology allows organizations to move information digitally, both within and beyond the organization's walls.

Key components of a digital nervous system

As with any automated system, there are five key components of a digital nervous system. Hardware, software, people, data, and procedures all play an important role in making a digital nervous system work. The proper technology must be used to increase the speed of information transmission within an organization. Hardware must be fast enough and big enough to transmit and store the information needed to operate the organization. Advanced software must take advantage of the hardware available and help humans organize the data into useful information and use it for collaboration.

The right people must have the right data at the right time to use in their daily tasks. This data must be used according to the correct procedures, which dictate the proper way to share and use data within an organization. Often, however, procedures stifle communication by adding organizational boundaries that are difficult for employees to cross and that make it hard to complete even the simplest tasks. Organizations must take care to avoid creating superfluous steps and signature tasks that reduce the effectiveness of a digital nervous system.

An effective organization performs three key functions: commerce, knowledge management, and business operations. An important step in establishing and using a digital nervous system is linking these three functions together to form an efficient business operation. These functions affect the three main elements of any business: customer/partner relationships, employees, and process. E-commerce involves automating business transactions with suppliers and customers. Businesses must be willing to trade information for time. Although there are certainly some security concerns about sharing mission-critical information with vendors and customers, it's important for organizations to recognize that their digital nervous system must provide information to all participants in the value chain, whether inside or outside the organization.

This sharing of information is at the core of knowledge management. Knowledge management involves having the right knowledge in the right place at the right time. As already mentioned, this concept extends beyond the boundaries of the organization. All parties in the value chain must have access to what they need. Having the right knowledge creates the ability to anticipate emerging needs, satisfy current needs, and get the information into the right hands everywhere in the organization. The right knowledge is the information that the worker—regardless of organizational level—needs to make good decisions and be productive.

Getting knowledge to the right place means having it the right person's hands for immediate use, not in a repository or paper file. Technology helps people find knowledge they can use and helps them use it productively. In fact, one of the most productive uses of technology that an organization can take advantage of is the gathering and routing of critical work information. Knowledge management technology includes both a push and a pull side. Knowledge workers must be given an incentive to ask for and use information, and the organization must be willing to provide the worker with the information needed.

To have knowledge at the right time involves having it available when it must be utilized, or having it slightly ahead of time to allow workers to digest it before using it. If it is to be applied in an area that is complex, it must be available soon enough to allow for the required analysis and thought processes. Speed of delivery is at least as important as speed of acquisition when it comes to managing knowledge.

Both e-commerce and knowledge management are targeted squarely at optimizing the business processes of an organization (see Chapter 9, "Microsoft's E-Commerce Strategy). E-Commerce is used to serve customers and acquire information quickly and efficiently. After that information is acquired, it must be used to create better products and services and to improve the efficiency and effectiveness of the organization's functions. A digital nervous system acts like a human nervous system in this situation and transmits the information needed by workers to do their jobs better, faster, and cheaper. By enabling an organization to be more agile and effective, a digital nervous system also helps complete the circuit from vendor to organization to customer and back. The Internet enables companies to use knowledge captured via e-commerce and use what they know to outmaneuver the competition.

Organizations must use the benefits gleaned from e-commerce and knowledge management to increase value in the value chain, to reduce cycle times and costs, and to raise customer service levels. They can use information available from a good digital nervous system to make and deliver products and services better than anyone else in industry. Sales, marketing, and other organizational business units must be optimized to achieve maximum revenues and profits. Good knowledge management systems will also help organizations determine how to balance resource requirements across bus- iness processes to maximize profitability.

A digital nervous system must be built on standard hardware and software, as well as standard procedures for people to follow when managing information. A digital nervous system makes end-to-end business solutions easier because the technology can link all the players in the value chain together and allow them to easily exchange critical information. It's important to develop a standard blueprint for technology and organizations. Organizations should work with their business partners to ensure that their hardware and software can communicate with each other and that information can be moved seamlessly.

One way of ensuring that communication is simple and easy is to create standards for hardware, software, and processes. Creating and enforcing standards can be difficult. Some of issues faced by those attempting to create standards for a digital nervous system include:

1. Gaining management buy-in. Some IS managers feel that the only real work is coding. Creating new standards may be the last thing a manager wants.

2. Helping customers understand that formal methods are necessary, even though the extra work may extend the elapsed time of the project. Users may also feel uneasy because they must sign off at certain times, limiting their ability to cause scope creep.

3. Convincing business partners to share their secrets. When all mem-members of the digital nervous system openly share information, each benefits by having a greater pool of knowledge and expertise available. In addition, barriers traditionally resulting from internal secrecy are demolished.

4. Persuading developers that structured methodologies don't take away their ability to do creative problem solving.

5. Helping the entire organization understand that process management is critical to optimizing and automating processes and methods.

Meeting these challenges is really just a matter of helping an organization understand that the benefits of a structured approach outweigh the costs (see Chapter 4).

The role of a digital nervous system in e-commerce

E-commerce should integrate with current systems and break down barriers between departments—from administration, finance, and marketing to order fulfillment and field force operations, and a digital nervous system provides this integration. Digital nervous system technology allows organizations to share information internally faster and more accurately. Real-time involvement of business partners and customers enables seamless supply chains and faster response to your organization's business transaction data.

This means that business partners and customers can compete more effectively in their own markets, as well as help your organization compete better in its markets.

E-commerce goes beyond a Web site. It is a comprehensive business solution that can integrate accounts receivable, sales statistics, inventory, and service orders to leverage a full range of business opportunities. Much of your existing technology can be utilized in an e-commerce solution to turn a Web site into a tool for operating more efficiently with your customers, improving your internal processes, and enhancing your relationship with business partners and customers. A digital nervous system provides organizations with the ability to communicate more quickly and accurately with all parts of the supply and value chains. Improved communication and faster and more accurate processing of business transactions result in better relationships through an improved exchange of information.

WHY IS E-COMMERCE IMPORTANT?

E-commerce is transforming the way products, services, and even information are bought, sold, and exchanged. E-commerce also changes the way organizations interact with customers and business partners (see Chapters 7 and 8). E-commerce involves making use of the Internet to penetrate new markets, discover or create new sales channels, and get closer to customers and business partners through communication channels. Some pioneers achieve real success for both small and large organizations because size matters less now; all organizations stand an even chance because they have access to the same types of resources. However, significant obstacles can pop during e-commerce initiatives (see Chapter 3, "The E-Commerce Obstacle Course").

Who Wins and Who Loses in E-Commerce?

Many organizations develop an online presence because of the myths and great tales of fame and fortune that circulate (see Chapter 2, "E-Commerce in Action: Reality and Myth"). Organizations that approach e-commerce with realistic, specific, and measurable goals or objectives will be the big winners. It's critical for organizations not to succumb to the myths and hype surrounding e-commerce because of the possibility of setting unrealistic expectations and unreachable goals. Organizations must also hire the right staff, whether permanent employees or consultants, because people are the primary resources on e-commerce projects. Staffing can be a major issue on e-commerce projects because of the Information Technology (IT) staffing shortage. Good training programs can assist organizations in developing Web-based skills sets for their staff (see Chapter 3).

Small businesses that approach the Web with strong strategies and resources can also be big winners. Because the Web allows any company to reach any consumer anywhere in the world, so businesses have a chance to catch up with or maybe even pass big businesses if their e-marketing campaigns are done correctly. Organizations that carefully manage and continuously improve their customer relationships, regardless of the organization's size, can also be big winners. As more consumers head to the Web, their expectations of service speed and accuracy will continue to grow. Organizations that meet or exceed those expectations will succeed, whereas organizations that fail to keep their customers satisfied will ultimately lose big. Customer relationship management (CRM) will be a key to whether or not an organization succeeds in the world of e-commerce (see Chapter 8).

When Will E-Commerce Have an Impact on Your Organization?

When can you expect to be affected by the move to e-commerce in the marketplace? Today! The reality is that nearly every organization in every industry is affected by e-commerce. Any organization that doesn't at least have some kind of plan for an e-commerce initiative is going to find itself significantly behind its competitors. In fact, some organizations may find themselves driven to the Web and e-commerce simply by a competitor's activities or by customer demand. Even some manufacturers that do not sell direct to consumers are already making plans to create Web sites to increase public awareness of their products and services. In some cases, an organization can manage or improve its image through the Web, even if it doesn't actually sell a product or service through its Web site. The bottom line is that sooner or later every organization will have some kind of Web site, if for no other reason than to communicate with and manage its relationship with customers and business partners.

Costs of ignoring e-commerce

Organizations ignore e-commerce at their own peril. Not moving to the Web means more than just staying in the dark ages of business technology. It means that organizations won't be able to compete as well in their markets because they won't be able to exchange information with business partners and customers as easily. Ignoring e-commerce amounts to ignoring access to information and other resources that competitors will have. Lack of information is an organization's greatest enemy and prevents it from competing effectively, particularly if an organization's competitors know something they don't! Organizations that ignore e-commerce will not receive as much outside information as those that implement e-commerce strategies with their customers and business partners, which means that they won't be able to make the same quality decisions. Making too many bad business decisions means no more business!

Many organizations now require their business partners and customers to operate electronically. If an organization is behind in e-commerce technology, it could very well lose the ability to do business with suppliers, customers, or other business partners. Organizations that ignore the move to e-commerce will also find themselves trapped in the current workstyle, while other organizations redefine or eliminate boundaries between themselves and their business partners. The boundarylessness of e-commerce allows organizations to structure themselves to be more efficient and use the best resources, regardless of location or affiliation.

Organizations that continue to operate on paper-based systems that are slow and inefficient will tend to lose market share to their competitors. Because e-commerce enables companies to reach larger customer populations more quickly via the Internet, those organizations that implement effective e-commerce solutions will also be able to compete more effectively for the consumers who fit the Web-based demographic. This demographic is made up of consumers who tend to be better educated and have higher incomes. They buy more goods and services via the Web, and those purchases tend to be of higher values. Organizations that gain market share of that particular demographic are more profitable over time.

Benefits of implementing e-commerce

E-commerce is a tool for reducing administrative costs and cycle time (see Chapter 4), streamlining business processes, and improving relationships with both business partners and customers (see Chapter 6, "E-Commerce Site Essentials"). An effective e-commerce solution can extend the reach of your business by increasing opportunities with customers, suppliers, and other business partners. Organizations that compete effectively in the e-commerce arena should therefore be able to make better decisions, which should enhance market position and, ultimately, profitability.

E-commerce techniques allow small businesses to have access to the same markets as larger businesses. Small organization can have instant access to international markets. Customers all over the world can access your Web site and buy your products whether your company has one full-time person or one thousand full-time employees. Small businesses can grow very quickly and can eventually take on larger businesses in their markets. Smaller businesses may also be able to provide a personalized experience for customers who come to their Web site more easily than larger businesses that have to deal with the bureaucracy involved in designing a Web site.

E-commerce can provide benefits beyond cost reduction (see Chapter

4). Electronic sign-offs can prevent inappropriate business transactions that can be missed in a paper-based system. Business rules can be implemented electronically so that systems won't accept transactions than have incorrect codes or insufficient electronic authorization (see Chapters 7 and 10, "Microsoft's E-Commerce Platform and Products"). Buying patterns can be tracked as well, which allows organizations to make better decisions about the product and service delivery. Giving the right information to the right people of the right time can dramatically improve the company's ability to compete in its marketplace.

Organizations that use e-commerce techniques and technology will also attract additional consumers because of a higher level of customer service. Organizations that move to the Web will be able to help their customers resolve problems faster, which will eventually lead to better customer relations and more customers. Organizations that customize the interactions of both vendors and customers will appear to be more attractive business partners, which ultimately enhances their market position. Some organizations will find that a majority of their customers prefer to conduct business via the Web rather than traditional methods, which means that organizations that can't keep up with the technology will find themselves in trouble.

WHO SHOULD READ THIS BOOK?

This book is primarily targeted at business and IT decision makers. This book presents a strategic look at, and high-level technical overview of, e-commerce. The material in this book discusses the application of e-commerce technology and solutions to business problems encountered in the world of e-commerce. However, IT and business project leaders and managers will also find this book useful for planning e-commerce projects because of the content that discusses potential obstacles encountered during an e-commerce project, as well as how to calculate return on investment numbers for those projects.

WHAT WILL YOU FIND IN THIS BOOK?

This book is divided into three parts. The first part provides an overview of e-commerce fundamentals, myths, and obstacles and offers guidance on how to justify e-commerce projects. The second part presents concrete, usable information on how to apply information technology to e-commerce and e-commerce best practices. The third part presents Microsoft's e-commerce strategy, platform, and products.

Part I: E-Commerce Changes Everything

Chapter 1 provides the business imperative for doing e-commerce projects, some background on e-commerce, and a brief history of e-commerce and its evolution. Chapter 2 provides specific examples of how e-commerce is being applied to business problems by various organizations, presents Web sites that represent best practice designs (also see Chapters 6 and 7), and debunks some common e-commerce myths. Chapter 3 discusses potential solutions to various types of obstacles encountered by organizations during e-commerce initiatives, including technology, global and cultural issues, legal concerns, and security problems. Chapter 4 provides various approaches to setting success measures for e-commerce projects and calculating return on investment (ROI) for those projects.

Part II: E-Commerce Business Solutions

Chapter 5, "E-Commerce Building Blocks" provides an overview of technical basics for e-commerce, including hardware, software, service providers, and interfaces and integration tasks. Chapter 6 presents a primer on Web site design best practices, including site elements, aesthetics, extranet designs, and content management. Chapter 7 provides both research-based and real-world examples of e-commerce best practices, including personalization and profiling, managing visitor perceptions, and managing business knowledge. Chapter 8 presents strategies for managing organizational brands online, leveraging real world brands, building partnerships, and acquiring and retaining customers.

Part III: The Microsoft Total E-Commerce Solution

Chapter 9 presents Microsoft's present and future e-commerce strategies, the BizTalk Framework initiative, and how e-commerce can be applied to knowledge management and business process optimization. Chapter 10 presents an overview of Microsoft's e-commerce platform and products. More on Microsoft's products can be found in Appendix C. Chapter 11, "Web Portals" discusses Microsoft's involvement in various types of Internet information portals, including the Microsoft Network (MSN), MSNBC, and others. Chapter 12, "Partnering" provides an over- view of Microsoft's partnering strategies that complement Microsoft's own strategies and product lines. In addition, the appendixes supply references to source material used in writing the book, a list of Web sites discussed in the book, and information on Microsoft's e-commerce products and services. The Glossary provides definitions for relevant e-commerce and technology terms.

Real World Examples

The examples in this book are based on the experiences of actual organizations and serve to illustrate the application of the concepts presented in the chapters. These experiences present concrete examples of how e-commerce solutions are being applied in businesses and organizations today. Each example is intended to help the reader better understand how to implement e-commerce strategies in actual situations.

Readers can visit the Web sites listed in Appendix B to see how e-commerce strategies are actually being implemented by the organizations mentioned and to see examples of successful Web initiatives.

Standard Features in Each Chapter

Each chapter has some standard features to assist the reader and provide a standard format for their convenience. These features include a mission statement, chapter wrap-up, a section of questions to help the reader take stock of his or her current e-commerce environment or situation, and a set of steps that form an action plan to help the organization move forward in the e-commerce arena.

Mission statement

Each chapter opens with a statement that summarizes the chapter content. The mission statement embodies the goal of the chapter the same way a corporate mission statement embodies the goals and values of a company.

Wrap up

The end-of-chapter materials begin with a Wrap Up section consisting of a list of summary points. The Wrap Up provides a concise summary of the chapter's content and presents an overview of the chapter's most important points.

Taking stock

Following the Wrap Up is the Taking Stock section, which consists of a checklist of five to ten questions that relate to that chapter's content. The reader can use these questions to perform a self-test of his or her organization's current need and readiness for new technologies. If the chapter presents one major phase in a technology development process, for instance, the Taking Stock feature would assess the reader's need for implementing strategies and adopting technologies used in this phase.

Action plan

Following the Taking Stock section and ending the chapter is the Action Plan, a set of three to seven steps that delineate the process the reader needs to take to implement the technology or phase that the chapter has presented.

FOR MORE INFORMATION

This book attempts to provide you with the information you need to understand, assess, and initiate e-commerce successfully in your organization. Of course, e-commerce business models and tools are evolving rapidly, and the Web is probably the best place to find out about the latest developments. A good place to start is Microsoft's home page at *www.microsoft.com*.

This an exciting time for organizations of all kinds. E-commerce puts forward both challenges and opportunities for everyone. May you and your organization slay the challenges and seize the opportunities for your success!

Part I

E-Commerce Changes Everything

Chapter 1

Go Online or Go Out of Business?

Electronic commerce is a critical business imperative to most organizations. Managers at all levels of an organization need to grasp the basics of e-commerce and to understand why it's important to their organization.

E-commerce has been around in various forms since the late 1960s, but since about 1993, new and constantly evolving technologies have enabled companies to perform e-business functions better, faster, and more inexpensively than ever before. The result has been an explosion of e-commerce activity. Today, even traditional brick-and-mortar organizations must at least establish a Web presence if they want to remain competitive. And a strong business case can be made that organizations that don't enter the e-commerce fray will eventually be left in the technological dust.

Simply using e-commerce techniques will not, however, necessarily lead to success. Organizations that currently suffer from inefficient processes, questionable product quality, or poor customer service will find that e-commerce enables them only to make the same mistakes faster and more frequently. On the other hand, organizations that are truly dedicated to excelling in these and all areas of their operation will benefit from electronic commerce because it will enable them to most efficiently build upon these capabilities.

UNDERSTANDING E-COMMERCE

To understand how an organization can operate successfully in an e-commerce environment, it's important to grasp at least the basics of e-commerce and the digital flow of information. For our purposes, this basic understanding comprises a definition of the term "e-commerce"; an overview of how e-commerce fits into the flow of information to, through, and from an organization by way of its *digital nervous system*; and a discussion of various types of e-commerce architecture and activity.

Electronic Commerce Defined

Many business leaders might think of e-commerce simply as the exchange of goods and services for payment over the Internet. But this view overlooks internal commerce and the competitive advantages that result from linking members of the supply and value chains (those people involved in the flow of goods, services, money, and information necessary to get products from raw material to consumers). In its broadest sense, electronic commerce encompasses any commercial activity that takes place directly between a business, its partners, or its customers through a combination of computing and communications technologies.

Because electronic commerce can help organizations to achieve business goals by using the most effective technology to employ the power of the Internet, e-commerce rightfully encompasses all of the activities that heighten a customer's interest before, during, and after a sale. In this way, e-commerce can be used to create brand equity and to improve an organization's public image, as well as to develop and strengthen direct relationships between an organization and its customers, distributors, suppliers, and retailers.

Benefits of e-commerce

In a useful way, the benefits of e-commerce help to define what it is. Electronic commerce:

■ Offers new ways to manage supply and value chains; to enhance manufacturing, logistics, and distribution systems; and to link business partners together in a seamless business operating environment.

■ Provides organizations and individuals with the ability to buy and sell products, services, and information on the Internet.

■ Automates business transactions and the flow of information between organizations.

■ Helps organizations cut customer service costs while improving the quality of service and increasing the ability of the organization to better manage the customer relationship.

One of the primary reasons e-commerce can provide these benefits is that many elements of commerce technology are standardized. This standardization provides a common language for the electronic exchange of commercial data. The technical standards for e-commerce data exchange are set by several agencies, but the two key organizations and their standards are the United Nations' Electronic Data Interchange For Administration, Commerce, and Transport (UN/EDIFACT) standard and the American National Standards Institute (ANSI) rules, known as ANSI/X12. The functional capabilities of these standard e-commerce technologies enable organizations to compress product-to-market time by streamlining the production process and by eliminating intermediaries. Customers can interact directly with the company, efficiency increases, and costs go down.

New business models and work styles

Electronic commerce has encouraged the development of new business models, new information-sharing practices in organizations all over the world, and a significant cultural shift. (See the Introduction to this book for further discussion of the "Web work style.") Brick-and-mortar businesses—those businesses using traditional storefronts or physical plants—are rethinking the way they do business. Retailers such as Barnes and Noble and Toys 'R Us have created "virtual" companies to gain a Web presence, and in some cases (such as Toys "R" Us), they have created entirely different operating companies or have spun off divisions to free them from the potential limitations of conventional business thinking.

Product and service vendors are also responding to the new "e-biz" model by creating software and services that allow organizations to entirely automate their supply and value chains. This brave new world of opportunity seems as though it's spawning thousands of new e-businesses every day. One has only to watch the stock market to see the large number of Internet-related *Initial Public Offerings (IPOs)* that continue to occur routinely. And with remarkable regularity, profitability has become a distant concern in many of these dot-com startups, whose IPOs have raised tens or sometimes hundreds of millions of investment dollars. For many organizations, e-commerce has fundamentally changed the rules of the game.

Technology and the Flow of Information Through an Organization

When an organization includes an e-commerce system as part of a larger, internal *digital nervous system*, e-commerce provides much more than just an electronic sale. A digital nervous system that integrates knowledge management, business operations, and electronic commerce allows an organization to communicate and accomplish its tasks digitally while simultaneously enabling the sharing of information throughout the organization. A digital nervous system significantly improves organizational thinking and collaboration via technology by connecting all computers in an organization and encompassing all computer-to-computer exchanges of information.

The flow of information through a business via a digital nervous system is as unique as the specific organization and its business partners. Yet, in order to capture and maintain a competitive advantage in its markets, the organization and its partners need to create these digital information systems.

E-commerce architecture

E-commerce systems also vary, yet every e-commerce system's technical architecture includes some standard elements. Figure 1-1 presents a simple e-commerce technical architecture diagram. (Don't let any of the technical jargon in the figure scare you off. Each term is covered in more detail in later chapters.)

In a simple transaction, a system user accesses the transaction server through a PC or workstation. The PC in organization A is used to update data in a database server. When the data is correct, the user tells the system to transmit the data via a Web server. To transmit the data, the Web server uses the transaction server to access the database through the database server. The Web server transmits the data over the Internet to organization B via the router. The Web server at organization B reverses the process that occurred in organization A. The Web server at organization B stores the data in the database through the transaction and database servers. A user at organization B can then access the data through a PC via the transaction and database servers.

FAST FACT: KEY E-COMMERCE TECHNICAL COMPONENTS

- Client or PC workstation
- Transaction server
- Web server
- Database server
- Database
- Router
- Internet communication line

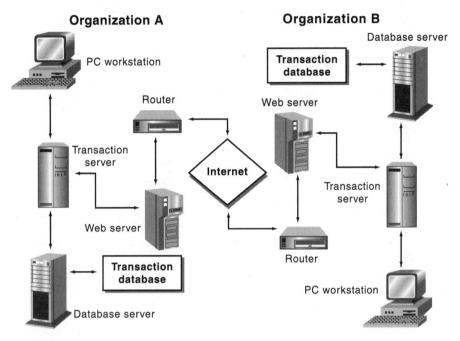

Figure 1-1. *A simple electronic commerce technical architecture*

Automating the supply chain

Various types of information flow up and down the supply chain using the technology depicted in Figure 1-1. The type of information transmitted depends on the type of transaction and the information that interacting organizations have agreed to share. Figure 1-2 depicts a sample information flow for a business-to-business supply chain.

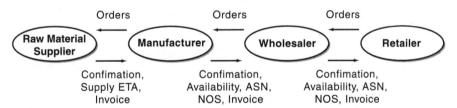

Figure 1-2. *Information flow for a business-to-business supply chain.*

The retailer places an order with the wholesaler. The wholesaler then consolidates orders from several retailers and orders the necessary products from the manufacturer. The wholesaler sends the retailer an order confirmation or acknowledgment and an estimate of inventory availability. The manufacturer may or may not need more raw materials, depending on inventory status. The manufacturer sends an order confirmation and a notice of inventory avail-ability to the wholesaler. The raw materials supplier provides an *estimated time of arrival (ETA)* for the materials needed by the manufacturer when the order is received.

When the raw materials are shipped, the raw materials supplier sends an invoice to the manufacturer. As the manufacturer produces the product, an *advance ship notice (ASN)* is sent to the wholesaler to allow the wholesaler to plan for receipt of the goods. When the product is shipped, a *notice of ship-ment (NOS)* and an invoice are sent. That process is repeated from wholesaler to retailer. As Figure 1-2 shows, many similarities exist among the types of data transmitted between each part of the supply chain. Standard electronic docu-ment formats make communication among supply chain members easier, more efficient, and more accurate.

The internal value chain

As we've mentioned, e-commerce includes internal operations. The value chain includes more than just product movement and adds ancillary and support services to the supply chain. Organizational departments such as human resources, marketing, accounting, finance, and legal must be involved in the flow of goods and services. Figure 1-3 shows how an e-commerce system might distribute information needed by departments within an organization (via an intranet) other than the core production and logistics groups.

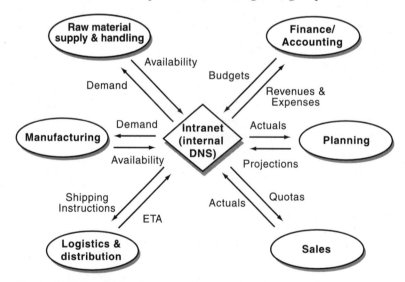

Figure 1-3. *Internal information flow to value chain members*

Your specific architectures and information flows will vary based on your industry, organization, workers, and business partners. One size does *not* fit all when constructing e-commerce technology solutions. Whether you use outside consultants or internal staff to construct your e-commerce platform, you must customize it to meet your business needs and *return on investmetnt (ROI)* requirements. However, it's also important to consult business partners with whom you'll be communicating to ensure that your technology is compatible with that of other members of your supply and value chains.

Types of Electronic Commerce

The two primary forms of e-commerce are business-to-business and business-to-consumer. Business-to-business e-commerce is used by businesses perhaps most commonly to improve communication within the organization and to cut the cost and increase the efficiency of business processes. Business-to-consumer e-commerce is used by consumers for the convenience of purchasing products or services over the Web. Businesses use business-to-consumer e-commerce to reach new markets and promote products and services. An additional e-commerce type, called *intra-organizational e-commerce,* comprises global organizations using electronic technologies to communicate between divisions or operating companies. The same technologies are used internally as would be used externally, but generally with more restricted access.

Many types of transactions and business functions can be completed via e-commerce. Common types include:

- EDI (electronic data interchange)
- EFT (electronic funds transfer)
- Purchases
- Marketing and promotions
- Customer service and billing
- Inventory management for global and multi-location entities
- Organizational communications (usually over an intranet, which is an Internet-technology-based internal network accessed using a Web browser)

Organizations can use a combination of any or all of these e-commerce strategies. All these forms of e-commerce should be interoperable and work together cohesively for the benefit of the organization.

Technical forms of electronic commerce

Electronic data interchange (EDI) is an older form of e-commerce, originating in the late 1960s. Standard EDI transaction formats enable organizations to exchange information via dial-up lines or dedicated leased lines. Some standard EDI transactions include advance ship notice (ASN) and notice of shipment (NOS). These transactions are transmitted up and down the supply chain in standard EDI formats.

Most people are familiar with at least one type of electronic funds transfer: an ATM (automatic teller machine) transaction. ATMs long have allowed people to deposit funds to checking and savings accounts, withdraw funds from those accounts, and transfer funds between accounts. If your bank is in New York and you withdraw money from an ATM in Sacramento, the bank that sponsors the ATM transmits a withdrawal notice to your bank. The two banks communicate using standard *electronic funds transfer (EFT)* formats to tell each other the account(s) affected by the withdrawal or deposit, the amount and date of the transaction, and other relevant information.

On a larger scale, e-commerce enables organizations to exchange money via the Internet or via *virtual private networks* (*VPNs*), which are discussed in Chapter 6 of this book. In this way, one organization can purchase goods from another by sending a purchase order over the Internet. The buying organization can pay for that purchase via the Internet by using EFT to transfer funds to the seller's account at the same or a different bank.

Business forms of electronic commerce

Purchasing as a business function has used EDI as its method for nearly 30 years. Now, EDI standard formats are being used to transmit purchase orders over the Internet. Marketing and promotion via the Internet are somewhat controversial because of spam occurring in the e-commerce industry. *Spam* denotes unsolicited (and typically, unwanted) advertising e-mail. A consumer who is interested in buying diapers may not be interested in receiving constant e-mails about new innovations in diaper technology or hot deals on diapers in bulk. Organizations must be careful about the quantity and frequency of promotional e-mail sent to consumers; otherwise, potential customers may feel irritated and turn away from a product or service. Lawsuits may also ensue.

Customer service and billing are probably the hottest business functions being conducted over the Web today. In many businesses and organizations, customers can carry out a host of customer service and financial activities, including checking order and shipment status, accessing account balances for such activities as cell phone usage, banking, revolving credit, and investing. Online bill presentation and payment is also growing quickly. TransPoint, a joint venture of Microsoft and First Data Corporation, (At the time of this writing, industry-leading CheckFree Corporation announced a merger agreement with

TransPoint, lending critical mass to online billing and payment.) allows bills to be presented and paid over the Web. Many banks now also offer electronic bill payment directly from customer bank accounts.

E-commerce also offers new ways for large organizations to manage inventory. Using VPNs rather than expensive leased lines, organizations can monitor inventory levels worldwide to prevent outages and eliminate slow-moving items.

Last but certainly not least is the use of the Web for organizational communications. Some organizations station field sales and service representatives all over the world. These field reps often feel disconnected from life at the organization's offices. E-mailed newsletters and organizational Web sites with information about current organization events help distant staff feel connected.

E-COMMERCE COMES OF AGE

The Internet was designed more than 30 years ago to serve the needs of the U.S. Department of Defense and other organizations and individuals working on defense-related research projects. The Internet was built to solve the key problem of communication between computers that were thousands of miles apart but needed to work together. The Department of Defense eventually opened its network to educational institutions and then to commercial users. Figure 1-4 shows a rough timeline of how electronic commerce has evolved from a simple exchange of information between government agencies to the World Wide Web of today.

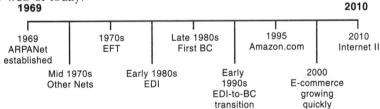

Figure 1-4. *Electronic commerce timeline*

1969: Technology Enables E-Commerce

In 1969, the U.S. Department of Defense established The Advanced Research Projects network (ARPANET). ARPANET was the first really viable inter-organizational network or Internet. In the 1970s, other networks such as Bitnet and Usenet sprang up as the technology became more public. In the same decade, banks began to use EFT over secure private networks to move money quickly and accurately. EFT made electronic payments possible and led to direct deposit and debit cards.

In the early 1980s, electronic commerce practices became widespread between organizations in the form of EDI and electronic mail. EDI allows companies to send and receive business documents such as purchase orders. As mentioned previously, the EDI formats are determined by ANSI and other standards organizations. Around the late 1980s, e-commerce became an integral part of business, although not over the public Internet. Around that same time, new e-commerce technology emerged, pushed by the Internet, but the technology was difficult to use; most work had to be done manually.

1992: The World Wide Web Is Created

In 1992, the World Wide Web arrived. The Web made the Internet graphical and relatively easy to use, compared to the level of technical skill needed with earlier technologies. Web technology supported information publishing and dissemination. The Web made e-commerce cheaper because small businesses could now reach large audiences easily. It also increased accessibility for all businesses and made international operation technologically easy (although culturally, it was still difficult).

2000: Expansion Is Exponential

Electronic commerce is expected to grow at spectacular rates. A 1998 World Trade Organization report put the value of e-commerce at $300 billion by the year 2001. According to the study, business will remain primarily U.S. domestic because of various legal and cultural problems. International trade over the Internet may reach only $60 billion, mainly generated from the United States. Also, Internet-based electronic commerce could account for as much as two percent of all commercial transactions in industrialized nations within five years.

FAST FACT: E-BUSINESS GROWTH
A *CIO Magazine* study concludes that business-to-business e-commerce will grow at roughly six times the rate of business-to-consumer e-commerce by 2006.

The business-to-consumer segment of e-commerce is advancing rapidly. A handful of studies have shown that the business-to-consumer arena is expanding faster than most organizations can keep up. Online sales to consumers are expected to become a significant portion of total consumer sales in the next few years for retailers and manufacturers. Today's online retailers expect the Internet to account for a steadily increasing percentage of revenue, with an 800 percent increase in the next three years. Manufacturers already selling online project that Internet revenue will represent 7 percent of total revenue by fiscal year 2001.

STUDY SHOWS MORE CONSUMERS SHOPPING ONLINE

In October and November 1999, Ernst & Young surveyed consumers and online retail companies in six countries. More than 3,000 worldwide consumers, of which 1,200 were U.S.–based, were surveyed online during the time period. Thirty-eight retailers were interviewed for the company portion of the report.

The survey indicated a strong increase in 1999 from the previous year in households shopping online and in those making more frequent and larger purchases over the Web. The percentage of retailers and manufacturers selling or planning to sell to consumers over the Internet also rose.

According to the survey, consumers are doing more online shopping than ever before. As a result, online shopping is growing quickly as a part of total retail activity. In 1999, the market for goods and services sold to consumers over the Internet reached $15 billion and is projected to grow at a rate in excess of 200 percent per year over the next few years.

In the U.S., a significant number of consumers (34 percent of households) are online, and half of those households (17 percent) have become online shoppers. If this powerful trend continues, online shopping could become a mainstream activity in the U.S. in 2000. A similar pattern of growth is taking place worldwide. The survey also found that the number of online purchases is increasing significantly. Thirty-nine percent of Internet buyers in the U.S. made 10 or more purchases between November 1998 and November 1999.

Remarkably, almost all retailers in the study said that either they are engaging in or preparing to engage in online shopping. The percentage of retailers selling online to consumers increased dramatically from 39 percent in November 1998 to 69 percent in 1999, while the number or retailers not yet selling but planning to sell online was at 31 percent. This means, in effect, that nearly all retailers will have some type of consumer e-commerce service in place by 2001.

The majority of consumer goods manufacturers surveyed don't sell online and have no plans to do so, but some—particularly smaller organizations—are preparing for direct electronic sales to consumers. Apparently, these manufacturers are not content to let retailers corner the online consumer market. According to the survey, a steady 43 percent of the manufacturers reported that they either are selling online or are planning

(continued)

Studies Show More Consumers Shopping Online *continued*

to do so. (This is the same percentage as in 1998). Even large companies with established brands that sell well through traditional retail channels are preparing consumer e-commerce initiatives.

WHY E-COMMERCE?

One of the primary reasons cited in news stories in *Information Technology (IT)* trade journals that many organizations get into e-commerce is that "everyone else is doing it!" Is this necessarily the best reason for spending money on e-commerce? Probably not. But if your competitors are doing it, shouldn't you? To take business-to-consumer e-commerce as an example, as we move toward a technology-permeated society, consumers increasingly will expect to be able to use technology—and the Internet in particular—to find the products and services they need at the best prices. Studies indicate that although consumers say that they might not necessarily purchase online, they will at least use the Internet as a convenient and efficient resource for comparison shopping and as a products catalog, even if the store they're viewing online is just down the street. This is important because consumers won't want to waste time physically going to a store that doesn't carry or is out of the item they seek, or if the item can be purchased significantly cheaper elsewhere. In this scenario, if you're not online, how will you let the consumer know what merchandise or services you have available?

Dramatic changes in telecommunications and computing technology in general are leading to the creation of new applications. Some of the applications are designed to bring consumers and organizations closer together; others are designed to help organizations work more closely to improve the efficiency of their supply and value chains. Many organizations that have previously been conservative in their use of computers are rushing to create an Internet presence, even if they don't sell their wares directly to consumers.

Small businesses can become international, and it makes sense for some of those businesses to do so. Economic and cultural boundaries are disappearing—in some market segments businesses must be global! E-commerce offers lower costs per business transaction, especially with respect to mailing and paper costs. Fewer mistakes occur in paperwork because fewer people handle the data. Customer satisfaction is heightened due to better access to order and promotional data. The old rules are breaking down. Companies now share information with competitors, producing "coopetition." Suppliers and buyers share information, though some corporate cultures make doing so difficult because of concerns about securing corporate secrets. And some functions, such as corporate procurement, formerly consisting of purchasing clerks, are now strategic (for more information, see Chapter 2).

FAST FACT: E-BUSINESS GROWS TOP LINE
A study by New York-based research firm Jupiter Communications indicates that organizations can show a 52 percent increase in revenue and a 47 percent growth in their customer base after just 12 months of doing business online.

Why Is E-Commerce a Business Imperative?

To survive, organizations must compete in an environment in which consumers expect more for less. E-commerce enables organizations to operate at lower costs while maintaining or even increasing revenues. E-commerce also can reduce business cycle times by increasing the speed and accuracy of transactions processed with fewer people. These results can, in turn, improve business partnership quality. Faxes and e-mail can be sent instantly, and document tracking should improve because e-mail and e-commerce transactions can be audited easily. These improvements can result in reduced inventory levels and fewer stock-outs. Organizations also can use e-commerce to communicate information efficiently to business partners, which allows all players in the supply and value chains to react more quickly.

E-commerce also can cut the cost of getting goods and services to consumers by providing convenient shopping methods (for example, online ordering). This method of shopping can reduce an organization's need to spend money on retail branches (also known as brick-and-mortar operations). E-commerce may also lead businesses to *disintermediation*, in which organizations eliminate the middlemen, thereby reducing inventory, distribution costs, and, eventually, price. Organizations can attract new customers through marketing and advertising with very small mailing costs. E-commerce also enables organizations to serve existing customers via customer service and support Web sites. Because the Internet reaches a diverse audience, organizations can even develop new markets and distribution channels for existing products.

According to Dale Kutnick, CEO of the Stamford, Connecticut-based The Meta Group, a research and consulting firm, some organizations think that if they're not in the direct-to-consumer business, they don't have to do e-commerce. Kutnick says that in reality, however, these organizations still need to make people aware of their presence. Even organizations that are not direct-to-consumer are part of the supply chain, and the consumer is at the end of that chain.

An organization's vendors and customers may also force the organization to go online. If your organization services direct-to-consumer organizations, they will most likely want you online. And non-direct-to-consumer organizations can use the Web to build brand awareness. (See Chapter 2, "E-Commerce in Action: Myths and Reality.")

Dwight Davis, an analyst with the Boston-based research firm Summit Strategies says that some organizations may be driven purely by customers, whether consumers or other businesses. According to Davis, the more sophisticated and aware of electronic commerce the customer, the more likely he or she is to want e-commerce-based business relationships or links. Competition may drive the need for visibility. If your competitors are doing e-commerce, you want to be seen in the same favorable light. Another competitive factor is low customer loyalty. Customers are likely to gravitate toward organizations that are perceived as more progressive.

What Forces Brought Us to This Point?

The Meta Group's Kutnick thinks that competition from traditional and nontraditional players, the opportunity to lower costs, and the opportunity to reach new customers faster and easier than ever before are just some of the factors driving e-commerce. Traditional competitors may be driving some organizations to e-commerce because they're realizing cost and efficiency benefits. Nontraditional competitors are sneaking up on big organizations, using e-commerce techniques that allow them to extend their business lines into areas they wouldn't normally be able to reach. Smaller businesses are doing what large, traditional, brick-and-mortar businesses do, only much better.

Combinatorial innovation

E-commerce enables multiple players to work together more easily, which allows large organizations to become assemblers rather than manufacturers, creating "The Virtual Enterprise." Also driving the adoption of e-commerce is the fact that organizations can innovate by combining multiple organizations' innovations, creating a new product (a system Kutnick terms *combinatorial innovation*). Combinatorial innovation means using the "best of the best" organizations to help you do what you do overall. By using the strengths of multiple organizations, everyone in the value chain wins.

According to Summit Strategies' Davis, the available technology may have been driving the move to e-commerce, but business seems to have snapped up the technology and used it. People naturally want to do things faster, and this technology has allowed us to go faster, accomplish more, and spend money more effectively. Using the technology to link multiple organizations into a single virtual enterprise provides organizations with the ability to do what they do best and outsource the rest. However, in this case, outsourcing doesn't mean losing the business benefits—just the business costs.

Customer forces

The expansion of e-commerce is being pushed along by many forces, including customer habit changes, online marketing, technology changes, and in general the sheer economics of the Internet market. Measured marketing, also known as *target marketing*, is becoming more and more important as the number of products available to consumers continues to grow. Using information gathered from the consumers themselves, e-commerce can use simple tools such as e-mail to target advertising and promotions to specific consumers.

To keep costs low and margins high, organizations need low-cost customer prospecting methods, and the Web is a reasonably easy way to capture many potential customers quickly. Through personalization software, organizations can establish close relationships with customers and develop customer loyalty more easily than through traditional channels. Marketing professionals are using the Web to create new ways of interacting with customers and delivering services.

Technological forces

Technology has made it possible to manipulate pictures, sounds, and movies, and to ship them painlessly to consumers. Communications, entertainment, publishing, and other industries are being forced into a situation of competition and cooperation because consumers want easy "one-stop shopping" for Web content. Creating content means using information publishing and browsing tools. These tools are only front ends that feed networked databases and data warehouses, which are used to improve corporate and individual decision making. Technology also facilitates the integration of an organization's business processes with those of other organizations. Easier delivery of data also means reduced cost and increased accessibility.

Economic forces

From an economic perspective, organizations are always under pressure to cut costs and stay competitive in their respective markets. E-commerce offers the opportunity (though not a guarantee) of lowering the cost per transaction and provides a mechanism to increase accurate electronic transactions with suppliers. E-commerce offers global information sharing and advertising at a low cost per customer and provides customer service alternatives to expensive call centers. Finally, e-commerce provides the capacity for small organizations to take advantage of economies of scale such as external integration with business partners through the automation of information transfer.

Ultimately, the demand for better, cheaper goods and services delivered faster will drive most businesses to some form of e-commerce. The Internet business model can offer ease of information navigation and use, ease of content publishing, and potentially new distribution models as organizations find ways to push new products and services out through the e-commerce pipeline. To do this, organizations must establish an "Internet-centric" business plan and provide both IT and business professionals with technology that enables new intra- and inter-business applications.

Why Doesn't E-Commerce Pay Off for Some Organizations?

Some organizations are participating in e-commerce but aren't receiving the expected payoff. Dale Kutnick indicates that the most likely problem is that unrealistic expectations were set when the program started, but there are other more specific problems as well. Kutnick states that often an organization's internal systems aren't integrated well enough. And some organizations can't or won't share the right information because of either technical or cultural problems—the culture can't or won't change with the technology. An e-commerce program is put in place but the culture won't use it. According to Kutnick, implementing the technology is difficult—automating internally is hard enough, but automating across organizations to link the supply chain members is harder yet.

Davis says that other problems include a lack of understanding of business-to-business or business-to-consumer e-commerce basics. Some organizations have no idea as to the complexity and difficulty of the needed infrastructure. Yet others suffer from hype-induced disappointment. With all the hype about how everyone *must* be online, organizations often develop a Web presence simply because some executive read about it on his or her last airplane flight. When the organization's Web site doesn't deliver on expectations, the "blame game" starts. And, of course, the executive who started it all never seems to get hit!

The Effect of the Internet-Based Business Model on Organizations

Electronic commerce has a profound effect on organizations. New business functions and technologies are changing the way organizations do business. Employees face a pace of change faster than at any other time in history. There are some key changes. According to Dwight Davis, e-commerce accelerates the integration of IT as an important part of business. Also, organizations are struggling with the need to open their systems to outsiders (vendors, customers) because of cultural and technological barriers. The pace of change in the Internet business world means that organizations must be extremely agile and be able to adapt quickly as the Internet business model evolves.

Organizations must continually reexamine their business components (Kutnick's term) and stay current, deciding on an ongoing basis whether to manufacture or outsource. Business components are the discrete functions that make up most organizations. Typical business components include human resources, accounting, purchasing, manufacturing, and so on.

Competitive analysis takes on new urgency and feeds business component management, even internally. Organizations can take advantage of new business opportunities, such as selling to other potential customers products that would normally be used internally. Other opportunities include buying products from other vendors that would normally be manufactured internally. E-commerce-ready organizations are more concerned about speed, efficiency, and flexibility than "snubbing" internal resources; these organizations realize that outsourcing functions to best-of-breed organizations is usually more cost effective than performing them internally.

How Electronic Commerce Affects Local, State, National, and International Economies

Recent estimates from The Meta Group show that the worldwide market for the business-to-business e-commerce alone will exceed $200 billion by the year 2000. The e-commerce phenomenon poses significant challenges, particularly within the context of international business integration. These challenges include the need to address socioeconomic parameters (such as the impact on employment), issues relating to the integration of e-commerce technologies into business environments, questions regarding market access and globalization, financial issues, and legal and regulatory requirements (for more, see Chapter 3, "The E-Commerce Obstacle Course").

Technology infrastructure needs

One of the major problems facing the world of e-commerce is that of achieving a critical mass of technology infrastructures for e-commerce deployment. Doing so requires the existence of adequate infrastructures in terms of affordability and accessibility for the target population (whether consumer or business), support of products and solutions from the IT industry, and the definition of geographical or industry sectors in which e-commerce will operate. Organizations must also consider the affordability of services, financial profitability, and potential of growth for the benefit of users.

According to the *Organization for Electronic Cooperation and Development (OECD)*, the goal of most nations and/or states is to ensure that e-commerce service providers can provide reasonably priced, value added service offerings.

Worldwide, genuine market opening will lead to increased competition, improved telecommunications infrastructures, more customer choice, lower prices, and increased and improved services. Confidence in the security of electronic payments is essential for the development of e-commerce. Otherwise, users will be reluctant to disclose credit card information or use the emerging electronic money technologies to purchase (for more on this topic, see Chapter 3).

Electronic commerce promotes worldwide competition

For some economists, e-commerce brings the world closer to the ideals of perfect competition. They argue that e-commerce will contribute to a further reduction of transaction costs, lower barriers of entry, and improve access to information for the consumer. Those who track government issues also know that the expanding usage of electronic commerce necessitates updating current trade legislation and regulations. The new environment must guarantee protection and security of transactions and privacy of exchanges, which means that law enforcement agencies will need to update their methods.

Businesses need to understand the potential benefits of electronic commerce in terms of cost savings, creation of new markets, and opportunities for the development of new products and services. Industrial organizations and associations should be encouraged to publicize case studies and to promote themselves and their benefits. Consumers are being made aware of the potential gains from e-commerce, including wider choices, comprehensive pre-purchase information, and potentially lower prices. E-commerce offers firms new ways to access their markets.

Sharper identification of new market segments is now possible using data-mining and market-tracking tools. Interactivity with the market and personalization of marketing will help to adapt the products and services to individual consumer requirements. The new concept of information brokerages is emerging. Easy access to valuable information is a strong requirement, together with the need for new technologies to build innovative intermediation platforms. An intermediation platform is a hardware- and software-based solution that brings parties with common interests (either commercial or social) together. New information brokerage services will be at the center of the new marketplace. The trend is a revision of existing value chains as electronic commerce brings new players into the game and creates new roles, with a consequent need for extraordinary amounts of information.

"INFONOMICS"—THE NEW WORLD ECONOMY

Dale Kutnick, CEO of The Meta Group, a Stamford, Connecticut-based analyst group, says that electronic commerce will cause governments to rethink taxation and regulatory policies. Organizations must think about nontraditional competitors from across borders, which will break down because of the Internet. Organizations now can buy from anyone, anywhere, as long as the seller has a Web presence. Information is becoming a bigger part of economies—hence Kutnick's term *infonomics* to describe the coming wave.

Infonomics is responsible for the capitalization of most Internet companies in the business-to-consumer market. Infonomics is also responsible for the perception that Internet organizations know their customers better, which will ultimately lead e-commerce-ready organizations to sell more "stuff." E-commerce-ready organizations have a propensity to use customer information more productively than they have in the past, which means that information, not manufactured goods, is the new most valuable item. Meta-products (data about products) are becoming more valuable than products.

As the market expands, new technologies will generate new jobs through the creation of start-up companies (in multimedia, in intranet building, in new communications products) through the creation of new professions (Webmaster, security manager, information net-manager, project and operations manager, attorney specializing in electronic commerce, and so on).

How Electronic Commerce Facilitates Global Knowledge Management and Information Sharing

E-commerce techniques provide the technological, business process, and cultural links between organizations that allow all members of the supply and value chains to work together. They can share and manage knowledge assets to better compete and personalize products and services to customers' needs. Global implementations of groupware products such as Microsoft Exchange allow organizations to share the information needed to make better decisions and process business transactions faster and more accurately at a lower cost than via paper.

The Meta Group's Kutnick indicates that e-commerce–ready organizations use the information gathered about customers to tailor service and product offerings to customers. Organizations can use e-commerce techniques to share customer demographic and satisfaction data with business partners, a strategy that allows a smoothing of the supply chain activities. E-commerce links business partners, which increases buy-in from all players in the supply chain.

Summit Strategies' Davis agrees that e-commerce supply chain automation helps organizations share globally. E-commerce also helps partners work together to deliver integrated solutions (for example, the MSDN Web site and Microsoft's solution partners). Organization Web sites allow exchanges and moderated discussions among business partners. Organizations can train business partners via e-commerce or Web-based education, allowing the supply chain players to work together in a directed, cohesive manner, which ultimately makes the supply chain seamless and smooth.

WRAP UP

- **E-commerce is redefining the business landscape.** This technology is changing the way businesses communicate internally, with their partners, and with their customers.

- **Many types of e-commerce already exist**. Common electronic commerce formats include electronic data interchange (EDI), electronic funds transfer (EFT), online buying, and electronic transmission of business documents between business partners.

- **E-commerce can make good business sense.** Reasons for implementing e-commerce include lower costs, increased revenues, faster time to market, more accurate communication with business partners both locally and internationally, wider access to larger markets, and the ability to target markets more narrowly.

- **A successful e-commerce strategy often requires an organization to undergo significant change.** Organizations and governments must change their culture and thought processes as well as their technology and business processes to succeed in the e-commerce world.

- **Building an e-commerce infrastructure requires a variety of hardware and software components.** Organizations communicate over the Internet using various types of hardware and software, including Web, database, and transaction servers.

Taking Stock

1. Does management recognize that speed, flexibility, and efficiency will be enhanced when tasks are no longer kept internal to the organization?

2. Is management willing and able to talk about outsourcing production of components?

3. Does management think about outsourcing *first* and then producing internally?

4. Can you logically disaggregate or disassemble your business into components such that an outsourcing decision can be made?

5. How well are you prepared to share information and processes with other organizations?

6. Are the organization's people willing to share information with others in the organization?

7. Do your business processes facilitate the sharing of information with business partners?

8. Is your data organized in a way that other organizations can use and understand?

9. Does senior management recognize that the business environment is changing and that using e-commerce is almost mandatory to stay competitive?

10. Does the company have any connections to other supply chain members? Are any planned?

11. Is the organization staffed for e-commerce (from strategy to implementation)?

12. Does management know where the organization stands in e-commerce relative to competitors?

13. Does management understand and appreciate how and why we got to where we are in the e-commerce world? Does management understand the evolution of electronic commerce and the forces driving it?

14. Is management willing to rip apart and reconstruct current organizational models?

ACTION PLAN

❑ Educate everyone in your organization—beginning with senior management—on the rapid pace of change in business today. Emphasize the role of e-commerce in remaining competitive in such an environment.

❑ Train managers on how to identify business components that can be outsourced or shared with business partners. Have them evaluate each business process for e-commerce opportunities.

❑ Talk to your business partners and customers about getting connected.

❑ Make a plan with your business partners to begin the collaboration process.

❑ Evaluate your organizational model and staffing plan and determine whether your organization is or can be e-commerce-ready.

❑ Do a cultural assessment to determine whether the organization's people are e-commerce-ready.

❑ Do a competitive analysis to determine where your organization stands in e-commerce relative to your competitors.

❑ Evaluate your organization's technology and data to determine whether they're well organized, easy to use, and ready to share. If they're not, determine the problems and fix them.

❑ Evaluate your organization's business processes to determine whether they're well organized, easy to use, and ready to share. If not, have systems analysts work through the problems to make your organization "e-ready."

Chapter 2

E-Commerce in Action: Reality and Myth

Many organizations begin electronic commerce initiatives with totally unrealistic expectations. To avoid this pitfall, organizational leaders and decision makers need to learn how successful organizations are using electronic commerce. Leaders also need to be aware of the myths surrounding doing business on the Web.

From purchasing to payroll, business functions are going online. Organizations are moving their applications and services to the Web, both on intranets and over the Internet. These Web applications and services enable organizations to share information faster and more accurately within the organization's walls and with external business partners. The lure of "better, faster, cheaper, and with fewer people" is the siren call of electronic commerce.

But e-commerce hype makes these benefits seem inevitable once an organization implements e-commerce initiatives. As this chapter explains, e-commerce doesn't always pay off in ways that live up to the hype. E-commerce infrastructures and applications are not as easy and cheap to construct as many people might think. However, as this chapter also makes clear, some organizations are doing e-commerce right and they are learning to do it better as they go. By studying businesses that have succeeded at e-commerce—and some that have failed— you can become better prepared to avoid the pitfalls and to help guarantee a successful e-commerce venture.

WHERE ARE BUSINESSES APPLYING E-COMMERCE SOLUTIONS?

Some form of electronic commerce is at work in almost all business functions today. Purchasing departments are using e-commerce to increase the speed and efficiency of acquiring products and services. Customer service departments are using the power of the Web to provide customers with 'round-the-clock service. Technology companies such as Dell Computer are using the Web to provide online help desk services. Marketing and sales departments are using the Web to push information out to customers—and potential customers—faster and more efficiently than ever before. So, how are the best companies using the Internet to improve their business functions?

FAST FACT: BUILDING AND BUYING EXPERTISE

An *InformationWeek* survey shows that more than 80 percent of organizations are sending staff to e-commerce–related training and that just less than 80 percent are buying expertise via consulting firms. This implies that many organizations are doing both.

Corporate Purchasing

Corporate purchasing solutions reduce paperwork and streamline purchasing processes by empowering employees to conveniently purchase and route appropriate approvals for their own office business supplies and other goods over the Internet. Supply chain management solutions link inventory, billing, and shipping between customers and suppliers to ensure more efficient supply/demand coordination. According to U.S Department of Commerce numbers, early adopters of Web-based corporate purchasing systems report saving a minimum of 25 to 35 percent in vendor sourcing and order placement in the first year alone. They also report cutting the cost of handling invoices by as much as 80 percent. Numerous surveys of corporate purchasing managers indicate that deployment of Web-based corporate purchasing systems will grow dramatically over the next two years.

FAST FACT: MICROSOFT CUSTOMERS PURCHASING ONLINE

Today, an average of 28 percent of Microsoft's enterprise customers have deployed Web-based corporate purchasing applications. By the end of the year 2000, this average is expected to grow to 42 percent.

Organizations are moving quickly to deploy Web-based corporate purchasing systems. Although each organization is unique, most organizations have similar objectives for doing e-commerce–based purchasing:

- Lowering costs by reducing administrative bureaucracy, inventories, and transaction costs.

- Gathering more detailed information on purchasing activity, which allows companies to find and terminate noncompetitive suppliers, negotiate volume discounts, and direct employees (buyers) to preferred vendors.

- Empowering employees by transforming corporate purchasing from a labor- and paperwork-intensive process into a virtually paperless, self-service application.

To automate its procurement process, MasterCard International is rolling out an enterprise corporate-purchasing solution based on Clarus E-Procurement and Microsoft BackOffice technologies that cut the average time required to fill purchase orders by some 70 percent and cut the cost of processing purchase orders by approximately 68 percent. Jim Cullinan, MasterCard's vice president of global purchasing, has been the driving force behind the electronic procurement project. "When I came in three years ago, everything was manual," Cullinan recalls. "Filing, processing, everything was a piece of paper that needed to be moved around."

Cullinan saw that by eliminating all that paperwork and automating the purchasing workflow, a corporate-purchasing application would not only reduce expenses and speed delivery but also leave buyers more time for studying purchasing patterns, evaluating suppliers, and exploring new ideas. MasterCard is a great example of using Web technology to automate the purchasing function, which saves time and money by eliminating paper and unnecessary approval steps. The shorter cycle times and ease of purchasing mean getting the right materials to the right people at the right time and at a lower cost than doing it manually.

Marketing and Promotions

Corporate identity and awareness programs, product and service marketing campaigns, and electronic product and service literature publishing are just a few examples of how e-commerce supports electronic marketing and promotions. Organizations can use the Web to accomplish the following:

- Attract new customers through marketing and advertising

- Serve existing customers via customer service and support functions

- Develop new markets and distribution channels for existing products

- Develop new information-based products for business-to-business and business-to-consumer e-commerce

Organizations do need to consider, however, who they're likely to reach via the Web, particularly with respect to consumers. Many consumers, particularly those new to the Web, don't know the specific names of the Web sites for which they're searching. Traditional advertising, such as print, television, and radio, can help build awareness of an organization's Web site. The same techniques can help build awareness for business-to-business Web sites as well.

Expectations are also changing, and organizations must be able to meet the new expectations they promote through e-commerce marketing. During the 1998–1999 holiday season, business partners and customers were forgiving of delivery and customer service issues on the Internet because they understood that it was new. During the 1999–2000 holiday season, there were high-profile reports of customer dissatisfaction with problems in these areas, even as Internet-based consumer order volumes were higher than ever. As the e-commerce market matures, consumer patience with these issues is likely to run out. Businesses and consumers are starting to see the Internet as an extension of or an alternative to ordering by phone or fax. An organization's customer service and professional image must be consistent across channels and business partners.

ELECTRONIC COMMERCE ATTRACTS FTC ATTENTION

It's absolutely critical for organizations to be careful when using e-commerce marketing techniques. The Federal Trade Commission (FTC) recently announced its 100th "Internet scam" crackdown and has begun to examine electronic commerce even more closely. Under such careful scrutiny, organizations must be certain that information about their products and services sent to potential customers (particularly consumers) over the Web cannot be seen as deceptive. The case law is still young and impressionable, and governments are anxious to "make examples" of early offenders. The FTC and the U.S. Department of Commerce are also looking into *online profiling*, the practice of aggregating information about consumers' interests, gathered primarily by tracking their movements online, and using the resulting consumer profiles to create targeted advertising on Web sites. The FTC is examining the implications of online profiling for consumer privacy and taking a close look at current e-business efforts

(continued)

Electronic Commerce Attracts FTC Attention *continued*

to implement fair and self-regulatory information practices. These issues must be carefully considered, and any organization should obtain legal counsel before initiating e-commerce services.

Customer patience and site reliability aren't problems for CBS SportsLine. This organization provides a high-quality site with extensive content. The content is well organized, and the site is easy to find. Online customers' demands for availability 24 hours a day, 7 days a week mandated that the company's information technology (IT) infrastructure be highly reliable and customizable. "Our audience is 'prequalified' because we know they are interested in sports merchandise, among other things, when they come to the site," says Dan Leichtenschlag, vice president of engineering and chief technology officer for SportsLine USA, Inc., the Fort Lauderdale, Florida-based publisher of CBS SportsLine. "To provide the level of service that drives sales and keeps customers coming back, we need a system that delivers database-driven marketing. This lets us analyze customer behavior and buying patterns so we can personalize The Sports Store for each visitor. This makes it a better, more convenient shopping experience."

CBS SportsLine uses Microsoft e-commerce tools to enable administrators to easily add, manage, and modify custom advertisements with targeted delivery, ad schedule management, and exposure limits. This efficiency helps generate greater ad revenue for the sites, as well as better leads from ad campaigns for advertisers. In addition, CBS SportsLine rotates ads for its own merchandise on the home page of The Sports Store. The marketing department at SportsLine USA makes rapid and frequent changes to the content. Using Microsoft e-commerce tools, scheduling a targeted ad, for example, at the beginning of a particular sporting event such as the World Series is easily accomplished.

Brand Management and Awareness

The Web enables organizations to get the word out faster and to larger audiences than ever before. However, merely making people aware of your organization's existence is not enough. You need to present relevant information that gets the point across. Implementing e-commerce using a digital nervous system can help organizations with marketing and advertising, brand name management, and the dissemination of product catalogs and sales information. E-commerce also makes product announcements easier and faster to deliver.

Many new advertising challenges have arisen, as described in the next section and covered in detail in Chapter 8, "Brand Management Strategies."

Some organizations such as Barnes and Noble and Toys 'R Us are splitting their brands into brick-and-mortar and e-commerce organizations. For business-to-consumer organizations, direct sales to customers become easier and faster but remain just as tough to manage as through any other channel. The brick-and-mortar and e-commerce organizations are managed separately, and the skill sets of the professionals are targeted at the e-commerce business requirements.

The Internet and e-commerce will take a long time to live up to their hype. However, e-commerce can assist organizations through both social and commercial channels by providing wide-open markets. On the Web, your image can speak louder than other forms of PR and advertising. Customers can talk to one another about your Web site, your image, and your organization more easily than ever, so image management is critical. How you represent your organization on the Web says as much—if not more—about your organization than what you say about it. Many organizations that slapped up Web sites in an effort to establish any kind of Web presence got slapped back by customers because their sites were difficult to navigate and offered nothing of value. Those organizations learned that it's better to take your time and do a site right the first time, because, as the saying goes, you never get a second chance to make a first impression—even in cyberspace.

BRAND MANAGEMENT MADE EASY

Two interesting examples of brand management on the Web are Microsoft and SAP. SAP is probably the best known and most widely used enterprise resource planning package. To promote the growth of its package and its customer base, SAP makes it easy for business partners and other Web sites to use SAP content by simply requiring the Web site, book, or other material to acknowledge that the content is not specifically endorsed by SAP. This simple policy protects SAP while allowing other Web sites to continue to increase the awareness of the SAP product line.

Microsoft knows that the more people who know about its products and Web site, the more customers it will acquire. Therefore, Microsoft allows other Web sites to use the Microsoft name, incorporate content about Microsoft products and services, and link to the Microsoft Web site. Web content authors and Web site organizations must follow specific Microsoft policies to be able to use the Microsoft name. These third-party sites must

(continued)

Brand Management Made Easy *continued*

use no more than 10 percent of direct quotes from the Microsoft Web site. They must comply with Microsoft's data privacy requirements for visitors to their Web sites. All mention of Microsoft products and all screen shots must be properly trademarked. These simple Web policies make it easy for other organizations to work with Microsoft, thus Microsoft continues to accumulate business partners. For more information, see Microsoft's business partner policies at *www.microsoft.com.*

Advertising E-Mail

Advertising e-mail is probably one of the most controversial aspects of e-commerce. Anyone who has ever found his or her e-mail inbox filled with junk e-mail knows how annoying this is. In the business-to-consumer sector of electronic commerce, many cases concerning deceptive use of e-mail advertising are currently making their way through the judicial system, with the disposition unknown at this time. Organizations must avoid deception in their advertising and allow consumers to easily unsubscribe to any advertisements they receive. A direct-to-consumer e-commerce business must carefully avoid getting a reputation as a *spammer*—a person or organization broadcasting unwanted messages.

The business-to-business sector is a different story. Advertising e-mail can be used constructively to increase brand awareness and to communicate new products and services to business partners. However, organizations must still be careful to not overwhelm their business partners with too many announcements, lest they be seen as spammers. There's a fine line between information and spam, and your business partners will usually let you know quickly where that line is!

FIRST IMPRESSIONS COUNT IN CYBERSPACE

For both business-to-business and business-to-consumer e-commerce organizations, ensuring truth in advertising is important. The Justice Department, Commerce Department, and other U.S. government agencies are actively investigating and considering regulation of the Internet. Each new Internet scam that pops up results in new calls for regulation. The only way for e-commerce organizations to avoid the heavy hand of government

(continued)

is to self-regulate carefully. Organizations and their business partners must work together to ensure that information disseminated about their products and services is as accurate as possible. Electronic commerce makes it easy for organizations to share the knowledge needed to provide accurate information about products and services. Consumers who doubt your organization's honesty may be lost forever.

The Microsoft WebTV Network has defined the next generation of advertising. The network's Click-To-Video ads enable subscribers to the WebTV Network to select an advertiser's banner ad and then view a full-screen, full-motion video TV commercial for the advertiser's product before arriving at the advertiser's Web site. The feature benefits advertisers by allowing them to seamlessly integrate their online and television campaigns and benefits audiences by giving them the choice of whether to watch the full ad. The ads are tailored to the consumer, based on the content of the Web site they are visiting.

Click-To-Video ads are simple for advertisers to execute and provide an instant advertising experience targeted directly at the specific subscriber on the WebTV Network. Advertisers submit existing banner ads and television commercials to the WebTV Network, where they're integrated into an advertising product that leverages the targeting capabilities of the Web with the full-screen impact of television. Subscribers immediately view the television commercial after selecting the banner ad, with no waiting required to download the video. Consumers don't have to select the ads but many do so voluntarily. This way, consumers aren't forced to receive or view advertising they don't want.

Inventory Management for Global Entities

Managing inventory in a global organization can be very difficult. Global organizations may have multiple divisions spread across several countries. A single division might even have facilities spread across multiple locations, in many countries as well. Ordering, storing, and tracking inventory globally presents a major challenge that can be answered by electronic commerce. The same challenges apply to organizations and their business partners. By using either decentralized or distributed inventory databases, organizations and their business partners can use Internet technology and e-commerce techniques to access those databases around the world, at any facility at any time.

By automating communication, business partners in the supply chain can access inventory information and order automatically as needed. E-commerce inventory management techniques also help ensure that inventory will arrive when needed. This means that suppliers can also improve their own internal efficiency by knowing inventory requirements in advance. Because there is no paperwork, business partners involved in a transaction can significantly reduce the time spent and increase the accuracy of the information exchanged.

H&R Johnson, a manufacturer of ceramic tiles, produces approximately 750,000 tiles every week from its headquarters in Stoke-on-Trent in the United Kingdom and sells its products through distributors worldwide rather than directly to the public. It relies on efficient communication and ordering to ensure that retail outlets have the necessary tiles in stock. For five years, the company had been using electronic data interchange (EDI) to automate the order and supply process with its larger distributors. But because of the cost and complexity of EDI, the company's smaller distributors found it difficult to implement the systems needed to communicate electronically with the manufacturer. Instead, they relied on fax and telephone to place and track orders and to check on stock availability. H&R Johnson recently began redeveloping its existing online ordering system, which automates stock control and ordering between the company and its worldwide distributors. It's expanding the system to create an end-to-end supply chain system by integrating the supply side of its business.

H&R Johnson conducted a survey to identify its customers' key requirements. The most apparent were the need for stock information, order-progress information, and order entry. To address these needs, Johnson worked with Alternative Business Solutions (ABS), a Microsoft Certified Solution Provider, to create an e-commerce solution. Using ACE (advanced client/server environment), from ABS, the two companies developed a Web-based supply chain system using Windows NT Server as a gateway to H&R Johnson's existing AS/400 system. The business-to-business system, which is based on the Microsoft BackOffice family of server applications, allows H&R Johnson's smaller distributors, which previously could not access the EDI system, to enter orders via the Web, check stock levels, and track the progress of their orders. But the new system offers additional benefits that go beyond replacing manual processes. Using e-commerce techniques offers H&R Johnson an alternative line of communication to suppliers. Now the company can see requirements and react by providing the necessary materials. Because customers participate in the order and delivery cycle and monitor progress online, nothing gets overlooked.

H&R Johnson recently decided to extend the system to include its own suppliers. A prototype was been developed that enables H&R Johnson's established suppliers to monitor internal stock requirements. With the new system, the company won't have to manually monitor stock levels and process orders. Although these materials are critical to its business, the company cannot hold large amounts of stock because of the inventory carrying costs. Improving the lines of communication with its suppliers lets suppliers take responsibility for anticipating when the stock will need replenishing.

Supply Chain Management

Electronic commerce can be used to link all the members in the supply chain for a seamless flow of goods, services, and information about purchases, payments, delivery schedules, and so forth. *Supply chain management* (*SCM*) has been a hot buzzword for the past 10 years, but linking many business partners manually has been extremely difficult. Everyone from the raw material supplier to the ultimate seller in the chain must be able to get accurate information quickly and easily about orders, shipping, and customer response to products and services. (See Chapter 1 for more information on automating supply chains.) Business partners must decide together which areas they will try to link first. Each partner then focuses on key internal groups that have the most to gain by adopting e-commerce. These groups will provide early successes and buy-in, which are the key to driving adoption throughout the entire organization.

Electronic commerce affects everyone's role in the supply chain. Each organization participates as a vendor in some segment of the global supply chain and acts as a customer in others. E-commerce helps the supply chain work more effectively and efficiently by lowering the cost of SCM activities, which can ultimately reduce prices to consumers. Because of the expanded marketing opportunities, e-commerce increases options available on products and services and speeds the delivery of products and services to the ultimate consumer. E-commerce also makes purchasing products easier for all customers along the chain.

Effective supply chain management involves integrating all supply chain activities into one solid system. An integrated supply chain system is flexible and adaptable. New business processes can easily be automated without a major revision of the original concept. Organizations must manage more than the flow of goods and services, though. Symmetry must exist between the paths followed by the physical items and the information related to those items. Where transformation, assembly, input, or output takes place in the physical system, e-commerce technology must store and process information to monitor, control, and re-optimize this physical operation.

E-commerce can help supply chain management teams determine how much of each raw material or intermediate or finished product should be processed at each facility. E-commerce can also help organizations decide which supply sources should be chosen. Working with their business partners, each player in the supply chain interactively determines the best production schedule, size, and sequence. E-commerce helps business partners share information that enables them to forecast demand most accurately for each individual customer.

Figure 2-1 shows how materials transfers correspond to information flows between business partners. This correlation guarantees a tight fit between the information and the physical products, services, or both. The organizational structure of each business partner must be built according to the business processes that are to be performed to reach the organization's overall goal. Over time, through external and environmental changes and technological advances, the business processes change and, consequently, the organizational design changes.

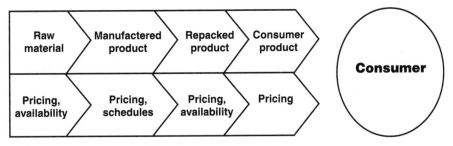

Figure 2-1 *Material and information flow from raw material to consumer*

Exabyte, a Boulder, Colorado–based maker of tape drive and tape automation backup equipment, found that its manual processes were slowing down and reducing the accuracy of its communication with business partners. The increasingly competitive marketplace, combined with shorter and shorter product life cycles, was straining Exabyte's manual partner-management practices. When launching new products, the company took too long to notify and train its business partners. Distributing leads to Exabyte's partners was too labor-intensive to monitor progress and track results. This resulted in missed sales, and the difficulty of tracking leads made future lead-generation programs difficult to justify. Exabyte decided that e-commerce offered a cost-effective and scalable way to interact with partners.

To solve these problems, Exabyte deployed "Exabyte Partner Central," a partner extranet that allows the company to exchange information selectively and securely with partners over the Web. Extranet solutions provide organizations with the ability to allow business partners to directly interact with the organization's systems. This solution automates and accelerates all the labor-intensive day-to-day tasks of partner management: administration, contact and lead management, publication and distribution of product and pricing information, product configuration, order management, performance tracking, and notification to partners of new programs. The technology platform consists of Portland, Oregon-based Webridge's Mainspan enterprise platform, integrated with Microsoft BackOffice technologies. This structure provides Exabyte with the development tools and flexibility to respond to changing market requirements without disrupting the flow of business.

With Exabyte Partner Central, business partners now have one place where they can always obtain the information and sales tools they need when they need them, and these tools are customized to reflect the partners' preferences and business relationships. To publish and target information quickly, authorized content creators use a browser and forms without the need for technical support resources.

Customer Relationship Management

Electronic commerce provides businesses with a growing, dynamic channel for efficient delivery of goods and services to consumers through the supply chain, in both business-to-consumer and business-to-business commerce. E-commerce enables organizations to market goods and services to consumers and businesses alike online in a more personalized, dynamic environment and will increasingly include the delivery of digital goods and software, electronic media, and information. Customers, (businesses and consumers) also look more frequently to the Internet for the delivery of services, including ticketing, reservations, and financial services. In short, e-commerce (business-to-business and business-to-consumer) has a dramatic impact on the way goods and services are managed, purchased, and sold from producer to customer/consumer. Electronic commerce provides organizations with these benefits:

- Increased speed and accuracy of information sharing between organizations and their customers.

- Improved relationships with customers. Organizations make fewer errors when taking orders and are able to deliver goods and services to customers more quickly and efficiently.

- Better management of the customer relationship using e-mail, online FAQ (frequently asked questions) lists, and automated problem-resolution systems.

- Faster response to customer orders, requests, and problems, which ultimately helps increase customer satisfaction.

A digital nervous system puts the customer at the center of this process. By using technology to deal directly with customers, businesses have the potential to deliver improved methods of customer service and the ability to help customers solve their own problems. As an organization's digital nervous system is extended beyond its walls, the organization begins to realize the benefits of using such a system for customer relationship management. One major benefit of using technology in this manner is closer customer interaction, enabled by the Web. Connecting all parts of the organization (and its business partners) and sharing customer information enable rapid collaboration and response around new customer opportunities or potential customer losses. By using the Internet to connect organizations to their customers and partners, provide improved access to information, and act quickly on customer/market feedback, an organization can better manage the customer relationship.

CitySearch, Inc., based in Pasadena, California, provides a complete and current community guide for its member cities, delivering searchable information on events, area activities, and local businesses to consumers via the Web. To help drive its success, CitySearch places great emphasis on customer relationship management—building and maintaining relationships with customers by offering superior sales, support, and customer service. From its beginning, CitySearch sought a competitive advantage in the fast-moving world of Web-based publishing. For this leader in a new medium, customer relationships are key to the company's success. To foster customer relationships, the company automated its customer service and telemarketing operations to pursue and manage as many sales leads as possible, while at the same time providing great customer support.

To capitalize on growing customer interest and to maintain quality service, CitySearch wanted a system that would enable the company to both tightly manage the sales process and offer a high degree of customer responsiveness. In addition, the company wanted to reduce the time taken to turn leads into sales, resulting in increased sales and more effective tracking of its marketing efforts. To meet this challenge, CitySearch created a customer relationship management solution that would place information quickly in the hands of the right staff and support sharing of customer data among sales and customer service personnel. They created a solution that integrated database marketing, lead management, and sales analysis using various "best-of-breed" vendors.

Customer Billing and Payment

As e-commerce grows, more organizations are looking to save time and money by billing and receiving payments from customers via the Web. The seller can save time and money by generating bills directly from its accounts receivable system, which can cut the estimated cost of billing between 35 and 50 percent. Jupiter Communications predicts that by the end of the year 2000, 20 million households worldwide will handle some form of their finances online. This study suggests that online billing will probably become the norm in the e-commerce world. Jupiter estimates that the average household spends 25 hours a year just paying bills and that by 2002 these households will be able to receive and pay bills online. This means that households will be able to save time, effort, and postage by paying bills online.

FAST FACT: BILLING AND PAYMENT BY THE NUMBERS

According to Jupiter Communications, less than 30 percent of households currently pay bills online. However, by 2002, that number is expected to more than double to 65 percent. Jupiter's research shows that the majority of consumers would prefer to pay their bills electronically through their banks, using either automatic withdrawal or e-banking techniques such as EFT (electronic funds transfer).

There are some significant issues with online bill presentation and payment. The first and probably most visible is consumer reluctance to surrender personal information online. Recently, lawsuits against online banks and catalog companies for selling consumer information have made consumers wary of providing any information via the Web. The second most visible problem is the complete lack of standards for the online presentation and payment process. In addition, competition in the field is causing many organizations to work together in small groups. This means that a consumer may not be able to pay all bills in one place. Because the whole purpose of online bill presentation and payment is increased convenience, little incentive exists for consumers to work with multiple companies to pay their bills, even if it's online.

Fast Fact: Consumers Don't Care...Yet

A Jupiter Communications survey shows that consumers rank managing finances online low on the list of online activities. In a survey of more than 2200 consumers, managing finances online was rated a 4 on a scale of 1–10. E-mail was the top use at a 9, followed by researching products and services at a 7 and reading news at a 5. These items represent the top 4 items as ranked by respondents in the survey.

Web-based bill delivery and payment require a unique combination of corporate and consumer software expertise along with efficient transaction processing and proven operating capacity. Online bill handlers such as

TransPoint introduced an end-to-end system for Web-based bill delivery and payment in 1999 and early in 2000 announced a merger agreement with CheckFree Corporation. Services like TransPoint and CheckFree allows billers to reach customers virtually anywhere over the Internet with graphically rich "e-bills" that also serve as powerful, interactive marketing tools. The graphics on the e-bills are similar to the fliers that often come in paper handbills. A credit card company might include a graphic or banner ad on the e-bill cross-promoting an airfare sale with an airline partner.

Online Help Desks

Online help desks are another useful feature of electronic commerce. Organizations can save huge amounts of money by providing online, automated help 24 hours a day, rather than using employees to answer individual customer questions. Since many customers ask common questions, providing a FAQ (frequently asked questions) section can save an organization significant time and money. During off hours, customers can check the status of orders, get answers to frequently asked questions, and have access to a knowledge base that can help them solve problems.

In the business-to-consumer arena, Dell Computer has one of the better examples of an automated online help desk. Dell's support Web page offers order status options, a file library, discussion forums, an online knowledge center, and even "Ask Dudley," a natural-language advisor powered by the search engine Ask Jeeves. (Of course, all these types of features should be incorporated into business-to-business help desks as well.) Dell provides the ability to get help for the customer's specific system and also provides assistance for ISPs (Internet service providers) that are members of DellNet. DellNet is a portal of sorts, similar to Yahoo!. DellNet offers news, weather, and other features to its subscribers.

Perhaps one of the most interesting features is the DellTalk discussion forum. Here, customers can ask questions of other customers, discuss problems with Dell service representatives, or send e-mail to Dell. Providing this kind of discussion group can often make customers feel more comfortable and it lets customers interact in a way that's both useful to the customer and informative to the vendor. Watching the activities and exchanges in discussion groups gives organizations a better idea of what's bothering customers, common problems with products, and new ideas from customers—if the organization is willing to listen. It's a good idea to assign a full-time moderator with whom customers in the discussion group can get comfortable. The moderator listens and helps the organization learn from customers in an environment more natural than a formal e-mail problem/resolution situation.

How Are Organizations Using Their E-Commerce Sites?

Some organizations are applying electronic commerce techniques to business solutions by "Webifying" almost all of their business functions. Conceptually, e-commerce is a great idea, but actually implementing e-commerce services on a Web site is a different matter. Some organizations have done well, while others have struggled. E-commerce is still a very new concept, and most organizations are working through trial and error. This section presents success stories upon which an organization can model its approach.

Product Catalogs and Online Buying

Online, information-only catalog Web sites were one of the first uses of e-commerce on the Web. Today, catalog companies provide full-color online catalogs, online purchase and return services, and 24-hour general customer service. Such traditional catalog companies as Fingerhut and JC-Penney now offer online purchasing and provide special deals for Web-based buyers and special "club" members. Even airlines offer specials, such as Northwest Airlines' (NWA) CyberSaver fares. Each week, NWA posts special Web-purchase fares that are essentially those seats left over for the coming weekend. Would-be buyers have an incentive to purchase via the Web because the cost of a ticket purchased through the Web page is $10–$30 less than the same CyberSaver ticket purchased by phone or in person. This is an example of an organization providing incentives to customers to use the Web because of the labor, time, and dollars saved when a customer doesn't call and require the services of the reservation staff.

Purchase Orders/Order Entry

According to an *Electronic Commerce Association (ECA)* study, only 5–10 percent of organizations are actually doing e-commerce–based purchasing in the business-to-business arena. Office Depot, a supplier of office supplies, is one of these businesses. Office Depot has built the complex profiling, permissions, and workflow required for allowing contract customers into their Web page. The company also provides an online order-entry process for corporate customers. With the exploding popularity of electronic commerce over the Internet, Office Depot decided to develop a Web site that enables a business of any size to order goods. The ability to access data from this system and display it in real time provides a higher level of service for customers shopping online, while not requiring Office Depot to change its internal business systems. The ability to integrate e-commerce activities with legacy systems and other back-end systems is a key requirement of any digital nervous system, and Office Depot managed to do it rather gracefully.

Office Depot created the site using the commerce components of Microsoft's Web server software, Site Server, and made sure that the site was both flexible and complete. This includes a shopping cart feature that enables Office Depot to integrate shopping cart functionality into the company's enterprise-wide product information database. Shopping cart functions allow site visitors to "add items" to a "virtual shopping cart." The items in the cart are "rung up" at the end of the shopping experience. The company also uses Site Server personalization and membership features for assigning and keeping track of customer IDs, and an inventory checking function that uses postal codes to compare the stock on hand at the Office Depot outlet closest to the customer's shipping address.

Merisel is one of the top three distributors of computer products in North America. In 1997, the company moved more than $4 billion worth of computer hardware and software through its 25,000 resellers to millions of end customers. Merisel built a World Wide Web site that intelligently communicates with reseller Web sites to check inventory and take orders. The result is instantaneous news of product availability and excellent customer service. To lower costs and improve customer service, Merisel implemented a digital nervous system that links customers with real-time inventory and order-entry systems. It's a state of the art e-commerce application called SELline II.

SELline II enables resellers from Canada and the United States to log onto a Web site, check product availability and location in multiple warehouses, check pricing, place an order, and check order status, all in real time. SELline II even allows an end customer to gain access to this information through a reseller's Web site—in effect, allowing Merisel to provide virtual inventory for its resellers. This is an example of digital nervous system technology bringing the Web to life for Merisel and its customers. Creating a digital nervous system is all about the true elimination of paperwork and the linking of business partners up and down the supply chain.

Logistics Control

Mayne Nickless Limited is an Australian-based international service company operating in health care and logistics. Mayne Nickless operates integrated health care services, contract and cash logistics operations, and time-critical express services. Mayne Nickless Logistics needed an advanced and comprehensive supply chain solution to satisfy the requirements of a key customer, Unilever, a large consumer packaged goods company, in Malaysia. The company sought a system that could monitor, manage, and report on product flow and integrate seamlessly with Unilever's enterprise resource planning technologies. Mayne wanted to increase accuracy, throughput, and cost efficiency.

Mayne Nickless Logistics deployed EXE Technologies' EXceed SCE software. The software allows businesses to optimize the operation of warehouses, distribution, and supply chain execution (SCE) elements. This solution enabled Mayne to meet and exceed Unilever's SCE requirements. It has produced measurable positive results in the areas of warehouse picking and dispatch, location control and stocktaking/allocation, load planning, delivery confirmation, replenishment, reverse drop sequencing, radio frequency capabilities, and product recall capabilities.

The solution was implemented at the centralized Mayne Nickless Logistics distribution center in Kuala Lumpur, Malaysia. This modern 200,000-square-foot facility specializes in handling dry consumer packaged goods and features approximately 30,000 pallet positions and 10 dock doors. The solution is part of Mayne's digital nervous system and uses Telxon RF (radio frequency) technology and advanced EDI capabilities to move inventory. Item movement is recorded by the Telxon system and fed into the warehousing system. EDI software allows Mayne Nickless Logistics to exchange information with Unilever electronically. This is a great example of how a digital nervous system can work both internally and with business partners.

Customer Service

A digital nervous system can provide a fast, easy way for an organization to help customers. Cinergy, one of the largest and most progressive energy providers in the U.S., is working on a three-year project called EDSIP, for Energy Delivery Systems Integration Program, that will showcase the power and flexibility of a digital nervous system. Cinergy sees EDSIP and the digital nervous system as key to its ability to streamline work processes, make better use of data, and deliver high levels of customer service—the very things that energy companies will have to do to flourish in a competitive environment as the energy industry is slowly deregulated.

The energy-delivery business is moving toward performance-based rates. The rates that energy companies will be allowed to charge will be based on factors such as reliability, customer satisfaction, and response time.

From the customer's perspective, EDSIP should improve Cinergy's level of service and reduce its response time. If multiple Cinergy field personnel respond to the same service request, they will be able to design facilities in real time using current records—working right from a job site. Cinergy employees will also be able to provide instant job status updates to customers. An employee back in a base office could use the system to determine that a gas meter has been installed and is ready for inspection. Schedulers will be able to manage crews more effectively. When an outage occurs, the information provided by EDSIP will help Cinergy quickly identify trouble spots and mobilize work crews, while accurately updating customers and the media on the current status. This is an example of a digital nervous system being used to run an organization more effectively and efficiently, which ultimately translates to better customer service.

Call Centers

Call centers are becoming e-commerce centers. In many cases, call centers are being relieved of their order-taking duties by Web sites and are better able to concentrate on customer service. But most customers will eventually want to talk to a person when there's a problem, or if they just aren't comfortable ordering over the Web. A digital nervous system is the perfect solution for linking call centers with back-end technology and creating a simple, easy way to enter call information, solve customer problems, and increase customer satisfaction. Most customer satisfaction problems result from incorrect or insufficient customer information processed within an organization. A properly designed digital nervous system ensures that information not only is accurate, but is available to those organizational staff who need it to serve the customer properly.

Few call center applications are more critical than the 911 emergency service. Founded in 1995 and headquartered near Philadelphia, LifeSafety Solutions developed a plan to enhance the national 911 public safety emergency system. LifeSafety Solutions used Sintaks Unlimited, a consulting and services division of Canon, USA, to develop 911Plus, a Web-publishing system that distributes critical information to emergency service providers. By using Web publishing to distribute the necessary critical information to emergency service providers, Sintaks has kept deployment costs to the minimum. 911Plus is a private intranet that saves lives by instantly delivering critical information to emergency dispatchers and rescue personnel when someone dials 911. Information such as directions to a victim's house, presence of hazardous materials, location of children or bedridden individuals, medical conditions, allergies, and medications are automatically sent to 911Plus terminals located in 911 call centers and other strategic emergency agencies.

A Windows NT workstation connected to the 911 call center computer runs a custom Visual Basic program that decodes the telephone number of the 911 caller. As the call is received at the 911 call center, the system creates a message that is then sent to the 911Plus "terminal" associated with the operator/dispatcher handling the call. The 911 dispatcher then browses through different critical information screens simply by touching the screen's icons or hyperlinks. The dispatcher can also query information by entering a subscriber's telephone number if someone else reports the emergency. At about the same time that the call is received at the 911 center, a customer service representative (CSR) receives a notification request. Notification lists, available at all CSR stations, automatically keep track of who needs to be called or paged and records each attempt in log files.

E-COMMERCE MYTHS

Electronic commerce has quickly become the Holy Grail of business. And like the Holy Grail in medieval times, myths and mystery surround it. Some experts say that electronic commerce is cheap and easy, whereas others say that it's too expensive and security isn't as good as it should be. As with most subjects, electronic commerce has its strengths and weaknesses. In general, electronic commerce initiatives offer many benefits for an organization, its customers, and its suppliers. It's important, however, to understand the realities of electronic commerce before starting e-commerce initiatives.

Like any major IT initiative, an electronic commerce project should be thoroughly planned, and return on investment (ROI) metrics should be created and calibrated before the project starts. Setting realistic expectations for a payback on an electronic commerce project is critical to both short-term and long-term success. Organizations must also educate themselves on the major issues surrounding e-commerce projects before they start. This can be done via consultants with e-commerce experience or by hiring experienced e-commerce staff as permanent employees. For example, an organization must understand that it is unlikely to be able to pull off a successful e-commerce initiative alone. Because most e-commerce projects involve players outside of the organization's walls, when planning the project e-commerce project teams must account for project activities that will involve people from other organizations. Organizations may not be used to involving people from outside their walls (except software and hardware vendors) when planning IT initiatives.

Fast Fact: Happy, So Far...
An *InformationWeek* study shows that 89 percent of organizations are satisfied with their progress towards transforming their business models from traditional to e-commerce.

Myth #1: It's Cheap, Easy, and Lucrative

According to Andrew Bartels, a senior research analyst with Cambridge, Massachusetts-based Giga Group, e-commerce will eventually be lucrative, but isn't yet. Besides, the Giga Group believes that looking at the Web as a specific source of income is the wrong approach and that organizations should be using e-commerce techniques to improve their business processes and cut the costs of acquiring, servicing, and selling to customers. In many cases, organizations doing e-commerce are getting orders through the Web that they would have received anyway, so the revenue isn't incremental. However, these companies are realizing considerable cost savings because the orders are more accurate, and the handling cost per order is lower because fewer human hands touch each order.

The Web also allows customers to order specific items, and organizations can build to order, which reduces unwanted inventory. In this way, e-commerce makes just-in-time (JIT) manufacturing easier and reduces the parts needed in inventory over time. This setup reduces inventory carrying and warehousing costs. The cost per custom order drops because a human isn't needed for each special order. Customer satisfaction goes up because customers are surer that they'll get what they want, and they can order anytime (provided that the Web site is up).

Bartels also says that e-commerce isn't as easy as everyone thinks. Putting up a Web site is easy, but it's much more difficult to integrate that front-end Web site into the back-end processes such as inventory, accounting, and so on. It's also hard to integrate customer data between the Web interface and other customer contact points such as telephone call or mail order. Creating a customer relationship management (CRM) database can solve this problem, but creating, managing, and forcing internal staff and business partners to use that common database can be difficult. Also, as the Web site grows, the user friendliness shrinks. A small, simple Web site can quickly grow into a jungle of Web pages that customers must hack their way through to find what they want.

Another major problem is that many organizations simply automate or "Webify" the bad manual business processes they already have. In this situation, the Web and its technology allow the organization to make the same mistakes much faster! Before moving business processes to the Web, organizations must perform a thorough systems analysis on those processes to determine their speed, efficiency, and accuracy. After the organization is sure that its data and processes are sound, those data and processes can be automated or shared with business partners via Web technology.

Myth #2: Everyone's Doing It

Although Many organizations are looking to do something, eventually, on the Web, not all are there yet. Giga's Bartels says that roughly 90 percent of large companies have Web sites that are more than just "brochure ware." About 25 percent have the ability to take orders, and 25 percent are using e-commerce to allow suppliers to order from them. About 80 percent are using their Web sites for customer service. Only 5–10 percent, however, are using e-commerce techniques to actually automate their supply chains.

According to Bartels, organizations that are already part of proprietary EDI networks are not embracing Web-based e-commerce yet because of performance, security, and a lack of standards for order transmission. Performance reasons include the potentially slower speed, the random nature of travel paths of information, and concerns about reliability. Many organizations doubt the security abilities of the Internet (this topic is covered in more detail in Chapter 3). However, eventually EDI networks will morph into Web-based networks, possibly using VPN (virtual private network) technology. No firm standards exist yet for Internet-based e-commerce, though ANSI EDI standards will probably be used.

CONSUMERS ARE BUYING THE WEB

Internet retailing grew at extraordinary rates around the world in 1999, according to a report released January 17, 2000, by Ernst & Young. In the U.S., a significant number of consumers (34 percent of households) are online and half of those households (17 percent) have joined online shoppers. If this powerful trend continues, online shopping could become a mainstream activity in the next 12–18 months. This growth pattern is also taking shape worldwide. Following the U.S. in percentage of households to shop online in 1999 are the United Kingdom at 10 percent, Canada (9 percent), Australia (5 percent), France (2 percent) and Italy (1 percent). Ernst & Young also found that consumers are making significantly more purchases online. Thirty-nine percent of Internet buyers in the U.S. made 10 or more purchases during the past 12 months. By comparison, Australians making frequent purchases are at 20 percent; Canada, the U.K., and France are at 15 percent, and Italy trails at 7 percent. Online retailing will continue this rapid growth trend in the years to come. Current nonbuyers who join the ranks of Internet shoppers will contribute significantly to online sales in the next year. A whopping 79 percent of U.S. nonbuyers plan to purchase via the Internet in the next 12 months. That number is even greater in other countries. Canada shows the largest potential, with 85 percent of nonbuyers intending to purchase in the next year; in the United Kingdom, 75 percent; Italy, 79 percent; and France, 80 percent. By the year 2002, U.S. online consumers will spend one-third of their total "shopping money" via the Internet. American online consumers, who currently spend 15 percent of their "shopping money" on the Web, will more than double that expenditure to 36 percent. This trend will be mirrored by online consumers in Italy, who will also double their Internet

(continued)

Consumers are Buying the Web *continued*

spending and will increase threefold in Canada, Australia, France, and the United Kingdom.

Retailers and manufacturers have problems in making online shopping work. Those businesses that sell or plan to sell online believe their biggest challenges are lack of corporate resources, alleviating consumer concerns for security and privacy, and the complexities of linking their site to other business processes. Organizations enjoying the most online success with consumers operate very differently from those that are struggling. In leading organizations, managers regard the Internet as strategic to the company's future. They see the need to leverage the company's brand in cyberspace and they spend more on marketing to attract consumers to their Web site.

Myth #3: Middlemen Are Eliminated

Is the middleman being eliminated? "Yes and no," says Bartels. Some middlemen, such as travel agents, can be replaced by automated reservation systems, such as Microsoft's Expedia. However, some middlemen, known as *brokers*, are emerging in situations where price is critical, or where a new market can be created. The reality is that *infomediaries*, who provide information about products and who locate the best choice or price, replace *intermediaries*, the traditional middlemen. For example, Priceline.com helps consumers set a price (essentially a bid) for an airline ticket or hotel reservation, and then the airline or hotel responds. eBay allows consumers to put items up for auction and bid on items in real time. These new middlemen are allowing consumers to do things they couldn't do before, in a way that's convenient for everyone.

Myth #4: All Products Become Commodities and the Playing Field Is Leveled

This is true to a point. A specific mobile radio, such as a Sony Walkman, may become a commodity because it doesn't matter where you buy it. That is, a known product, with consistent quality, can be purchased through any Web site. However, don't expect that "If you build it, they will come." Products that are still differentiated through quality or uniqueness, or on which organizations depend for mission-critical operations, are unlikely to become commodities. An example is the automatic teller machine (ATM) in the consumer banking industry. ATMs are unlikely to be replaced by Web-based e-commerce because you can't withdraw money or make a deposit on your PC at home (although cash smart cards are coming). In addition, consumers are queasy enough about giving information over the Web that the ATM will likely be around for a while.

Myth #5: Brand Building Is Easy on the Web

"Brick and mortar" isn't dead yet. Organizations that have brand strength and are well known are unlikely to go away or lose money simply because they don't have a Web presence. Offline brand awareness and strength (as mentioned in Chapter 8) is just as important for small startups as it is for Fortune 500 companies. Don't expect "Martha's New Bran Cereal," sold only through the Web, to replace FiberOne from General Mills overnight. Software can be delivered via the Web, but even consumer trust in a specific brand of software takes time. Products that are critical to businesses or consumers will take longer to gain brand strength. It's pretty hard to test-drive a car over the Internet.

On the other hand, organizations that produce and/or deliver commodities such as books, videos, and so on can build brand strength quickly. Organizations whose products can be delivered and described completely digitally can also succeed faster over the Internet than can consumer-packaged goods such as food, clothes, and so forth. Amazon.com built its brand in just three years. It's one of the most widely recognized brands and has made its name through both Web-based and traditional advertising. They still move product via "brick and mortar" warehouses, so they are not entirely in the information commodity business. Organizations that are completely "virtual" (including product delivery) are still a few years away.

WRAP UP

- **Almost all business functions can benefit from some form of e-commerce.** From purchasing to call centers, electronic commerce can provide organizations with new ways to automate business processes and reach customers and business partners. Electronic commerce provides organizations with the means to share information, build brand awareness, and improve relationships with customers.

- **E-commerce can improve the accuracy and speed of information exchange with internal and external business partners.** Electronic commerce provides organizations with the ability to quickly share information with business partners. Electronic commerce also reduces the number of times humans touch information, which reduces errors.

- **E-commerce can lower the cost of customer service, purchasing, and other functions, but organizations shouldn't just automate bad business processes.** Organizations must evaluate their current business processes and organizational practices in light of new technologies. Electronic commerce is more than just technology—organizations must also change the way they think about information sharing and knowledge management.

- **Organizations must be careful with customer service and advertising to prevent further governmental regulation of e-business.** The Federal Trade Commission (FTC) and other government agencies are closely watching the Internet. Organizations must understand the laws in each of their operating environments to avoid government intervention. Ethics and legal issues must be considered when beginning e-commerce initiatives.

- **E-commerce can help organizations improve their relationships with customers through improved customer service.** Electronic commerce techniques are helpful in managing the customer relationship. Using e-mail to keep in touch with customers and profiling customers to better understand their needs helps bring organizations closer to the customer.

- **The flow of information through a digital nervous system must parallel the flow of goods and services.** Organizations must thoroughly understand how their supply and value chains work before they try to automate them. Working with business partners helps organizations understand their place in the supply chain and helps them get closer to business partners. Digital nervous systems help link organizations to the business partners.

- **Organizations must be aware of the myths associated with e-commerce and create initiatives with realistic expectations.** The hype surrounding electronic commerce is overwhelming. Organizations must carefully evaluate electronic commerce strategies against the organization's goals and objectives. Getting advice from consultants, analysts, and other experts can help organizations navigate the electronic commerce obstacle course.

Taking Stock

1. Within your organization's business processes, where do you see opportunities for automation or e-commerce techniques?

2. What are your business partners' e-commerce-ready capabilities?

3. Are your organization's business processes slow and clumsy because of excessive paperwork?

4. Do employees complain about not being able to get supplies or resolve customer problems easily?

5. Do your customers frequently complain about your customer service being too slow or not available at the right times?

6. Do you have trouble tracking inventory across locations or divisions?

7. Are your competitors streamlining operations and using their Web sites effectively? Are you?

8. Does your supply chain seem too slow end-to-end? How fast can you get a product from your supplier to your customer? Is that fast enough to beat your competitors?

9. Do you and your business partners share information about products and services?

10. Does your organization know the laws concerning e-mail advertising? Are your organization's attorneys e-commerce-ready?

ACTION PLAN

❑   Evaluate your organization's Web site in terms of functionality, ease of navigation, clarity of content, and aesthetics.

❑   Do a thorough analysis of your business processes to find areas for improvement. Processes that are slow or ineffective should be reengineered prior to automation.

❑   Check your employee suggestion box. If you don't have one, start one. Then see where automation or an intranet could reduce internal bureaucracy.

(continued)

Action Plan *continued*

❏ Think of what your business partners might know that you would want to know and vice versa. Offer to meet with them and start sharing the knowledge.

❏ Assess your customer response time by looking closely at customer complaints. Where customer service availability and problem resolution time is an issue, see whether e-commerce techniques can help.

❏ Learn federal and state regulations regarding e-commerce, and spam in particular. If you don't have time to do so, be absolutely sure your lawyers do.

❏ Look for ways in which e-commerce can help reduce costs by moving activities from human hands to e-commerce applications.

❏ Reexamine your organization's role in the value chain. Look for ways to adapt your business model to Web-based e-commerce.

❏ Sketch out a digital nervous system for your organization and its business partners. Try to see the "big picture" and how you might be able to link up with them via the Web.

Chapter 3

The E-Commerce Obstacle Course

E-commerce initiatives typically present organizations with significant challenges and potential obstacles. Decision makers need to face these challenges and find ways to overcome any obstacles.

Implementing successful electronic commerce services is *not* as easy as most people might think. Many obstacles exist and they all revolve around the three major pieces of the e-commerce puzzle: money, technology, and people. Because competitors might force organizations into electronic commerce initiatives, justifying the costs of such an initiative by the return on the investment is sometimes difficult. Sometimes the costs of avoiding e-commerce are greater than the cost of initiating e-commerce. Web technology is still developing. Significant problems exist with the interoperability between systems used by organizations and their business partners, as well as between front-end systems that exist on the Web and back-end transaction-processing and legacy systems. Electronic commerce also necessitates major changes in an organization's culture and to the whole of the business world. Organizations must be prepared to change the way they think about customers, suppliers, and their business environment. Finally, electronic commerce exposes organizations to new security and legal risks that did not exist in the business environment before the innovations of e-commerce. All these changes can be overcome, but planning and determination are needed to implement the best practices.

COST/BENEFIT ANALYSIS

Analyzing the costs and benefits of an electronic commerce initiative requires understanding the direct costs of planning, implementing, and maintaining the initiative, as well as the opportunity cost of not doing the initiative. If a competitor is moving services to the Web and receiving the usual publicity benefits, can your organization realistically afford not to at least establish a Web presence? The cost of an electronic commerce project must often be justified in terms of more than hardware, software, and labor costs. If your customers expect to be able to access your organization through the Internet, you may be forced to add a Web presence or risk losing those customers to your competitors. Analyzing the benefits or return on investment of an electronic commerce initiative is equally tricky. Many organizations never realize huge gains in revenue as a result of simply building a Web page (see Chapter 4, "Measuring Success") but often they can at least keep their current customers—which can be a difficult benefit to measure.

Cost

Costs are obstacles in any initiative, but e-commerce initiatives are slightly different because of the unknowns associated with both the technology and marketing strategy. Many costs are associated with moving to an e-commerce-based business model, and those costs can vary widely from one venture to another. As the e-commerce business model evolves, new costs for various types of hardware, software, and business processes will emerge while other costs will disappear. Costs for paper and fax supplies, for example, will dwindle as more organizations move to paperless business practices. Right now, companies are struggling to create new business models to take full advantage of the Internet rather than to emulate business models in physical space. For these organizations, it's an exciting and somewhat frightening time, in part because there are not many examples of companies making money from their e-commerce sites.

Many costs associated with e-commerce projects include those for hardware, software, data, procedures, and personnel. Hardware costs include:

- PC clients
- Web and transactions servers
- Routers and other network equipment
- Purchased and built bandwidth
- Leased lines and switching equipment

Other hardware costs can be incurred based on redundancy and reliability needs. Many organizations also purchase or lease hardware to get through peak usage times, and because such hardware is not always fully utilized, the lease expense can become a loss.

Software costs include:

- PC operating systems
- Server operating systems
- Network operating systems
- Firewall software
- Transaction processing software
- Web server software

Other software costs may be incurred depending on the organization's industry, location, and type of e-commerce initiative. Data storage costs include disk space, backup and recovery, offsite storage costs, and memory upgrades. Costs associated with procedures primarily revolve around reengineering business processes so that they are better aligned with e-commerce initiatives.

Personnel costs include recruiting, hiring, training/retraining, and resolving ongoing human resource management issues. As mentioned in the "Staffing for E-Commerce" section, hiring, training, and retaining e-commerce professionals is a difficult, expensive process. Employee turnover and replacement of current staff are among costs that aren't easily visible. The recruiting process can likewise be difficult and expensive because the number of *information technology (IT)* college graduates in the U.S. is declining slowly while the demand for future employees is increasing exponentially. Some organizations in the U.S. are now starting their recruiting process at the high school level to find students with potential before their competitors do.

Other costs are sometimes difficult to identify. Addressing a changing corporate culture resulting from a move to Web-based transactions often requires hiring professionals experienced in managing such change. Those professionals cost money, as do the programs they design and implement. Also, the cost of running dual or hybrid operations (physical sites, Web channels, Web sites, and call centers) can be high. The combined cost of hardware and software can run into millions of dollars even for mid-sized organizations.

How Does Electronic Commerce Add Value?

One of the obvious barriers for a firm's entry into e-commerce is a measurement problem of its Web activities and the return on this investment. (For more information, see Chapter 4, "Measuring Success.") Companies are unsure about the number of people visiting their Web pages and how many individuals they can reach through the Web. Thus, a basis for making investment decisions can be elusive. The success of the Web-based business model is still in question and a firm's success on the Web is dependent on accurate information about consumer needs and target markets.

Cost justifying the evolving model

Electronic commerce project managers are frequently asked to justify the large costs associated with these initiatives. Because the e-commerce business model is still evolving, setting meaningful metrics is troublesome for an organization to do. The only metric may be the customer's access expectations, even if the organization can't sell its products or services over the Web. One potentially helpful guideline is the concept of improving supply-chain relationships through e-commerce technology. That is, if e-commerce initiatives can improve relationships with customers and vendors by meeting their expectations for an organization's Web presence, those e-commerce initiatives are worth the money spent to create them.

As mentioned in Chapter 1, there are some specific value-added features of electronic commerce in the business-to-business arena. Increased accuracy and speed as well as lower costs per transaction between an organization and its vendors and customers are significant achievements through e-commerce. The hard-dollar savings of those benefits, however, may be difficult to measure. For example, if an organization moves from paper-based invoicing to electronic invoicing, a major saving is likely to revolve around invoice accuracy (as matched to a purchase order). The electronically generated and mailed invoice will likely match the purchase order more often, which reduces the amount of work required to reconcile discrepancies. Thus, the clerical staff that reconciles invoices and purchase orders will have less work.

So, can you reduce clerical staffing levels? It depends. Electronic reconciliation methods are still in their infancy, and artificial intelligence systems have failed to show that they can outperform people in the realm of fuzzy logic and reasoning. If true reasoning is required to work through an invoice/purchase order reconciliation problem, a person is still needed. Further, a vendor or customer will more likely want to work through the problem with a person than through a computer. Even with the assumption of reduced overall labor needs, how can you show specific productivity increases? You might be able to show a reduction in the hours worked by clerical staff or in the rate of hiring. However, if fewer employees are available for customer and vendor service, goodwill may drop because of the frustration of trying to resolve a problem through a computer.

Separating hype from real value

If you think this cost-benefit analysis sounds somewhat convoluted, you're right! Much like the hype in the 1950s and 1960s of robots completely replacing humans in all manufacturing jobs (which hasn't fully happened), the ROI hype surrounding e-commerce that's touted in the IT and business trade journals is more symbolism than substance. It's critically important for organizations to understand both the explicit and subtle implications of e-commerce-based business and to understand that return on investment (ROI) may be difficult to measure in the short-term. Organizations must take a strategic view of e-commerce and realize that e-commerce–based business models will evolve and mature over time in much the same way that quality measurement evolved over the past 50 years. Eventually, hard metrics will be available with which e-commerce projects can be measured. For the present, considering implicit savings and closely monitoring the numbers at a high level to spot opportunities to reduce transaction and decision support costs are important.

Table 3-1. VALUE MEASUREMENTS AND OBSTACLES TO ACCURACY

Value Measurement	*Obstacle(s) to Accuracy*
Productivity	Requires extreme drill-down to determine hard cost savings; may not be worth the effort
Goodwill	Difficult to measure; can change rapidly over time
Revenue	May not be incremental; may mix new customers and customers transferring from telephone to Web-based ordering
Cost Savings	Similar to productivity, but even harder to determine which costs, if any, were eliminated
Hits-to-Orders Ratios	Site activity tracking tools are relatively immature; may not account for site performance problems or crashes
Customer Awareness	Almost impossible to measure, although market research studies can help

Consumer packaged-goods companies, such as General Mills and Pillsbury, do not use their Web sites to sell directly to consumers but rather to communicate important information about their products. Such companies also use their Web sites to communicate financial information, such as annual reports, and to recruit employees through career opportunity listings. They also provide online access to press releases, continually updating their customers and vendors on important happenings in the organization. Measuring the return on the investment of time resources required to create these Web sites, however, would be very difficult; the value is more subtle than an ROI report and revolves around the continuous buildup of goodwill fostered by increased access to the organization. Although accounting procedures exist that allow organizations to recognize the value of goodwill, it's difficult to measure that value in hard dollars for Web sites.

As mentioned in Chapter 2, "E-Commerce in Action: Reality and Myth," Web sites may not always produce incremental revenue. Many organizations trumpet vast increases in revenue from their Web sites sales, but what you don't hear is what percentage of that revenue is above and beyond the revenue generated by the company through other means. Customers may simply use the Web to order products or services instead of calling the organization directly. In such cases, revenues could be tracked as customers switch from direct call to Web site purchasing. However, these revenues can be mixed with new customer orders as well, so the measures will not likely be accurate.

The believability factor

Even if accurate measures were available for both business-to-business and business-to-consumer e-commerce, some business people may not be convinced by such data. Metrics may not be interesting to decision makers. An executive may believe that sales are made on the basis of price rather than on the Web response time to an order. Even if presented with information indicating that consumers will abandon an order after a set time, an executive might believe the data but consider it unimportant. Metrics may not touch on important issues, such as risk management. The use of metrics assumes a view of rational decision making that may not prevail in the real world of business. This is not to say that business people are irrational (although some are) but rather that commitments of resources are made for many reasons, and factors that affect decisions are often subtle. Hype may rule over reason.

TECHNOLOGY ISSUES

Of the numerous technical challenges to e-commerce, most fall into two major categories: *interoperability* and *interfaces.* Interoperability in this context refers to how an organization uses technology to communicate with external business partners. The term *interfaces* as used here refers only to the communication between internal systems within an organization. The Internet, as an interconnection of networks (computer, telecommunications, wireless, and others) and as a veritable cornucopia of content, services, and applications, may significantly improve the way people use information in their jobs and in their daily lives. The Internet can do this by bringing vast amounts of information and greatly improved services to everyone who is connected. These benefits, however, hinge on the ability of Web systems to communicate with each other within an organization, as well the ability of an organization to communicate accurately and quickly with its business partners. A true digital nervous system tightly integrates organizations with their business partners, allowing a smooth exchange of information. Such an exchange takes a tremendous amount of interoperability.

Electronic commerce applications require the interoperation of communications, data management, and security services. Many different types of companies, including value-added networks (VAN) suppliers, systems integrators, hardware vendors, and software vendors, will provide these services. The IT industry must ensure that e-commerce will be reliable and that the components can be assembled, maintained, and upgraded at a reasonable cost. Organizations must develop technologies, measurement tools, testing services, and interoperability demonstrations to ensure that components satisfy the current and future requirements of e-commerce.

Interfaces to Legacy, ERP, and Other Systems

Electronic commerce systems typically interface with most of the other systems in an organization. Because most organizations have many stand-alone systems with individual data requirements and formats, an organization may need to write many interfaces from the e-commerce system to other transaction-processing systems. Enterprise Resource Planning (ERP) systems simplify the development of interfaces because most ERP systems have standard interfaces and data formats for all the different functions in the ERP package. Still, interfaces must be written from each of the electronic commerce systems to the ERP system, which may have one or more interface formats.

Chapter 1 presents a diagram showing a simplified technical hardware architecture. That architecture looks relatively simple from a hardware perspective, but many pieces of software run on the hardware, all of which must exchange information with the Web server and with each other. Designing and developing those interfaces can be complex and time consuming, and achieving optimal communication between each of the software pieces and the Web server is a significant challenge. Figure 3-1 presents some typical interfaces from Web servers to other servers.

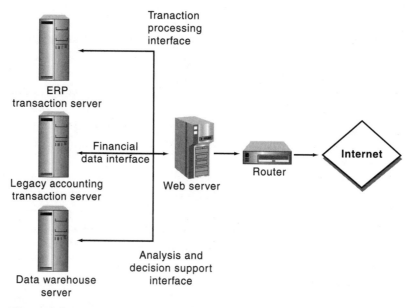

Figure 3-1. *Web server interfaces within an organization*

As shown in Figure 3-1, interfaces must be established for each organization between core ERP transaction processors, legacy systems, data warehouse or historical analysis databases, and the Web server. These interfaces must be tuned to allow fast access via the Web to provide accurate data on a timely basis. Making internal systems work together is a required first step for any e-commerce initiative. Until an organization's internal system interfaces and access are stable and correct, providing business partners with the kinds of information needed to make e-commerce work effectively and efficiently is nearly impossible. Electronic commerce technical issues are covered in more detail in Chapter 5, "E-Commerce Building Blocks."

Interoperability

The nature of e-commerce requires cooperation and flexibility among business partners, as well as the development of an international electronic marketplace that is secure, open, affordable, and easy to access and use. Achieving these qualities requires the establishment of standards for the interoperability of communications networks, information and data exchange, and security services. One agency helping that effort in the U.S. is the National Institute of Standards and Technology (NIST). NIST is active in research and development for electronic commerce as well as in efforts to increase public dialogue on electronic commerce and standards issues. NIST assists the private sector with the development of the technical underpinnings for interoperability and works to coordinate and facilitate the standards process. Other NIST activities include the establishment of an Electronic Commerce Integration Facility (ECIF) to assist in the removal of barriers that are currently preventing the transition from paper-based commerce to e-commerce and to help advance technology in order to permit the development of future electronic commerce applications. As mentioned in the next section, "Going Global," international agencies are also working toward similar goals.

The ability of an organization to communicate electronically with its business partners is at the core of e-commerce. As mentioned previously, communication issues will arise between business partners with different hardware and software, organizations and consumers in different countries, and business partners in different countries. The operation and scope of networks require virtual network services (VPNs), certified quality of services and data communication, and flexible bandwidth (upon request). An organization's set of obstacles to communicating with other computers is enlarged when that communication is international. Figure 3-2 shows some of the obstacles faced by organizations when expanding globally via the Web.

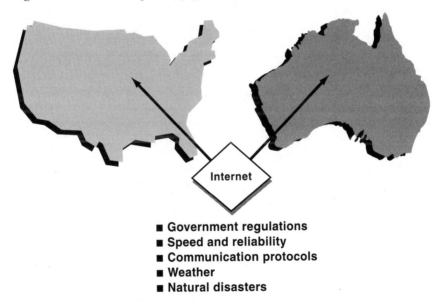

- Government regulations
- Speed and reliability
- Communication protocols
- Weather
- Natural disasters

Figure 3-2. *International data communication obstacles*

International data communication obstacles include government regulations, communication lag times, outages, routing issues, and data communication protocol matching. The use of advanced transmission media, such as fiber, microwave, and radio technologies, normally provide exceptional quality that will typically exceed performance expectations, but expectations will continue to increase, and technology must keep pace. Meeting reliability and quality standards will depend on the implementation of advanced technology by service providers. This technology includes the use of network management tools to rapidly identify and correct service problems. Organizations, their business partners, and governments must work together to minimize downtime through the proactive monitoring of networks and managing of providers. You can find more information on the basics of electronic commerce technology in Chapter 5, "E-Commerce Building Blocks."

GOING GLOBAL

E-commerce has developed at a spectacular pace. Organizations must work to maintain an environment in which the potential of e-commerce can be realized. Achieving this environment, however, requires cooperation on key issues between the private and public sectors to guide the development and implementation of electronic commerce policies and on basic policy approaches to major issues. These issues include cultural, geopolitical language, trade, and financial matters. The role of organizations such as the Organization for Economic Cooperation and Development (OECD) is to address questions of where and how principles and approaches might best be formulated and implemented.

Cultural and Language Barriers

Sometimes, cultural and language barriers aren't just a problem, they're the law! The Georgia Institute of Technology learned that lesson fast. The Association for the Defense of the French Language and the Future of the French Language (ADFL) went to court to force Georgia Tech Lorraine, the American college's French outpost, to translate its Web site into French. A 1994 French law bans advertising in any language but French. In addition to targeting Georgia Tech, ADFL is demanding that business Web sites also be in French. Georgia Tech eventually decided to offer a French version of its Web site to avoid any further problems. Organizations need to determine what languages their Web sites must offer before starting to do business in a specific country.

Some nation states have great public concern about the content of some of the information distributed and accessed on the Internet. Disagreeable or detrimental content is not more prevalent than beneficial content on the Internet, but people who distribute and access disagreeable or detrimental material on the Internet enjoy the same advantages offered by the Internet as other users do. With the benefits of e-commerce come the intrinsic difficulties of coping with content judged to be detrimental. The development of electronic commerce can potentially be impeded by illegal and harmful content issues when users fear unwanted content and network service providers fear the liability they expose themselves to if they are expected to be responsible for the content that flows across borders.

When in Rome...

A business must enter the new market using the native language, abiding by the local customs, and dealing in the local currency. In other words, a business should make it as simple and as comfortable for the consumer or business partner to conduct business with it as possible. Even though much global business is conducted in English, using the local language in advertisements will persuade other nationals that you are serious about gaining their business and will make understanding your message easier for them. An awareness of the culture of the country where you are conducting business will also allow you to avoid some of the classic blunders that we have all heard about regarding words that don't translate directly and idioms that make no sense or even cause offense in another language. Although traditional methods for addressing these issues may not be as feasible in the electronic environment, advances in technology are offering new ways to resolve some of the issues.

Tastes matter

Perhaps the most significant cultural barrier amounts to differences in tastes. What may be offensive in one country may be acceptable in another. Before venturing beyond their own nation's borders, organizations must determine what symbols, words, and approaches to business are acceptable in the countries in which they plan to do business. For example, Americans value openness in doing business. American business people are considered extremely blunt by some other cultures, such as the Japanese, in whose country business is transacted on a more subtle level. Learning local customs before establishing a presence can significantly reduce the number, significance, and severity of cross-cultural adjustments needed during the course of transacting business.

The Changing Geopolitical Landscape

Issues of public policy and the changing worldwide geopolitical landscape are major barriers to e-commerce. In an OECD study, respondents saw public policy barriers as "very strongly" or "strongly" hindering the emergence of electronic commerce. The policy work being done by international governing bodies serves the purpose of educating national governments and industry as to the challenges of electronic commerce, creating an environment conducive to international electronic commerce, and avoiding protectionist actions by the national governments. The different approaches are aimed at ensuring interoperability in terms of national and transnational legal environments and of technical infrastructure.

Fast Fact: International E-Commerce Resources
- World Trade Organization: *www.wto.org*
- Organization for Economic Cooperation and Development: *www.oecd.org*
- CommerceNet: *www.commerce.net*
- National Institute of Standards and Technology Information Infrastructure Task Force: *www.iitf.nist.gov*
- United Nations International Computing Center: *www.unicc.org*

Even borders once thought to be stable are changing. The breakup of the Soviet Union, the problems in the Balkans and the Middle East, and other geopolitical changes offer a constantly changing environment in which to operate. Organizations must be prepared to roll with the punches and be flexible concerning with whom they are willing to do business while maintaining legal and ethical operating standards. In some cases, technology-based tools will offer ways for organizations to protect themselves. There are mechanisms for verifying information, such as labeling systems that certify that a business partner meets certain good standards of business. Other mechanisms exist for notifying organizations of the legal jurisdiction or venue for resolving disputes arising from a transaction. Still other mechanisms allow organizations to access messages that describe their rights in the context of electronic transactions.

Organizations must expect and plan for geopolitical problems. If an organization's e-commerce business does not require a physical presence in a specific country, a geopolitical upheaval may not require much adaptation. Staying up-to-date on the issues involving the countries in which you do business, however, is prudent. Contingency and business continuation plans in place to deal with such problems are also useful. If your organization has an international relations department, its job is to know what is going on in all the countries in which you do business on a continual basis. As more organizations go global through electronic commerce, they will most likely want to hire international business experts and establish such departments.

Trade Rules

Trade rules and laws offer significant challenges to businesses in the international e-commerce environment. Many international organizations are working on setting up standard trade laws, but at present, each country has its own quirks and oddities in trade laws. The motto "Be Prepared" serves best here. Organizations must thoroughly research trade laws and restrictions in target countries before beginning business operations with business partners or consumers in the country. Consulting attorneys that specialize in international trade is a wise move. Some international law firms even offer expertise in specific countries and provide current expertise on specific problems and solutions in a particular country.

The United Nations Commissions on International Trade Law (UNCITRAL) created a model law that supports the commercial use of international contracts in electronic commerce. This model law establishes rules and norms that validate and recognize contracts formed through electronic means. It also sets default rules for contract formation and governance of electronic contract commerce and defines the characteristics of a valid electronic document and an original document. Because electronic signatures are key to the completion of e-commerce–based business transactions, the law provides for the acceptability of electronic signatures for legal and commercial purposes and supports the admission of computer evidence in courts and arbitration proceedings.

The UNCITRAL Model Law on Electronic Commerce was adopted and endorsed by the General Assembly in 1996. This instrument is in the process of being implemented as part of national legislation in many countries and is generally regarded as a useful reference by legislators throughout the world. UNCITRAL continues monitoring the technical, legal, and commercial developments that underline the Model Law. In line with its training and assistance activities, the UNCITRAL secretariat provides technical consultations for governments and other organizations involved in preparing legislation based on the UNCTRAL Model Law on Electronic Commerce.

The World Trade Organization (WTO) created the Agreement on Trade-Related Aspects of Intellectual Property Rights (TRIPS). This agreement aims to ensure the adequate protection and effective enforcement of intellectual property rights and the impartial resolution of disputes between WTO members about such matters to the mutual advantage of both producers and users of intellectual property. The areas of intellectual property that the TRIPS Agreement covers are the following:

- Copyright and related rights
- Trademarks, including service marks
- Geographical indications
- Industrial designs
- Patents
- Undisclosed information, including trade secrets and test data

This agreement guides organizations in their business operations and serves as a model for trade problem resolution.

Tax and Other Monetary Issues

One issue has emerged as the most significant tax-related barrier to electronic commerce: state sales and use taxes on the buying and selling of goods and services over the Internet. An overwhelming majority of organizations see this issue as one of the most significant barriers to electronic commerce, and it shows in the lobbying actions directed at the Congress of the United States as well as other governments around the globe. Lawmakers everywhere are trying to figure out where a transaction takes place when it occurs over the Web. In addition, touching on the issue of confusing and duplicative tax regulations in the nontraditional business world of the Internet, other major tax barriers include:

- Foreign taxes, such as VAT (value-added tax) and other transaction taxes

- State franchise or excise (non-income based) taxes

- Other federal taxes (excise taxes)

- Tax laws that range from simple to utterly convoluted

Most organizations see a strong hindrance to the growth of e-commerce presented by these tax barriers.

The taxman is confused

The development of electronic commerce also has the potential to create a parallel banking and payment system outside conventional banking channels. A key issue for organizations and governments is how the development of electronic commerce relates to the current tax system. This issue includes principles of direct and indirect taxation, as well as increased opportunities for tax avoidance and evasion and issues of tax administration. Consistent approaches at the international level are urgently required to ensure the effectiveness of taxation laws in this new environment. The OECD identified the following issues and is working with governments to reach an international consensus on general principles:

- Issues relating to the OECD Model Treaty on Income and Capital

- Issues relating to transfer pricing

- Issues relating to consumption taxes

- Implications of tax administration and tax compliance

These issues must be resolved quickly because governments risk losing potential revenues or even control over the flow of goods and services in and out of their state or country, and organizations could be hit with devastating retroactive taxes if governments cannot come to terms quickly.

Jurisdictional rules applying to taxes and tariffs are generally based on concepts of physical geography, such as the place of supply or residence of a taxpayer. Electronic commerce is not bound by physical geography, and it may become difficult for taxpayers and governments to determine jurisdiction and revenue rights. For consumption taxes, action is needed to avoid double or nontaxation. The availability, reliability, and completeness of commercial records generated in an electronic commerce environment, including those from electronic payment systems, are also issues of concern when such records are needed to ensure that taxation and tariffs have been appropriately and fairly applied.

Taxing information?

Many forms of taxation and tariffs are levied on physical goods. The capability, in electronic commerce, to create electronic substitutes, such as electronic books, presents challenges for revenue collection. The existence of electronic products also raises issues of fairness between the taxes and tariffs imposed on physical goods and electronic substitutes. Bypassing any or all of the traditional middlemen between producer and consumer raises serious issues for the collection of taxes, particularly withholding taxes.

The use of intranets by multinationals and collaborative groups increases the prevalence of transfer pricing and the difficulty of detecting such behavior. Organizational tax attorneys and accountants must stay current with the laws that apply to all areas in which the organization is operating and to the products and/or services the organization provides. The predicted growth of international e-commerce, much of which may be undertaken by smaller, less sophisticated businesses, may mean that the number of unintentional breaches of international revenue laws will increase. Organizations must be prepared to deal with the legal challenges presented by new sales methods and distribution channels.

Organizations and their local governments must review existing taxation arrangements, including concepts of source, residency, permanent establishment, and place of supply, and modify the existing arrangements or develop fair alternatives if required. Governments will want to ensure that electronic commerce technologies, including electronic payment systems, are not used to undermine the ability of revenue authorities to properly administer tax law. However, in fairness to businesses, governments must provide a clear and equitable taxation environment for businesses engaged in both physical and electronic commerce.

Exchanging currency information

In addition to taxes, foreign currency exchange rates also affect monetary conditions for global e-commerce initiatives. Economic statistics, politics, and social conditions are among the factors that drive the foreign exchange market and affect the relative value of the U.S. dollar against other currencies. These rate fluctuations have a direct impact on the amount you will pay or receive for goods and services sold in a global economy. It's extremely important to monitor exchange rates and use hedging techniques if your organization does a significant percentage of its business outside your home country. For more information on currency hedging techniques, be sure to consult a qualified financial professional. Corporate foreign exchange services are available through banks and foreign exchange specialist providers.

LEGAL ISSUES

Legal issues regarding e-commerce are often difficult to resolve. Because cyberspace doesn't really exist as a physical place, where should legal issues be resolved, and who should have the right to adjudicate those cases? The case law for e-commerce is still immature and incomplete. Both national and world courts have a long way to go before they can set any standard international laws governing e-commerce. Although normal contractual and international business laws still apply to e-commerce business transactions, arguments continue at various levels of the judiciary as to where and how e-commerce should be regulated, including whether e-commerce can be regulated at all.

Treat the Net with the Same Respect as Paper

According to William Henney, a Minneapolis-based business lawyer, the laws for conducting business via the Internet are essentially the same as via mail or fax. The exchange of goods and services for consideration (that is, money) works the same as regular commerce. The basic definition of a contract applies whether the contract is established over the telephone, in writing, in person, or communicated electronically. The same basic problems potentially exist as well. If the goods are not adequately described—the buyer didn't receive the expected goods or services—then the buyer must have recourse. If the seller can't deliver as promised, then the buyer shouldn't be responsible for paying for damaged or undelivered goods.

The twist is the lack of a paper trail that is usually associated with business transactions. Many organizations don't treat electronic commerce transactions with the same caution and respect that they give paper transactions.

According to Henney, business people must understand that certain laws apply to business transactions regardless of the medium in which they're conducted, and those laws cannot simply be tossed aside because of the new electronic frontier. Attorneys must understand that electronic commerce, although similar to paper-based commerce, has some unique characteristics. Organizational attorneys must stay up-to-date with judicial decisions regarding electronic commerce. This includes their own local, state, and national courts, as well as international courts and the courts in the countries in which they do business.

Fast Fact: E-Commerce Legal Tips

- Educate your attorneys on international law.
- Contact governments well ahead of doing business in their country to avoid accidental infractions.
- Check with regulatory agencies often to stay current.
- Write contracts that encompass all possible requirements.
- Treat electronic commerce transactions like normal transactions.

According to Henney, business now can be conducted via point-and-click processes, and sufficient laws aren't in place in the U.S. and other countries to protect consumers and businesses in this environment. In addition, legislatures and courts are behind in establishing precedences. Because courts are typically more sympathetic toward consumers, businesses must be proactive. For all electronic business transactions, businesses must safeguard their interests by basically treating those transactions as the same as paper transactions. The language and electronic forms should look the same and cover the same issues as a contract sent via mail or fax.

Who are You?

One example of the unique legal problems associated with e-commerce is the growing problem of identity theft. For example, a criminal can easily configure a new PC to be recognized as a different user. This new identity, including a stolen name, address, and social security number, is then used to buy goods and services over the Internet. The victim can potentially be saddled with paying for items he or she didn't purchase or receive, and the seller can be stuck with an inventory loss. Organizations must be sure to identify with whom they're dealing, either by telephone or in person, before beginning routine transactions over the Web. Organizational attorneys must learn to recognize the new issues brought about by the move to electronic commerce, particularly those concerning data privacy (see Chapter 7, "E-Commerce Best Practices").

PLAYING I-GAMES

The Internet gambling issue easily demonstrates the difficulty of resolving e-commerce legal tangles between international governments and establishing guidelines that are enforceable across national boundaries. Proposed regulatory approaches for Internet gambling range considerably: from fully supporting it as a desirable industry to banning any form of online gambling. But by the very decentralized nature of the Internet, enforcing a total ban on Internet gambling would seem impractical. Today, many organizations run Web-based casinos and use software to prevent cheating at Internet games.

Suppose that someone is caught gambling over the Internet. If the casino is based in a country that allows Internet gambling, and the player lives in a country that doesn't, which country's laws take precedence, who's held accountable for the crime, and in which country do you press charges? If the transaction took place in cyberspace, who decides whether a crime was committed at all? This and such similar issues as copyright and privacy will take years—maybe even decades—to resolve. In the meantime, an organization's attorneys must stay current and involved in issues relevant to their business.

Governments can assist their national businesses and help ensure the continued expansion of e-commerce as an efficient, effective form of commerce. Governments can help e-commerce grow more smoothly by taking the following steps:

- Remove existing uncertainties affecting the legal status of electronic commerce transactions

- Enforce laws concerning electronic commerce and paper-based commerce equally

- Provide an open playing field for all forms of technology

- Facilitate access to and the use of authentication and encryption technology

- Coordinate laws and other regulatory issues with other governments

Organizations must work with governments to champion the cause of e-commerce and simultaneously recognize that e-commerce must be treated like any other form of commerce. Although some businesses may find this collaboration with government inconvenient, it will ultimately protect both buyers and sellers by ensuring standard commerce laws.

SECURITY

Security is probably the biggest worry for organizations participating in electronic commerce. Oddly enough, although organizations are worried about it, few really know what precautions to take to avoid the problems mentioned in the previous section. According to Bill Boni, Director of the Dispute Analysis & Investigations department of the Financial Advisory Services Division of PricewaterhouseCoopers in Los Angeles, people still think locally and don't understand that risk can come from anywhere. Organizations still think that "it can't happen here" and have no idea that threats come from outside their borders. Also, often no controlling legal authority has single oversight capability for e-commerce. For example, suppose that someone from an Eastern European country hacks into your Web site in New York. What is the law enforcement authority in control?

According to Boni, the other common problem is management denial that insiders pose such risks. The most common cause of big break-ins and breaches in most organizations are employees or contractors who are currently on-site. Management must be careful when hiring professionals to work on electronic commerce projects. Background checks, security monitoring, and past employment reference checks are important steps to ensure the hiring of trustworthy employees. Organizations should, however, thoroughly check federal, state, and local laws to ensure that their screening practices are in compliance with common statutes.

It Could Be an Inside Job

Insiders represent the biggest threat through the use of so-called back doors, or their special accounts, to steal from an organization. Experimentation and accidental oversights can also cause problems. A security officer could forget to secure something. Poor security planning also can cause problems. (For more information on security planning, see Chapter 10, "Microsoft's E-Commerce Platforms and Products.")

Consumers are actually less at risk than businesses. To prevent insiders from stealing from the company, you should monitor and strictly control access, making sure that access is terminated after the work is done. Provide access only on an as-needed basis. Also, reduce the number of people have the opportunity to wreak havoc by granting only high-security access to the smallest possible number of people.

Larry Kanter, a partner in the Financial Advisory Services division of PricewaterhouseCoopers in Dallas, Texas, says that organizations do fear hacking but that management often outwardly downplays the danger to avoid alarming shareholders and other employees. Transaction interception is also a major concern.

Physical security is equally important. You need to prevent anyone from using your PC for illegal use. Thieves (yes, an insider or employee!) often simply walk into a security professional's office and use that employee's PC for miscreant purposes.

Disgruntled employees taking passwords is yet another major problem. To minimize this risk when an employee leaves the organization, be sure to terminate his or her security access as soon as possible.

Transactions are Safe, but Does the Consumer Agree?

The fear of transactions being intercepted or of the data being copied is overblown. The security mechanisms in place take care of transaction issues. Encryption prevents hackers from reading data. Also, hacking directly into the landline hubs from telephone companies is difficult. It's not as easy as people think to intercept or copy information as it's transmitted over the Web. An individual would have to gain access to the telephone lines and switches and install a program that would actually capture the data during transmission. Such an accomplishment is extraordinarily difficult and unlikely. From the consumer's perspective, however, the possibility seems real; therefore, one of the biggest obstacles hindering the growth of electronic commerce remains transaction security.

Protected plastic

Many consumers do not feel that their credit card information is protected if they use the Internet to make a purchase. The three major credit card companies—MasterCard, Visa, and American Express—have joined in an effort to make secure online transactions a reality. Third-party companies are also trying to develop systems for secure Internet transactions. One company is developing an encryption system that would encrypt the consumer's entire order and make it unusable until it was decrypted at the company (acting as a service bureau) and then sent to the consumer's bank for processing.

Credit card thefts are protected via the cardholder agreement. Visa's cardholder agreement protects the cardholder by allowing 45 days for the report of a theft or fraudulent use of the card. As long the cardholder notifies Visa within that time period, he or she has no liability. Even purchases outside the country of origin are protected, provided that the cardholder follows the rules. The lesson is that organizations must clearly state, preferably in writing, the rules by which their customers (whether business-to-business or business-to-consumer) must abide. In the business-to-business arena, these agreements should be delineated in writing in a paper contract before business transactions have begun.

One approach that seems to be gaining popularity is the development of an electronic currency. In this technology, which is based on public/private key encryption, the consumer creates both keys using a difficult-to-solve algorithm. The public key is given to anyone the consumer does business with and the private key is kept private. When consumers make a purchase, they must send the amount of the purchase along with their private key code to their bank. When the bank receives the request from the vendor with the consumer's public key code, it compares the information with the consumer's data; if they are correct, the bank pays the vendor electronically. For more information, see Chapter 10.

STAFFING FOR E-COMMERCE

Perhaps one of the most difficult challenges in implementing electronic commerce is the IT staffing shortage. Various studies show projected shortages of IT staff ranging from 15 to 60 percent over the next five years. Without proper staffing, electronic commerce projects can't happen at all. Organizations have several options to remedy this problem, including training, retention management, and outsourcing (contracting) the work.

Most organizations are starting to realize that training can be an attraction for new employees, as well as a turnover reduction method for current staff. Two major reasons for making training a priority are the overall IT staffing shortage and the expense of turnover. With the ratio of jobs to available IT professionals reaching 6:1 in some regions, training provides a relatively simple way of creating new IT professionals. Plus, morale will climb as IT employees learn new skills and are continually challenged. Organizations that offer current, exciting training opportunities have an easier time attracting highly experienced IT staffers. Turnover is expensive because new employees can take up to a year to become truly knowledgeable even if they are technically capable. It's much less expensive to keep current IT staff that know the business and train them on the latest technologies. Other considerations include the cost of hiring replacements for people lured away and the hidden costs of missed deadlines. At least one study estimates that the cost of replacing an experienced IT professional averages $20,000.

A major decision is whether to build the training program in-house or to purchase training. Organizations must establish criteria for the "make or buy" decision and honestly evaluate the skills of their internal staff. Using professional trainers can have advantages over subject-matter experts such as business end-users or software specialists. Purchased training, particularly in the form of a packaged solution, must be modified for a particular organization and sometimes even for a specific group of staff. Evaluating an organization's training capability before making this decision is important.

GETTING MOTIVATED

Motivation programs are another way to obtain and retain staff. Motivating employees may well be the most difficult part of a manager's job. Motivation is hard to define and often varies by individual, making motivational programs difficult to design and implement. Jill Spiegel, founder and CEO of Minneapolis-based Goal Getters and a nationally known motivational speaker and author of several books, cites two general rules for any motivational program:

1. **Keep employees involved.** When employees are involved in the design of a motivational program, the programs tends to succeed more often than those in which employees are merely players.

2. **Recognition often means more than money.** This rule may seem contrary to reality, particularly given soaring IT salaries. However, as long as employees are paid at or above their market value, recognition by peers and supervisors has a lasting impact on an employee's attitude and productivity.

If an organization simply lacks the financial and human resources to make an e-commerce project work, it may have to outsource the development and possibly even the maintenance of the system. Outsourcing a strategic asset or process is usually a bad idea and should therefore be a last resort because e-commerce is definitely a strategic action for most organizations.

If e-commerce systems are outsourced, strict disclosure agreements should be signed with the outsourcer to protect the organization. The outsourcer must be held to the same security and privacy standards as internal employees. Organizations should also try to learn as much as possible about the outsourcer's work before hiring. Also, if the outsourcer were to go out of business, the organization obviously must be able to continue operating the e-commerce system. The organization needs to have the outsourcer continuously transmit necessary information to the greatest possible extent.

WRAP UP

- **Costs and benefits are sometimes hard to quantify for e-commerce initiatives.** Opportunity costs and an organization's competitive environment must be factored in. If an organization's competitors go online, they may be forced to do create a Web presence to remain competitive, even if hard dollar benefits aren't gained.

- **An e-commerce technical architecture is complex and can take large amounts of time and resources to create and refine.** An organization's internal systems must be stable and accessible before attempting to connect with business partners. This includes both transaction processing systems such as ERP software and analytical systems that use data warehouses.

- **Cultural and language e-commerce barriers may constitute legal issues as well.** Some nation states such as France have strict language and cultural laws that must be obeyed. Organizations must be aware of these laws when targeting international consumers and businesses.

- **Geopolitical changes can make it difficult for organizations to work with foreign governments on e-commerce initiatives and infrastructure.** Some nation states have governments that are constantly changing leaders. Organizations may wish to partner with well-established businesses in countries where stability is an issue.

- **An organization's attorneys and accountants must understand the legal, trade, and monetary issues associated with the nation states in which the organization operates.** Trade laws continue to grow in diversity and complexity, and exchange rates fluctuate minute-to-minute. Organizations must understand these issues and plan for them.

- **Security issues include more than technology.** Organizations must keep a watchful eye on their own employees. Many security breaches are caused by disgruntled employees. Organizations must follow strict procedures when monitoring, regulating, and terminating employee system access rights.

■   **Training and motivational programs play a valuable part in reducing turnover and attracting new IT staff for e-commerce initiatives.** The IT staffing shortage is unlikely to get better in the near future. Organizations that offer varied incentive programs that offer career and monetary advancement, as well as benefits such as telecommunting and flex-time will be better able to attract and retain high-quality IT staff.

Taking Stock

1. What are your organization's goals and measurable objectives for your e-commerce initiative?

2. Are your organization's technical architectures and information systems stable enough to share with your business partners? How could you make them more stable?

3. Do the people responsible for e-commerce initiative(s) know the cultural rules (spoken and unspoken) of the regions in which you operate?

4. What exactly are the security processes and technologies used in the e-commerce system?

5. How will your organization test the safeguards to ensure that they work?

6. How are you managing employee access to e-commerce systems and transactions?

7. Do you eliminate temporary passwords when a specific project is completed?

8. Do you know the background of your Web developers?

9. Do your lawyers stay up to-date on the latest case law on e-commerce?

10. Are your lawyers changing and adapting to e-commerce as quickly as they should be?

11. Are your lawyers enforcing the same rules on electronic transactions as they do on paper transactions?

12. Do you listen to your lawyers regarding the safeguarding of e-commerce transactions, or do you disregard their advice because e-commerce is "totally different" and the rules don't matter?

ACTION PLAN

❑ Create a technical architecture vision that is detailed enough for its costs to be identified.

❑ Establish a long-term e-commerce plan that contains contingency plans for the obstacles your organization is likely to face in its e-commerce initiative.

❑ Write a list of measurable objectives for your e-commerce initiative and distribute it. Hold professional staff to those objectives when determining costs and benefits.

❑ Hire an international marketing relations expert or find a consulting firm that offers those services.

❑ Determine which nations and regions you are targeting or in which you're already operating. Find out what their cultures are like.

❑ Add multilanguage capabilities to your Web site.

❑ Educate your staff to reduce culture-centric attitudes.

❑ Ensure that security is more than incidental to an e-commerce project plan.

❑ Ensure that operational controls are planned according to best practices.

❑ Have clearly defined processes and procedures for discovering and response plans for reacting to breaches and anomalies in customer and/or system behavior that could become breaches.

❑ Stop thinking locally; realize that you must operate on a global basis and adhere to a wide range of evolving laws and policies and cultures.

❑ Set up an education plan for your lawyers and accountants to help them stay current on legal and monetary/trade issues.

Chapter 4

Measuring Success

The e-business model is still evolving, and many unknowns surround both the costs and benefits of electronic commerce. In this environment of uncertainty, it is imperative that business leaders establish e-commerce goals and objectives and that they measure the success of their e-commerce initiatives.

Electronic commerce must be measured. As mentioned in Chapter 3, however, the decision to begin an electronic commerce initiative may not always be driven by hard costs and benefits. And, even if hard benefits are identifiable, the e-commerce business model is still not mature, so organizations may have a difficult time making investment decisions. Historically, organizations have made IT funding decisions in isolation without really justifying them in business terms, other than through basic return on investment (ROI) calculations. Today, if an organization does not invest in e-commerce, it may go out of business. Still, some organizations may not exactly know how to quantitatively justify the project. A great deal of uncertainty surrounds questions of which metrics to use and how to apply them to electronic commerce initiatives.

WHAT CRITERIA MUST E-COMMERCE SOLUTIONS MEET?

To choose success criteria for an e-commerce project, you first should evaluate the markets in which your organization operates. The ability to derive incremental revenue, market share, and cost savings are important factors.

However, you must also evaluate your competitors. If your competitors have caused customers to expect Internet access to businesses in your industry, you may not have a choice about whether to invest in e-commerce. However, you can still measure the success of your investment if you've gathered and set the proper metrics and have an appropriate method of evaluating the project against those metrics.

Bruce Temkin, Research Director of Business E-Commerce at research analyst group Forrester Group says that organizations must learn how to make funding decisions for electronic commerce projects. Today, most organizations don't understand how to decide whether to invest in an e-commerce project because funding these projects is not like funding other IT projects. According to Temkin, organizations don't know how the business will look at the conclusion of the project, therefore knowing what ROI measures to set is difficult. Still, it's important to come up with some rationale, both quantitative and qualitative. It's also important to clearly define and manage expectations. A project can be technically successful, meet its financial objectives, and still be considered a failure if the customer is unhappy with the result.

Gathering Requirements

Much like other IT projects, the first step in determining success measurements for an electronic commerce project is to define the project's requirements and expectations. Gathering requirements is a process that most systems analysts have been through on numerous occasions. The key is that e-commerce project teams clearly define the requirements based on the expectations of senior management and end users. E-commerce technology is still a new experience for most managers and users. Gathering requirements for an e-commerce project involves interviewing organizational staff who are directly and indirectly affected by the new system.

Defining expectations

The management of expectations from highest to lowest level within an organization is a key element in managing the shift to e-commerce-based business processes. IT projects, whether initiated by business or IT staff, frequently evoke unrealistic expectations, both high and low. IT remains poorly understood by the majority of organization staff and has a reputation for big promises and small deliveries, so its projects are especially prone to the factor fear, uncertainty, and doubt (FUD). Clear and concise information must be provided regularly and frequently throughout the e-commerce initiative to ensure that expectations are realistic. Delivery should always be planned to be slightly better than that promised in terms of timing and cost. Almost nothing is technically impossible in the world of IT, but projects must always be justified to fit a solid business case.

The goal for electronic commerce projects is to select or develop that which is both beneficial and cost effective.

Gathering expectations early is critically important. Many organizations start their e-commerce initiatives without really clarifying their expectations for the project. This lack of clarity almost certainly dooms the project to failure. Unless the requirements and user expectations are defined ahead of time, the finished product cannot possibly meet those requirements and/or expectations. The e-commerce project team must know who the audience is, what it wants, and what the team can deliver. Some keys to a successful e-commerce initiative are the following:

- Communicating accurate project information on a timely basis
- Prioritizing goals and objectives
- Planning for success
- Competitive analysis
- Budgeting

You must also manage the expectations of your business partners as well as groups within the organization. E-commerce initiatives affect people outside the organization as well as within. Business partners must understand and agree with the goals and objectives of the project. They must buy in to the project because their support and cooperation is critical to any electronic commerce initiative. Feedback from customers may also be useful. If you are a business-to-consumer Web business, you're wise to consider your customers' expectations when you're beginning an electronic commerce initiative.

Because the technology is new, some staff members won't be able to clearly define their expectations. The project team, and analysts in particular, must lead the interviewee through the process of defining the requirements. The team should take into account the fact that information crosses departmental or functional boundaries. Some information that a user or manager needs comes from other parts of the organization, so the project team must talk with managers and users from many parts of the organization. When interviewing users and managers, the project team shouldn't focus solely on how to reduce costs rather than add value. The team needs to recognize the forces that are driving the organization to the Web. Cost may become a non-issue, particularly if an organization's competitors are the force behind the e-commerce project. Be sure that you and the team you assign understand the real forces driving the need for e-commerce before you start an e-commerce initiative.

Staff from the Minneapolis-based HomeSource, a home products and services provider, knew that they needed to carefully manage the expectations of their business partners, customers, and investors. HomeSource's information technology group worked with the board of directors and senior managers to ensure that they understood exactly what the e-commerce initiative would provide. The IT group created a set of the best practices based on other companies in similar industries. However, because HomeSource was the first e-commerce business of its kind, some questions arose about how they would communicate with their service providers. The HomeSource IT group worked with their business partners to develop a complete set of specifications so that all parties involved understood how their system worked.

E-Commerce requirements

The requirements-gathering process for Web-based commerce systems is somewhat different from that of other IT projects. Most system development methodologies, which are geared primarily to one customer, don't cope well with two diverse sets of requirements. In Web-based development, IT personnel must have the tools to combine and reconcile both sets of requirements, particularly if external requirements-identification techniques are used in a marketing environment (for example, a Web site for selling something). Further, as electronic commerce expands, a standard approach to Web-based development is needed.

STRUCTURED INTERVIEWING HELPS REQUIREMENTS GATHERING

Structured interviewing is generally thought of as a method of gathering information using specific techniques to elicit objective, measurable responses that can be diagrammed where appropriate. A structured interview contains questions presented in a systematic, highly precise manner. Its purpose is to enable the interviewer to obtain uniform data that can be reflected back to the interviewee, diagrammed, compared, summed, and, if it is quantitative, subjected to additional statistical analysis. The form of a structured interview, as well as the approach used, will vary according to how the information from the interview will be used. For example, a structured interview used for the requirements phase of a project will differ from the form used for design, testing, and so on.

The major reason that systems do not meet user expectations after development is the lack of requirements that are complete, accurate, and clear. A major difficulty facing the systems analyst in requirements identification is the lack of a technique that helps to elicit requirements accurately from the system user. Structured interviewing results in requirements

(continued)

Structured Interviewing Helps Requirements Gathering *continued*

that establish the foundation for essential business systems to be developed, enhanced, integrated, and implemented. Structured interviewing helps establish the foundation for gathering essential information that the organization requires. It also aids in generating enterprise-wide consensus for e-commerce initiative requirements. If the requirements are nailed down well, the e-commerce initiative has a better chance of providing realistic return-on-investment analysis for the expenditure.

The structured interviewing process involves five steps:

1. Plan the interview.

2. Perform the interview.

3. Analyze the information gathered, creating diagrams and narratives.

4. Walk through the materials created with the user.

5. Evaluate and improve the process.

The primary purpose of the interview planning process is to narrow the topic of the interview to a bite-sized chunk that can be covered in an hour or less, although some group interviews may be longer. Performing the structured interview requires the same skills as any other interviewing process. The key for the interviewer is to listen. The interviewer should stay with the user and not think ahead or try to suggest solutions. The analyst then analyzes the interview notes and sketches the diagrams in pencil. The analyst notes any missing steps or pieces and follows up with the user. When all pertinent information is known, the analyst creates the diagrams and narratives, paying attention to detail. The walkthrough is planned like the interview, with an agenda and an established time frame. The e-commerce team should avoid becoming defensive during the process and instead recognize that walkthroughs do not represent a personal critique of their work—they function only as a means of verifying information. Evaluating and continuously improving the structured interviewing process ensures that both the process and deliverable quality will improve, thus reducing errors, project times, and costs over time. In the continuous improvement process, business and IT professionals check communication problems to ensure that the process gets better over time. Continually improving structured interviewing skills over time eventually reduces project costs and increases project quality.

Deciding on the requirements for an e-commerce initiative means asking the right questions of the people who will be deciding the success of the project. Some important questions to ask include:

- What is your business mission?

- What are your business goals? (This may not be measurable.)

- What are your business objectives? (This must be measurable.)

- What factors do you believe are critical to the achievement of your goals? (See the later section, "Identifying Critical Success Factors.")

According to Temkin, many executives and senior managers have difficulty coming up with unambiguous answers to these questions. Temkin says that the more specific the question, the more likely you are to get a clear answer. Thus, he advocates asking questions such as:

- What are the objectives in terms of specific numbers for revenue, cost, market share, and so on?

- Which business units will be involved?

- What would happen if the initiative failed?

- How large is the scope of the project? Does it cover multiple business units and departments?

- Is it internal only or does it involve business partners as well?

- Which business partners are part of the project?

- What metrics, measurable objectives, or expectations do your business partners have for the e-commerce initiative?

Classifying the project in terms of the clarity of the project expectations is beneficial. The lower the level of clarity, the higher the risk of failure (see the section "Calculating and Managing Risk," later in this chapter). Expectation management is one of the most effective ways to prevent successful projects from being viewed as failures.

The competitive forces model

One way to look at the requirements from many sides is through the lens of Michael Porter's Competitive Forces model, depicted in Figure 4-1.

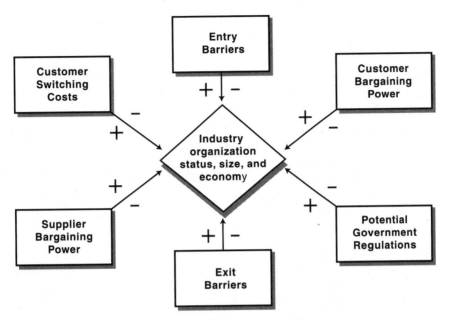

Figure 4-1. *Michael Porter's Competitive Forces model*

Porter's model contains five key competitive industry forces, plus government regulations that affect an industry, its status, size, and economy. Each force may exert a positive or negative effect on an organization. Those forces are as follows:

■ **Entry barriers** Obstacles that an organization faces when it attempts to enter an industry, or when it is creating and selling a new product or service. Entry barriers include financing, labor, and intellectual property patents.

■ **Exit barriers** Obstacles that an organization faces when it attempts to exit an industry or to stop production of a product or service. Exit barriers include contracts already in force, customer expectations, and government regulations.

■ **Customer bargaining power** The force that customers can exert on the organization because of their ability to either purchase from other organizations that sell the same product or service, or to simply go without the product or service.

■ **Supplier bargaining power** The force that an organization's suppliers can exert on the organization because of the scarcity of the product or service the supplier sells, the suppliers price, or the logistics involved with getting the product or service to the organization.

■   **Switching costs** Costs that customers or suppliers must incur when changing their business from one organization to another.

These five competitive industry forces plus government regulations affect each organization in different ways. However, the general theme of e-commerce initiatives should be to target these forces in a way that is beneficial to the organization. For example, an e-commerce initiative may enhance the organization's ability to increase market share quickly. This raises the entry barrier for other organizations that might want to enter the same market. An e-commerce initiative might reduce the cost of a product or service to a customer. This reduction increases the customer's switching costs (the cost of moving to and working with another organization), thereby reducing the customer's bargaining power.

Organizations also need to account for time when they're choosing e-commerce criteria, because this is a very dynamic business-operating environment, and the business model itself isn't settled yet. Because an e-commerce initiative may be driven by a competitor's actions, time is often a factor in an electronic commerce project. If the project can't be completed in a time frame that allows the organization to accrue competitive benefits, the return on investment may be less than anticipated. In this case, time to market for the project is critical. Entry barriers, government regulations, and the evolving nature of a specific industry can affect project timelines.

HomeSource used Porter's competitive forces model extensively when developing its IT strategy. Because the business was the first of its kind in its industry, staff members knew that they had to set the entry barriers as high as possible. They looked at e-commerce best practices and developed a set of specifications that would allow HomeSource to exchange data as quickly and accurately as possible with business partners. Because HomeSource cooperates so closely with its service providers to provide goods and services to customers, its suppliers typically don't exercise much power. HomeSource continues to increase its customer base, and as of this writing, HomeSource's technological strength had ensured that no other organizations had moved into its space.

Documenting and communicating requirements

After the requirements are defined, they must be clearly documented and communicated to all team members. Although many methods of documenting requirements exist, three basic pieces of information are necessary in any requirements documentation (see Table 4-1). A clear statement of the requirement itself is the first and most important. The next important piece of information conveys the driving force behind, or business justification for, the requirement. Finally, a statement of the consequence of failing to meet the requirement is needed.

TABLE 4-1. REQUIREMENTS SAMPLE

Requirement	*Business Case or Driving Force*	*Consequence of Failure*
Ease of communication with business partners	Need for business partner cooperation	Business with business partners may refuse to use system
Ease of communication with customers	Raising entry barriers, increasing customer loyalty	Lost market share to other organizations
Sophisticated reporting capabilities	Government regulations	Fines or other government-imposed penalties

These pieces of information must be communicated to all parties who are involved with the project. The requirements must also be frequently revisited so that project team members continue to use them as a guiding force over the course of the project. The original requirements for projects are often forgotten in the heat of crises and challenges that go along with most any project. Constantly revisiting the requirements keeps them in the back of each team member's mind, which helps team members to continue to target all the project activity aimed at meeting those requirements.

Translating Requirements into Success Measurements

Although some requirements aren't easily measurable at first blush, all the requirements must eventually be translated into some kind of measurable objectives. In some cases, a specific numeric goal may be associated with a requirement. For example, if the objective is to increase electronic commerce transactions by 20 percent, that objective can be measured fairly easily. In other cases, a requirement may be considered successful when it is completed. For example, a user may need the ability to cancel a transaction before transmitting it. This action is verifiable but does not have a specific numerical objective associated with it.

Other requirements may be hard to verify or quantify. User and business partner satisfaction with the system may be difficult to measure. The project review phase can help by utilizing satisfaction surveys that use seven-point Likert scales to measure customer satisfaction with the new system. In any case, translating requirements into some kind of success measurement is important for judging the success of the project. Surveys should be sent to both internal customers and business partners to check their satisfaction with the project results. Because financial calculations and customer service surveys may be required for a specific e-commerce initiative, the project evaluation/review phase can be quite lengthy.

One method of translating requirements into success measurements is to chunk work into milestones and deliverables by 60–90 day segments. Then, ask three questions at the end of each period:

1. Did you complete the deliverable?

2. Is the deliverable doing what you thought it would?

3. Is the impact what you expected? (This may or may not consist of a numeric measurement, depending on the metrics set.)

The metrics against which the requirements are measured must describe a future vision, which would itself be part of the measurement process. For example, if your goal was to shift customer inquiries from phone to Web, you might be to measure whether your customers and suppliers use the Web site more than they call you? Business partners and customers must also accept your solution and agree that it adds value to the flow of goods and services up and down the value chain. Business partners must be consulted early in the process to ensure their agreement to both the requirements and the metrics against which the requirements will be judged. One method of translating requirements into success measurements is to attempt to quantify each requirement. Table 4-2 provides an example of how requirements can be translated into quantifiable measurements.

TABLE 4-2. QUANTIFIED REQUIREMENTS AND MEASUREMENTS

Requirement	Measurement	Acceptable Range
E-commerce system must transmit complete, valid business transactionsness	Error rate between the organization and its business partners	Minimum 90% accuracy
E-commerce system must complete transmission of batch data in overnight batch window	Transactions/hour	Minimum of 100,000 transactions/hour in 8-hour batch window
Business partners must be satisfied with e-commerce system	7-point Likert scale-based satisfaction survey	Minimum of 85% overall satisfaction rating on survey

Even if competitive forces are driving the e-commerce initiative, quantifying the success of the project may still be possible. Market share, inventory turnover, and overall revenue are all ways of measuring an organization's competitive ability in its marketplace. Although quantifying requirements may often seem difficult, doing so will ultimately pay off because the project team will have a solid return on investment to show senior management and shareholders.

JUDGING SOLUTIONS

Judging the quality or viability of a specific solution or alternative involves estimating each solution's ability to meet the quantified requirements. Each of the quantified requirements must be analyzed for priority and impact. One requirement may be drilled down into several needs at a more detailed level, or may remain at a general level. Those needs are then prioritized with the help of the system's future users and its business partners. Each solution is then evaluated against the prioritized needs list.

Analyzing Needs

Analyzing and prioritizing the needs of an electronic commerce initiative is easy if the requirements are clearly defined. That is, the e-commerce project team understands the business requirements and the users understand at least the basics of the technology that will be used for the initiative. Of course, both sides must understand their own pieces, but the cross-understanding ensures that expectations will be met when the system is completed. According to the Forrester Group's Bruce Temkin, e-commerce projects are different from many IT projects because the business and technology are so tightly linked. Also, the effects of a project error or problem reach far beyond the walls of the organization. A significant failure or missed requirement can greatly affect the organization's relationship with both business partners and customers.

In determining the level of difficulty, impact, and priority of a specific requirement or need, the project team reviews present procedures and systems against the requirements and goals for a new system. The team must evaluate the organization's volume of data, number of users, reporting requirements, and current configurations to make the most sensible solution recommendation. The team must define the needs and develop and execute a well-considered plan to either upgrade or replace current software and hardware for the e-commerce initiative. The team can use its members' experience as a starting point and then build a unique requirements package based upon management focus and budget.

The management focus and budget will also dictate the prioritization of the system needs. Obviously, needs that are central to continuing operation of the organization and its business are top priority. However, some needs that have seemingly little financial impact may reach the top of the list because of competitive and market pressures, or because of customer or vendor requests.

The product requirements are divided into two types, functional and operational. The requirements can be further divided into such categories as "mandatory" and "nice to have," or perhaps categorized according to the degree of impact, such "high," "medium," and "low." The needs analysis typically results in a form resembling Table 4-3.

TABLE 4-3. SAMPLE NEEDS ANALYSIS

Requirement	Driving Force	Type	Impact	Severity of Non-Completion (1=Low, 5=High)
Accurate transmission of transaction data	Business partners, customers	Functional	High	5
Financial reporting completed	Government, auditors	Functional	High	5
System must have 99% uptime	Business partners, customers	Operational	High	5
Screen design must aesthetically pleasing	Customers, internal users	Functional	Moderate	3

Each organization will want to further refine the requirements in its own unique ways to reach the correct decisions concerning the project (see the section "Evaluating Solutions" that follows). In any e-commerce initiative, however, considering the impact on the following is important:

- System users

- Business partners

- Customers

- Government reporting requirements

- Operational ease of use

- Organization finances

- Organization industry position and market share

- Current technology configurations.

Each organization must determine how best to proceed while keeping in mind these and other factors. A comprehensive project plan and requirements definition is the only way to eliminate or at least greatly reduce the possibility of hidden or missed needs.

Evaluating Solutions

Judging the alternatives should include factoring in speed, risk, proof of concept (has this been done before?), which options meet strategic options (80 percent of goal with low risk is better than 90 percent with high risk), and others. When more than two alternatives exist, these alternatives need to be ranked. In instances when only two alternatives exist, a comparison analysis may not be necessary because the costs and benefits developed for the report are sufficient to make an informed assessment. If a comparison of alternatives is necessary, the report should highlight the respective benefits to provide management with an assessment of the alternatives.

If no numerical method of comparing alternatives is available, an organization can begin by listing each alternative in order of least cost or greatest savings, followed by the benefits the alternative provides. However, if the benefits are the more critical consideration in selecting the project, the benefits should be ranked and the associated costs should be shown in the column next to the benefits. When analyzing the alternatives, opportunity costs need to be compared. Although the largest investment may provide the greatest number of benefits, investment costs may be too great for the alternative to be accepted. Therefore, the alternative that normally maximizes benefits at the most reasonable investment is the most likely to be adopted.

The analysis and evaluation should be formally presented to management in a report that is complete but concise. One format that seems to work well contains a one-page executive summary of the process, followed by the details. The document should include the following sections at minimum:

- Executive Summary
- Need Statement
- Requirements
- Functional Evaluation
- Operational Evaluation
- Recommendation
- Management and Support Considerations
- Financial Analysis
- Financial Spreadsheet

The report may need to be edited for sensitive information before being shared with outside parties such as business partners, but they will eventually need to see it. Alternatively, a nondisclosure agreement may solve this problem. The financial analysis process is detailed in the section "Measuring a Solution's Success," later in this chapter.

The report should contain some kind of a one-page evaluation form that ranks the alternatives according to the quantified criteria. This form contains numerical rankings of each potential solution, and a point total that clearly delineates the winning approach. A discussion of the ranking can also follow, but the numbers themselves should be compelling enough to tell the full story.

DETERMINING DECISION-MAKING FACTORS

The two major categories of decision factors are critical success factors and risks. Identifying critical success factors means determining the resources required to ensure the success of the project. Identifying and managing risks is also an important part of any project, but is particularly important to e-commerce initiatives. Managing risk on an e-commerce initiative involves identifying potential failure points both inside and outside the organization. This process of identification can be particularly difficult, and depends heavily on the cooperation of business partners.

Identifying Critical Success Factors

Critical Success Factors (CSF) are determined by an organization, or teams within an organization, to define success, identify driving forces and needed resources, and determine direction. Ideally, CSFs are measurable characteristics, conditions, and variables that, when properly sustained and managed, have an impact on organizational success. If a CSF isn't measurable, it should at least be easily recognizable. For example, a critical level of funding is measurable. Management commitment may not be measurable, but it is easily recognized. E-commerce teams can adapt the concept to identify the characteristics, conditions, and variables critical for planning, developing, and maintaining successful electronic commerce practices, programs, and activities. The CSF process is useful for the following:

- Identifying e-commerce-specific elements, practices, structures, and requirements that are considered critical to the success of the program

- Focusing team members' attention on specific implementation issues

- Bringing to light issues that must be elevated to senior management

■ Identifying the potential impact of the e-commerce program or initiative on all employees

The major benefit of identifying CSFs early in the project is avoiding unpleasant surprises later in the project.

As mentioned in Chapter 1, it's important to cover all the pieces of any IT project, including hardware, software, people, data, and processes. In e-commerce initiatives, organizations must also consider competitor actions or reactions, customer actions or reactions, and vendor viability. Some typical critical success factors for e-commerce initiatives include:

■ Securing a buy-in from management and business partners

■ Establishing a realistic list of system expectations, including reasonable, accurate forecasts of capital needs based on complete project life-cycle cost analysis and a realistic list of benefits such as productivity increases, cost savings, or incremental revenues expected

■ Keeping development in the hands of the organizational staff and using consultants to provide expert advice and address specific development issues

■ Tailoring the system to the organization's business

■ Keeping all relevant organizational business areas and business partners informed and involved throughout the development and implementation of the system

■ Building on the strength of existing systems without duplicating effort

■ Training staff on available and new technologies to promote the transfer of knowledge and a smooth transition to the new systems and functions

Obviously, each organization's success factors will vary, based on their size, industry, and organizational culture. However, look at e-commerce initiatives at organizations that operate in a similar way is useful. Industry groups, conferences, and analyst group reports are all good sources of information concerning factors that are critical to the success of e-commerce initiatives.

Calculating and Managing Risk

Calculating and managing risk for an e-commerce initiative is a complex process. e-commerce teams must account for factors inside and outside the organization, some of which may be beyond the control of the team. Besides the risks or potential failure points on the project itself, it's also important to consider the risk involved with doing the project at all versus not doing the project (though these days, the latter is not truly an alternative).

Risk management alternatives

Thousands of books are available to be consulted on various types of risk management and calculation techniques. Each organization, however, must decide how to manage its own project risks based on the specific project and the organization's culture. Some common risk management techniques include:

- **Option theory** What are the costs and benefits of each option, and how do ROI calculations compare for each option? Can multiple options be used to hedge risks?

- **Opportunity cost management** What's the risk of *not* doing something? For example, if your competitor implements e-commerce initiatives and you don't, what happens as opposed to what's the hard ROI of the project?

- **Outsourcing vs. insourcing** What is the impact of using existing in-house resources, adding in-house resources, or hiring resources on a contract basis?

- **Managing human resource risks** How do you manage the reactions of your staff to the e-commerce initiative? Change management can help here.

- **Managing technology risks** Is the technology to be used proven or new? If the technology is proven, is it new to the organization's staff? Is management committed to providing the funding necessary for creating a solid technological infrastructure?

It's important to consider risks surrounding the main pieces of any IT project, such as hardware, software, data, procedures, and people. As mentioned in Chapter 3, "The E-Commerce Obstacle Course," many potential obstacles to a successful e-commerce initiative can arise. Some specific risk areas include:

- The adequacy and availability of infrastructure for the cost-effective use of electronic commerce

- Adoption of international standards relating to the transmission and content of electronic messages

- The adequacy and interoperability of software for electronic commerce messages

- The adequacy and competency of support from software suppliers

- The availability of cost-effective ways of transmitting electronic commerce messages to meet individual requirements (for example, the availability of reliable Internet and value-added network suppliers)

The introduction of effective facilities for linking current EDI systems with other forms of electronic commerce will go a long way to mitigating some of these risks because EDI is a fairly established form of e-commerce. For the time being, however, each organization must be well aware of the potential failure points and utilize effective strategies for countering the risks.

The risk management process

Risk management consists of identifying potential losses associated with the project, the uncertainty of the project's outcome, and the consequences of making various choices about the project. Three general activities related to risk management are the following:

1. Identification

2. Assessment

3. Management/mitigation

Three basic areas of risk can be identified on an e-commerce project. Project-related risks are related to the management of the project and include issues such as personnel, requirements, and complexity risks. Technical risks include system implementation and capacity issues. Business risks include market share losses, loss of competitive advantage, loss of trade secrets, and government regulatory issues.

Identifying the risks is half of the battle. The more risks that are identified early in the project, the fewer unpleasant surprises the project team encounters during implementation when it can least afford them.

After the risks are identified, they must be assessed and rated. Risks are rated based on how likely they are to occur, their severity, and the scope of their impact on the project. Estimating how likely a risk is to occur can be difficult. Consultants and other individuals or groups who have already been through the process can be valuable resources of information on how often potential failures actually occur on e-commerce projects. The severity of the impact is closely linked to the scope of the impact. A severe risk means wider impact (that is, affecting more parts of the project or organization) and higher costs to resolve the potential failure.

FAST FACT: TOP 10 E-COMMERCE FAILURE RISKS

1. The project has an unclear or ambiguous mission statement.

2. The project does not have a sponsor or clear business case that shows a clear payback for one or more units of the organization..

3. Project specifications and documentation are vague and not detailed enough.

4. The project is due to be delivered in one big chunk.

5. The project team does not have the experience necessary to do the project.

6. Some project team members are not committed to the project.

7. The project plan does not include time for holidays, vacations, or sick days.

8. The project plan includes no knowledge transfer plan for when consultants leave.

9. The project schedule was dictated by management without regard to the amount of work required.

10. Customer, business partner, and management expectations are completely unrealistic.

Source: Software Project Survival Guide, *www.construx.com/survivalguide*

The theme of risk management and mitigation is the idea that the best defense against failure is preparation. Contingency plans should be created early in the project and should be updated frequently as the project progresses. Good project management practices dictate that team members communicate the status of the project on a regular basis. The frequency of the communication should be based on the level of risk of the project. E-commerce project managers must continuously keep themselves informed of all activities on the project, even little ones. Frequently, problems that seem small when they first become visible snowball very quickly into disasters.

Evaluating the project status against the risk list at regular intervals is useful. Doing so can prevent risks and potential failure points from staying hidden until they become critical.

The staff of HomeSource knew they were venturing into uncharted territory. They also knew that the risk of failure was high because numerous service providers had to work together to enable HomeSource to provide good customer service. That's why they continually kept their business partners and senior management apprised of the project's progress as it moved toward completion. The risks identified early in the project were constantly revisited to determine whether the project was experiencing any of those risk factors. By carefully managing each step of the project, the IT managers were able to avoid the pitfalls they had identified. However, they did have a complete contingency plan and several alternative approaches to complete the project in case of failure.

MEASURING A SOLUTION'S SUCCESS

The best metrics balance customer needs, internal (operational), and financial issues, and continuous improvement goals. Customer-oriented metrics measure how the organization meets the needs of its customers compared to before the e-commerce initiative. Of course, a baseline measurement prior to the e-commerce initiative is needed to determine any true value. Operational metrics determine the impact on the organization and its ability to operate day-to-day. Financial metrics determine the value returned on the total cash investment of the e-commerce initiative. Continuous improvement programs are typically set up after the project and help the organization to continuously evaluate and improve the e-commerce system(s).

Deciding Which Measures to Use

The primary purpose of any set of measures is to determine whether each requirement was met. It's also important to balance the risk versus the reward for each measure. The quantified requirements list presented earlier in this chapter will be of great assistance in deciding on metrics to use. Some common e-commerce metrics include:

- Customer satisfaction
- Business partner satisfaction
- Number of new customers
- Customer attrition
- Product availability
- Cost of promoting products

- Profit margins
- Incremental revenue
- Cost of acquiring new customers
- Product distribution costs
- Inventory turns

Any measure used must be directly relevant to the purpose of the project. The e-commerce team, with the users, must determine the specific goals and objectives of the e-commerce initiative. The requirements and needs analysis are factored in here, and may dictate the measurements directly. However, there are "indicators" as well as critical success measurements. If the purpose of the project is to increase market share, then market share comprises one of the critical success measurements. Inventory turns becomes an indicator, but not the critical success measurement.

Measurements can also be weighted. In this case, market share may count twice as much as inventory turns. Weighting, however, sometimes complicates the measurement process. Debates can arise about which indicators should be weighted, and how much. It's important to keep the critical success measurements as simple and clear as possible.

Calculating ROI

Organizations can have a difficult time determining whether the money they've invested into an e-commerce effort is producing a positive return. The Internet has baffled many analysts because of its constantly changing nature. A Web site may impact an organization's marketing, distribution, manufacturing, customer service, and other areas. As mentioned in Chapter 3, many organizations mistakenly look only at online sales revenue for a justification of their presence on the Internet. Others have failed to have any consistent online marketing or customer service strategy and, consequently, may have a truly amazing slice of cyberspace that contributes little, if anything, to their objectives.

Costs

A number of costs can be associated with developing and maintaining a Web site. Forrester Research claims that corporations could, in the first year, spend as much as $300,000 for a purely promotional site and $3.4 million for a transactional site, that is, one that can conduct service or sales transactions with visitors. Another industry analyst, International Data Corp. (IDC), is more conservative with its estimate of $1.3 million for a transactional site. The fees paid to telecommunications companies and/or Internet service providers, as well as fees to design the site, contribute to these numbers.

Hardware costs include servers, clients, network devices, communication lines, and possibly satellite services. Software costs include everything from client operating systems to packaged e-commerce software solutions. Services include consulting, Web hosting, Internet access, domain name registration, and subscriber-based services. Interestingly enough, the largest cost associated with e-commerce initiatives is labor. Hardware and software prices are dropping while labor costs (such as salaries) skyrocket because of the IT staffing shortage. It's sometimes more cost effective to train current employees than to hire new ones.

Benefits

An e-commerce initiative can result in many and types of return, both financial (hard) and intangible (soft). The soft benefits are every bit as important as hard dollars. If your revenues are high but customer satisfaction is low, it's just a matter of time before revenues follow customers out the door. Some soft benefits that can be realized through e-commerce include:

- Improved customer relations

- Reduced or better used human resources

- Potential knowledge gathered via customer interaction with the Web site

- More accurate data for all business partners (this can be measured, but it's difficult)

A Web-based sales site may be to somewhat reduce order entry staff but may need more customer service staff to solve problems because of customer entry errors. Potential revenues may increase as a result of a reduction in lost demand because customers don't have to wait on hold. Also, more free advertising comes about because of accidental finds via Internet search engines. Resources used for order taking can be used elsewhere, including capital and redistributed human resources.

Many organizations use financial measures as the only measure of success for an e-commerce initiative. Finances only improve, however, if either costs decrease or revenues increase—and that follows the relationship between an organization and its business partners and customers. An important but often neglected focus is on customer-oriented benefits. Organizations must focus on improving customer relations by enhancing market insights, optimizing customer service, enabling quick reaction to changes in the market, and reducing the time-to-market for new products and services. Customer service can be improved through the use of the Web by allowing the organization to provide answers to their customers 24/7. This is true of both business-to-consumer and business-to-business e-commerce systems.

By receiving customer and even vendor feedback more often, an organization can increase its ability to anticipate all of its business partners' needs. Organizations can obtain current information about customers and improve their ability to communicate the customers' needs within the organization. Many organizations also find that they create the ability to access customer data more quickly than in older decision support systems because they can use middleware to move data from operational systems to data warehouses in real time. By capturing large amounts of data in a data warehouse, organizations can provide more intelligent and timely responses to customer inquiries.

Doing the numbers

Despite the numerous soft benefits, most senior management teams want to know the bang for their e-commerce buck. Basic ROI calculations depend on the economic life of the investment, which is the span of time in which the inflow of economic benefits exceeds the feasible alternatives. Because of the pace of change of technology, one can assume that the hardware will be replaced after five years. Software upgrades are released by most software companies regularly, so one can assume that the software will be upgraded after two years, which is typical of system software upgrades; the upgrade does not, however, cause a radical change in the computing environment. The salvage value for both hardware and software amounts to nothing at the end of their economic life. Quantifiable benefits include:

- Product and process improvements
- Better insight into planning and controlling the organization
- Cost reduction/avoidance
- Enhanced revenue/competitive edge (measured by market share)

All these items must be factored into the ROI mechanism chosen. Costs and benefits (cost savings) are major considerations in determining the merits of the initiative. The decision does not depend entirely on the benefit-cost ratio of the initiative because nonmonetary (intangible) benefits should also be given consideration. However, the net costs of a system are an important factor to consider. Costs and cost savings alone do not provide an accurate evaluation of a single project or a basis for selecting among projects; they fail to account for the time value of money. The costs and cost savings of any project occur at different points in time. E-commerce projects typically incur large costs early on without any cost savings until the very end. Management must have a basis for comparing these different net cost savings and for evaluating costs incurred now against benefits achieved later.

In developing this basis for comparison, an organization must take into account the time value of money. In making any decision about when to spend money, management usually has some preference. If managers have a strong preference to spend the money now, then they may proceed with the project even though less money is available. A weak preference toward spending in a specific operating period (such as a fiscal quarter) implies that more will be at hand money to spend when the investment is finally made. Evaluation of future costs and cost savings of a project is more meaningful if all future dollar amounts are converted to a current dollar equivalent. Management can then compare investment options, accounting for both the magnitude and timing of the costs and cost savings for each option.

If a net present value (NVP) approach is taken, present value focuses on cash flows and therefore eliminates depreciation. The five-year projection of average savings of operating costs, which are related to the investment, implies that each year, the same dollar amount will be saved. This influences the net present value of the cash flow and therefore affects the ROI. The expected payback period varies for each organization and the specific e-commerce initiative.

Two popular measures in use today are economic value added (EVA) and total shareholder return (TSR). EVA is the spread that the operation earns over its cost of capital multiplied by the amount of capital invested. Its advantage over other calculations is that it relates directly to stock valuation. The present value of all future EVA likely to be generated by an organization plus the value of its invested capital is equal to its intrinsic value. In some cases, the intrinsic value and stock price (for publicly held companies) are linked. If an organization is privately held, an internal valuation must be calculated to determine whether EVA is indicating positive or negative results. TSR also works best with publicly held companies, though internal valuations can be calculated for privately held concerns. TSR basically measures the actual return on a shareholder's dollars. So, if a shareholder invests $1 today and receives $2 tomorrow, TSR = 100%.

These are both long-term measures, and won't be evident for quite a while after the e-commerce initiative is complete. Some cost savings may be more evident more quickly. Labor savings is one metric that may appear fairly quickly. Reduced duplication of effort and less time spent correcting mistakes are benefits that can become clear immediately after implementation. Faster access to information may result in productivity increases. Even if head count is reduced, productivity increases occur where additional output can be achieved with the same level of effort. Sales may go up as well, but they count only if those sales are incremental (that is, not sales that switched from phone to Web). Overall, ROI for e-commerce is a wait-and-see process.

To calculate ROI, HomeSource used TSR. Internal stock had been issued and each employee knew how many shares he or she had. So, all the employees involved in the start-up had a very personal stake in the project. The project was designed to reduce the amount of labor required to complete each transaction to an absolute minimum. In addition, the system had to operate 24 hours a day, seven days a week, with very large amounts of data. HomeSource calculated its return on investment by dividing net income by the total number shares. In some cases, determining which customers were recruited by the Web site versus which customers saw radio and TV ads and called the 800 number was difficult. To compensate, HomeSource asked customers how they heard of HomeSource.

WRAP UP

- **Organizations must clearly define their ROI expectations.** It's extremely important to define and quantify requirements, and if possible, expectations, and doing so clarifies success measurements.

- **Organizations in general, and electronic commerce project teams in particular, must be very thorough in the requirements gathering process to determine what's important to the organization.** Requirements and project needs must be prioritized based on management's focus and budget.

- **It's important for electronic commerce project teams to generate multiple, measurable alternatives.** Potential alternative solutions should be compared on an equal, numerical basis.

- **Critical success factors (CSFs) define those forces or resources that must be present to ensure the project's success.** CSFs are identified by examining critical resource needs, and planning contingencies in case those resources aren't available.

- **Managing project risk involves identifying, assessing, and mitigating potential risks.** Risks should be detailed thoroughly before the project begins to avoid unpleasant surprises later in the project. Managing and mitigating risks over the life of a project requires experience and vigilance from all team members.

■ **Only success measures that are directly related to the project's requirements and expectations should be used to evaluate the project.** It's easy for organizations to use political agendas to measure project successes. By identifying and getting agreement on what determines project success early, electronic commerce teams will have a better chance of being recognized as successful on their projects. ROI mechanisms must be chosen that reflect project requirements and expectations.

■ **In some cases, it may be difficult to determine whether the e-commerce initiative is producing incremental revenue.** Unless sales from Web sites and brick-and-mortar are separated early, organizations will have difficulty recognizing whether the Web site is having a measurable impact. It's important to create some kind of identification process for Web-based sales.

Taking Stock

1. How well are the requirements for your organization's e-commerce initiative defined?

2. Are critical success factors identified? Are they concrete and easily understood?

3. Are management expectations realistic?

4. Are the expectations quantified?

5. Are the success measurements relevant and realistic?

6. Have all relevant risks been identified?

7. Have the project team members done an e-commerce project before? If not, have you hired qualified consultants?

8. Is a contingency plan in place or being created?

9. Have appropriate ROI metrics been established? When does ROI measurement begin?

10. Have all stakeholders been identified? Have each of them "bought in" to the project?

ACTION PLAN

❑   Check the project requirements to make sure that they can be easily and accurately measured.

❑   Make sure the priorities assigned to the requirements reflect the organization's needs and goals.

❑   Check the CSFs to see whether the necessary resources can realistically be available when they're needed.

❑   Create a contingency plan in case of failure.

❑   Share your ROI calculations with your business partners.

❑   Meet with all senior management and business partners to clarify their expectations of the e-commerce initiative.

❑   Test calculate the ROI for the project. Do the numbers make sense?

❑   Check your expectations of the e-commerce initiative again. Are they realistic?

Part II

E-Commerce Business Solutions

Chapter 5

E-Commerce Building Blocks

E-commerce technology consists of computing devices connected over various types of communication lines and networks using software to communicate and to process business transactions. Decision makers need at least a basic understanding of e-commerce technology to help them make informed e-commerce decisions.

To manage e-commerce initiatives, you need to understand at least the fundamentals of e-commerce technology. Chapter 1 of this book presents a simple technical architecture for business-to-business e-commerce initiatives (see Figure 1-1). Yet, even in this simple architecture, many pieces of hardware and software, both inside and outside the organization, need to work together to enable business-to-business and business-to-consumer exchanges of transaction data. To extend an organization's digital nervous system beyond its own walls, an organization must first link all of its own systems together and ensure stable, accurate data- and transaction-processing capabilities.

HARDWARE BASICS

Various combinations of computer hardware can work together to make electronic commerce happen. However, most e-commerce–oriented hardware performs one or more of the following four tasks:

1. Store data

2. Process data

3. Communicate/transmit data

4. Route data (some routing devices might also transmit data)

Generally, servers store and process data. Routers, bridges, gateways, hubs, and switches communicate and/or route data. An organization can purchase this hardware and house it on site. Alternatively, Internet service providers (ISPs) and Web hosting providers (WHPs) provide organizations with the hardware and software to perform all four tasks remotely with minimal hardware and software required at the organization's physical site.

Serving Up the Web: Web Servers

A Web server is a computer that provides Web services for other computers connected to it via a network. A Web server runs software that tells it how to deliver, or serve up, Web pages when they are requested by other computers. Sometimes the term *Web server* encompasses hardware, software, computer operating system (OS), network operating system (NOS), and Web site content. If the Web server is used for internal purposes only, it's called an *intranet server*. A Web server offers various services, including:

- Authentication (a security measure intended to validate a user or transaction)

- Transmission of Web pages or data

- Processing of data or Web pages (depending on which programs run on the Web server)

Figure 5-1 shows a simple Web server exchange: a Web server sends documents to your computer when you request them over the Internet. This process is initiated when you click a link or type in an Internet address, or Uniform Resource Locator (URL). Your PC then transmits that request to the Web server that corresponds to the link or URL you entered (for example, *http:// microsoft.com*). The Web server then uses the URL to find the requested information on its hard drive or other storage device, assuming the URL specifies more than just the name of the server (for example, *http://microsoft.com/business*) and transmits it back to your PC.

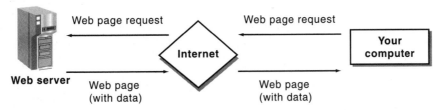

Figure 5-1. *A Web page request process*

A Web server is solely devoted to serving documents that are requested by *clients* (computers that request services from the Web server). The client computer receives the document, which contains content and formatting information, and then interprets this information and renders the document on its screen. This operating model reduces the amount of work performed by the server in order to maximize efficiency and accommodate several clients simultaneously.

Web servers use large amounts of memory and hard drive space, and they require high processor speeds. In some cases, they require multiple processors to provide the throughput necessary to keep busy sites running. (This use of multiple processors is called *parallel processing*.) Designing the proper system for an Internet server can be difficult because usage on the Internet is expanding at an exponential rate. This level of usage demands servers with higher levels of scalability, performance, and availability. Such platforms must be fault tolerant and have high reliability. Good Web servers incorporate additional features, including:

■ Redundant hard drives

■ Multiple processors

■ Redundant power supplies

■ Self-monitoring and self-correcting hardware and software

■ Temperature monitors and other Internet survival gear

The combination of these components helps ensure that a single-component failure will not cause the system to lock up or shut down. The goal is to make the system as reliable as possible in order to keep information flowing on demand.

Processing Transactions: Transaction Servers

A transaction server's basic duty is to process business transactions according to the business rules established by an organization. A transaction server has traditionally processed business transactions for internal users. However, transaction servers are now required to handle both internal and external requests. Many organizations now have separate, highly secured transaction servers to handle Web-based transactions because of transaction volume and security concerns. A Web transaction server receives requests from, and sends information to, the Web server as required. A Web server functions this way for both business-to-business and business-to-consumer business transactions.

A transaction is an activity or request. Orders, purchases, data changes, additions, and deletions are typical business transactions. Transactions update one or more files or databases and serve as both an audit trail and history for future analyses. Transaction volume is a major concern in configuring transaction server sizes and speeds, and transaction servers in general must be powerful computers to handle what are typically high processing needs. Figure 5-2 shows how a transaction server completes a transaction.

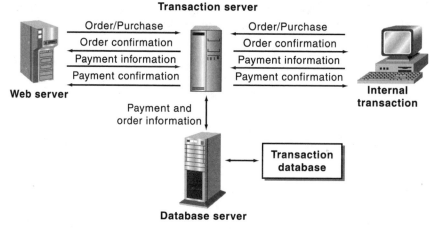

Figure 5-2. *The transaction process*

The transaction server doesn't care whether the transaction process originates via a Web server or within an organization. In Figure 5.2, an order or purchase request is sent to the transaction server either via the Web (and Web server) or through an internal network (for example, an incoming telemarketing salesperson). The transaction server checks for sufficient inventory, pricing, and so on, and sends an order confirmation. The transaction server also sends a request for payment. The customer or salesperson enters the payment information and the transaction server confirms that the payment was received and validated.

The transaction server communicates with the database server (discussed in the next section) to add, delete, and modify orders. The transaction server may need to add a customer if the customer is new, or change customer details if the customer has moved or changed his or her payment options. The transaction server runs the programs that tell the database server how to handle the data. The database server fulfills the transaction server's requests for information and updates the database with customer, order, and payment information sent by the transaction server.

The transaction server may need to communicate with an organization's business partners to validate payments if the payment is made via credit card. If the organization ships directly from its suppliers (called *drop shipping*), the transaction server may also need to check with business partners to see whether sufficient inventory is available to fulfill an order and to check current pricing. As e-commerce expands, this type of verification will become more common, and transaction servers will become less often owned by one particular organization or department and more frequently owned by an entire supply or value chain.

Maintaining the Data: Database Servers

A database server is a computer in a network dedicated to database storage and retrieval. The database server is a key component in a Web environment. It holds the database management system (DBMS) and the data. As shown in Figure 5-3, requests from clients (which may be other servers) trigger the database server to search the database for selected records and pass them back over the network. The database server also controls the updates of the database. In a Web environment, database servers must be able to serve many clients simultaneously. Web sites in the business-to-consumer market may receive thousands of hits each hour. The database server must be able to serve the transactions fast enough to provide good response time to users.

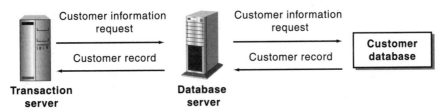

Figure 5-3. *A database server process*

In a simple exchange, the transaction server asks the database server for customer information. The database server provides the customer record based on the search criteria set by the transaction server. That data is passed back to the transaction server, which then passes it on to the Web server or to the client PC. A database server may also have preset routines that it runs to keep data clean and accurate. Such routines are called *stored procedures.* Stored procedures are usually run when a trigger is activated. A *trigger* is a mechanism that initiates an action when an event occurs. Events can include reaching a certain time or date or receiving a particular input value. A trigger causes a database routine to be executed, which updates the database.

Network Communications

The core of electronic commerce is the ability to communicate over both internal networks and the Internet. Various communication devices enable people to exchange information between computers. Internal communication devices may link one computer to another computer, or they might link computers to database, transaction, or Web servers. Some communication devices also provide security capabilities, as in the case of a router's access lists. These devices can be hooked together, or they can work independently to move data over internal and external networks.

A network is composed of a group of computers. A network may be as simple as two computers linked with communications circuits or as complex as a worldwide system with thousands of terminals, fiber optics cables, satellite links, and more (such as the Internet). There are two basic types of networks: local area networks (LANs) and wide area networks (WANs). LANs typically consist of clients and servers within an organization or within a department in a large organization. Several local area networks may be hooked together to form a WAN as shown in Figure 5-4. The Internet is actually a global WAN that consists of many large, linked WANs.

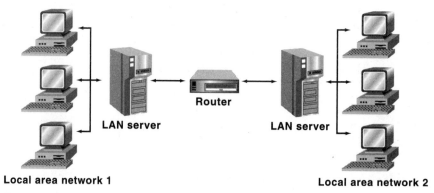

Figure 5-4. *Two LANs connected to form a WAN*

In a LAN, stand-alone computers are integrated into networks where they share access to the resources of other computers. In the LAN environment, each computer can share secondary storage and input and output devices on the system. Each machine is also equipped with communication facilities and specialized software and programs that enable network operation and provide security and access controls.

If only two devices (such as a client and a server) are to be tied together using a single communications link, then only a simple network architecture or design is required. Most communications networks are not simple, point-to-point networks. WANs involve dozens or even hundreds of devices connected to one or more communication links. Early network architectures had a central computer to control switching, contention between competing devices, and message timing. However, using a computer just to handle traffic flow added cost and complexity and often slowed down the system.

Routers

A router is a device that forwards *data packets* (units of information) from one network to another (as depicted in Figure 5-4). Based on routing tables (lists of addresses, permissions, and so on) and routing protocols, routers read the network address in each transmission and make a decision on how to send it based on the most expedient route (determined by traffic load, line costs, speed, bad lines). Routers are used to segment networks to balance and filter traffic for security purposes and policy management. Routers are also used at the edge of the network to connect remote offices. Routers can only route a message that is transmitted by a routable protocol such as that of the Internet (IP=Internet Protocol). Because routers have to inspect the network address in the protocol, they actually process data and thus add overhead.

Most routers are specialized computers that are optimized for communications. However, router functions can also be implemented by adding routing software to a file server. Some operating systems, such as Windows 2000, include routing software. The operating system can route from one network to another if each is connected to its own network adapter, or network interface card (NIC), in the server. Routers form an integral part of a corporation's digital nervous system, connecting the networks in an enterprise to the Web and the Internet, as depicted in Figure 1-1 in Chapter 1. This architecture strings several routers together via a high-speed network topology.

Bridges

Bridge is a rather old name for a device that connects two LAN segments together, which may be of similar or dissimilar types, such as Ethernet and Token Ring. A bridge was originally used to regenerate or boost network signals on large networks. A bridge is inserted into a network to segment it and to keep traffic contained within the segments to improve performance. Bridges actually build and maintain address tables of the nodes on the network. By monitoring which station acknowledges receipt of an address, bridges keep track of which nodes belong to which segments.

A bridge must be connected to two (or more) networks. It takes data from one network, holds it temporarily, and then re-transmits it to the second network. It forwards the data in this way only when the data frame needs to travel across the second network in order to reach its intended destination. A bridge is often used to go between token ring and Ethernet or other networks that use different technologies. Bridges can be slow and can cause big problems with data transmission if they are used improperly.

Hubs

A *hub* (see Figure 5-5) is a single-threaded communication device. That means that only one device at a time can use the wires in the hub. It's a central connecting device in a network that joins devices together in a star configuration. *Passive hubs* are simply pass-through units that add nothing to the data as it's transmitted, and they do not require power because they are simply connections. *Active hubs* regenerate the data bits in order to maintain a strong signal, and require power to do so. Some newer hubs are intelligent, modular, and customizable. This allows for the insertion of bridging, routing, and switching modules within the unit. A hub may even possess a CPU and network operating system, which means that the hub becomes a file server or type of network control processor that performs complex function as networks grow.

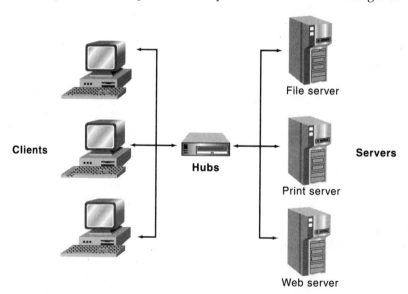

Figure 5-5. *Hub connecting multiple devices on a network*

The hub acts as a connector for multiple devices on a single network and manages the flow of information from computer to computer. This network of devices includes clients, various types of servers, and other devices such as printers and fax machines.

Switches

A *switch* is a multithreaded hub that forwards data packets between different computers based on some type of lookup table that contains data handling and forwarding instructions. The function of a switch is similar to that of a router. In effect, a switch is a traffic cop that determines which packets are allowed to pass between different users on different ports. A switch can typically provide a nonblocking service, meaning that traffic can pass between different pairs of source/destination sites without impacting other user traffic. A switch allows multiple user connections to occur simultaneously.

The functionality is very similar to a bridge or a router, in that all three devices provide a means to filter and forward data packets between users on a network. Additionally, like a bridge, all ports connected to a switch are considered part of the same physical network. Switches can be thought of as multiport bridges. Most switches are complementary to routers, with both devices working as a team. Plus, there is a trend toward sophisticated software functionality for switches. A switch can host multiple logical networks among groups of physical networks, thereby enabling several LANs to be associated with a single physical router and saving money on hardware while maintaining good security and other access control.

Gateways

A *gateway* is more a concept than it is a specific piece of hardware. A gateway connects a network to other networks. Various devices can function as a gateway, including routers, switches, and hubs. A modem can also be a gateway if the modem is connected to a network server, and multiple computers are connected to that server as well.

A gateway is essentially a computer that performs communication tasks between different types of networks or applications. A gateway may be internal or external to the organization. For example, a gateway can connect an IBM-compatible PC network to an AppleTalk network within an organization. Gateways convert one network protocol (or language) to another during data transmission. Sometimes routers can implement gateway functions. An electronic mail, or messaging, gateway converts messages between two different messaging protocols.

DSL SERVICE SPEEDS UP INTERNET ACCESS

Digital Subscriber Line (DSL) technology has begun to revolutionize consumers' access to the Internet by making high-speed Internet access a reality. With this broader bandwidth capability becoming increasingly available at costs only moderately higher than dial-up accounts, organizations are becoming able to provide more complex content with higher-quality results. DSL can make streaming audio and video, online browsing, software downloads, and online financial transactions happen faster and more seamlessly than with standard dial-up Internet connections.

DSL technology uses standard copper phone lines to send a digital signal between two points. But because telephones use low frequency transmissions and computers use very high frequency (VHF) transmissions, the telephone line can be effectively divided into high- and low-frequency delivery channels. Because the computer signal stays digital, DSL allows a much faster data connection than traditional dial-up access even though DSL goes through the public switched telephone network. DSL connection speeds vary, but in general, DSL allows computers to connect to the Internet at a minimum of 256 Kbps downstream (when data is received). This is about 9 times the speed of a 28.8K modem! Upstream DSL speeds (when data is sent), begin at about 64 Kbps.

Depending on an organization's needs, DSL might even be viable as an entry-level broadband e-commerce technology. With DSL, organizations don't necessarily need to lease dedicated, high-speed access lines to get high-speed service. DSL Internet hookups allow fast speeds over ordinary phone lines, saving significant monthly dollars. To check for availability of DSL service in your area, you might begin with your local telephone company.

SOFTWARE BASICS

Each piece of hardware in an electronic commerce configuration requires software to run it. Server software runs a server much the same as an operating system runs a PC. Web servers, transaction servers, and security devices all require software. Web server software allows the Web server to communicate with both internal computer resources and the Internet. Transaction-processing software processes both business-to-business and business-to-consumer transactions. Security software prevents unauthorized access to computing resources.

Web Server Software

Selecting server software for a high-quality Web business can be a daunting task. Many options exist in the areas of operating systems, applications, communications, and administration. The goal is to provide a fully functional Web server capable of offering enhanced features and capabilities to clients. The selection of the software must be tailored to the needs, vision, and budget of the enterprise. The purpose of a Web server is to provide information through a well-defined access mechanism. The Web server allows clients to request information and serves up the pages as requested (as shown earlier in this chapter in Figure 5-1).

Serving documents involves more than just sending files over a network connection. The presentation of the information and the interpretation of hypertext markup language (HTML—the language used to create Web documents) are left completely to the client. The server controls the storage and retrieval of documents and their transfer. The Web server is also responsible for providing encryption and authentication, and often allows for integrating dynamic documents. A Web server together with a browser program (that is, client) constitutes a client-server system.

Web server software is the key piece in a Web business architecture. Web server software today ranges from a very streamlined and simple feature set available for free on the Internet to a robust, feature-rich application from major software vendors, costing up to hundreds of thousands dollars. The Web server has communication software that allows it to communicate over the Internet. Because the administrative functions of the Web server software are of paramount importance in ensuring the smooth operation and maintenance of Web business service, it must be simple to configure, administer, and manage on a daily basis.

The most important consideration in the area of Web server management is performance. A very active Web site may receive hundreds of thousands of hits per day, so the number of users who can access the system simultaneously becomes a factor in the selection of high-performance Web server software. The server software should provide performance measurement tools and utilities to enable the system administrator to monitor the system, gather statistics, and provide information about usage trends to management. Good Web server software has load-control capabilities, which enables the software to better utilize the system resources to provide a higher quality of service for anyone accessing the site.

Processing Web-Based Transactions

As described earlier, transaction server is the application program that actually processes the information request, order/purchase, or other business transaction.

If the transaction server is multithreaded, it usually allocates a thread for each client. A good alternative to multithreaded transaction servers is to use a set of single-threaded processes, all of which are running the same program. This is often called a server class. The system dispatches the calls to the server class to a particular server process. The system usually also balances the load across the servers in the server class.

Transaction server software processes transactions as they are received over the Web, as shown previously in Figure 5-2. Also called *online* or *real-time* systems, transaction servers update master files and databases as soon as transactions are received over communications lines. They also send confirmations to the sender. Organizations increasingly rely on computers to keep everything up-to-date all the time. Transaction processing is often called *online transaction processing*, or OLTP. If a business depends on computers for its day-to-day operations, the computers must stay up and running during business hours.

Web transactions are usually processed using the Secure Electronic Transaction (SET) industry standard. This transaction-processing facility can be used to provide a secure transport mechanism between customer, merchant, and bank, without the merchant receiving sensitive information such as the customer's credit card information. Third-party payment providers provide custom solutions to support SET for an organization's business partners and banks. With digitally secured transactions, organizations can provide better service and support to consumers and business partners.

Browsers

A *browser* is the software that acts as an interface between the user and the Web (both internal and external). It is a client-side program that communicates with a Web server using formalized protocols that provide access to various types of information. It can be text-based or graphical, though almost all browsers are graphical now. The browser acts as an interface between the user and the information stored on Web servers connected by the Internet. Browsers are also referred to as Web clients because in the client/server model, the browser functions as the client program. The browser contacts a Web server and sends a request for information or for Web pages. It then receives the information, usually in the form of a page, and displays it on the user's computer.

A graphical browser, such as Microsoft Internet Explorer, allows users to view images on their computer, point-and-click with a mouse to select hypertext links, and use drop-down menus and toolbar buttons to navigate and access resources on the Internet. Users may also access the World Wide Web, and multiple media including hypertext, photographs, sound, video, and so on that can be fully experienced only through a graphical browser. Browsers often include plug-ins, which are software programs that are needed to display images, hear sounds or run animation sequences. Java, ActiveX, and RealAudio/Video are examples of such programs. The browser runs these applications when a user selects a link to a resource that requires them.

Browsers are also fast becoming the preferred interface for transaction-processing systems accessed through the Web. Organizations are using browsers such as Microsoft's Internet Explorer to access legacy systems and Enterprise Resource Planning (ERP) software to provide a standardized interface for both internal and external customers. A browser makes operating software easier because a single interface appears for all packages. This reduces learning times and increases ease of use. For business-to-business electronic commerce, an organization can use a browser to provide a well-known, standard interface for business partners to use when accessing the organization's systems over the Web. Software vendors such as SAP and Oracle are using browser-based interfaces for their applications.

Security

Security consistently ranks as the primary concern of both business-to-business and business-to-consumer electronic commerce. Several types of security features are available for electronic commerce. Some security measures involve software whereas others involve a combination of hardware and software. The secure sockets layer (SSL) is the leading security protocol for electronic commerce. With SSL, the browser sends its public key to the server so that the server can securely send a secret key to the browser. The browser and server exchange data via secret key encryption. SSL is a fairly secure data transmission method.

A *firewall* is a security concept that can be implemented in several ways and at several points along a network as shown in Figure 5-6. It can be implemented in a router that filters out unwanted packets using an access list, or it may use a combination of technologies in a computer. Firewalls are used to separate a company's public Web server from its intranet. They are also used to keep internal network segments secure, as in the case of national security research labs. A packet filter runs on a router and blocks traffic based on an address. A proxy server acts as a relay between two networks, breaking the connection between the two. If a firewall is implemented as a standalone device, it usually runs on its own computer, because if it gets hacked, an organization wouldn't want any other data or programs easily available to the hacker. An organization's public Web server is outside the firewall, but intranet servers and all internal computing resources are inside the firewall. A Web server can also have security features such as authentication or login scripts.

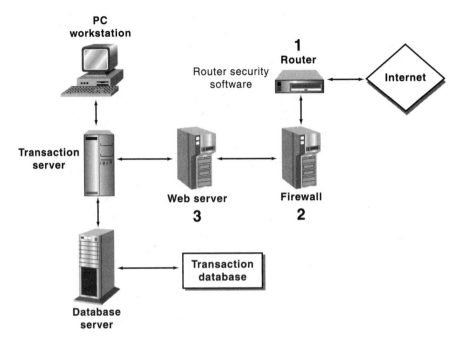

Figure 5-6. *Three-point security*

EXTERNAL SERVICE PROVIDERS

Various types of external service providers are available to organizations considering electronic commerce sites. Internet service providers (ISPs) offer simple, easy access to the Internet. Web hosting providers offer access and also provide organizations with the ability to store their e-commerce Web sites on the service providers' server. Application service providers host applications such as ERP software packages that can be accessed via the Web. Organizations must balance the need for control with the cost when considering these options.

Internet Service Providers

Internet service providers, or ISPs, provide access to the Internet via either telephone landlines or dedicated leased lines. ISPs handle administrative tasks such as obtaining and managing Internet addresses, maintaining connections to regional, national, and international Internet hubs, and routing and managing traffic. ISPs hook into regional telephone companies (telcos), which themselves link into major backbones that traverse the U.S., connecting major metropolitan areas. A national backbone connects major telcos to each other, and international lines and satellite hookups provide worldwide access.

Internet service providers offer organizations that do not wish to manage their own Internet access a valuable service. Good ISPs offer reliable Internet access, administrative services, blocking of objectionable content, and usage of monitoring reports. These services allow organizations to concentrate on their own areas of competence without worrying about the technical details of Internet access. Some telephone companies offer similar access services, although the organization must then manage its own Internet devices.

Web Hosting Providers

Some ISPs offer Web-hosting services. These services allow organizations to place the Web sites on the service provider's Internet server. The service provider manages the content and the directory structure. The organization is responsible only for creating and maintaining the content. Most Web hosting services process your application to the InterNIC (one of several organizations that allow you to register domain names) and manage the address. Most Web hosting Web sites are backed up daily, and they usually have servers housed in an environmentally sound and secure environment.

Larger companies also have systems protected with an uninterruptible power supply that is backed up by an on-site power generator. Web hosting services often have a sophisticated network architecture that is supported by redundant communication lines providing optimal connectivity. They offer reports such as Web site access statistics showing hits to your pages. They may also offer programming services such as server-side programs for dynamic Web pages and password-protected areas of your site. They usually offer various levels of traffic per month and a pre-allocated amount of Web disk space. Service providers that host e-commerce sites may also provide shopping cart software, real-time credit card processing, SSL Server, and even RealAudio and RealVideo servers for multimedia business-to-consumer Web sites.

Application Server Providers

An Application Server Provider (ASP) is an organization that hosts software applications on its own servers within its own facilities. Customers access the application via private lines or the Internet. They are also called commercial service providers. ASPs are similar to the service bureaus of old, such as ADP, which began by processing payroll for many organizations. ASPs host or run various types of software at their site so that organizations do not have to buy the hardware needed to run the application. Organizations can save significant amounts of money by simply using the hardware and software that the application service provider already owns. However, the organization loses control of the application and is dependent on the application service provider for system reliability and maintenance services.

Some software companies do not allow ASPs to host their software. Software companies lose the revenue associated with each license that would have been sold to individual customers. Historically, it has not been viewed as being in a software company's interest to work with an ASP, although some companies are now doing just that in order to reduce their after-sale support requirements. An ASP might face significant licensing issues that require the permission of the software company. An organization could potentially find itself in the middle of a battle between the ASP and the software company. This conflict could cause significant problems for the organization's day-to-day operations.

INTERFACES AND INTEGRATION: LEVERAGING EXISTING SYSTEMS

As mentioned in Chapter 3, companies must learn to use their existing systems with newer Web-based e-commerce systems. Legacy and ERP systems must both be accessible via the Web. Some organizations build client-server-based Web systems to allow Web access to older legacy systems. Writing interfaces for ERP software is also very difficult. Building these interfaces can take a great deal of time and money. However, the effort is necessary if business partners are to share their information with each other in an automated supply chain.

Bringing Legacy Systems to the Web

Legacy systems are truly the backbones of most organizations. These systems have been built over a long period of time and contain historical data that is very important to organizations. Even if an organization has an ERP system in place, the legacy system still contains valuable information that must be made accessible through the Web. Client-server and Web-based software tools, such as Microsoft's open database connectivity (ODBC) software, are available that allow organizations to link their Web server systems with backend legacy databases.

When interfaces to the legacy system are required, organizations must take into account the expected life of the legacy system, particularly if systems are likely to be replaced. Interfacing with legacy systems includes converting data from the existing systems for use on the Web. Editing programs are required to support programmatic or manual cleansing of data. The organization must understand that their business partners may not want to access data the same way that the legacy system has it organized. Flexible access interfaces must be built to make the legacy data easy to use.

Organizations are likely to face many issues when bringing legacy data to the Web. Encountering the problem of missing, obsolete, and just generally dirty data is a common experience among organizations just getting started in Web-based development. (Data is considered dirty if it has inconsistencies or errors within it.) One Web developer at a large direct mail company found that the Web-to-legacy interface project took nearly four times as long as originally anticipated because the data in the legacy systems was of such low quality. Business partners and customers may want to view the data in ways never envisioned by the organization. In such a case, the data may need to be reorganized or the organization may have to provide a significant toolset that business partners and customers can use to find the information they need.

Interfacing with ERP Systems

Most ERP vendors have announced that they will put their existing client/server applications on the Web by providing a Web interface to them. Others have new applications that are specifically built as Web-enabled. An application built for the Web must consider the technology. The software must be easy to use and must support security models and existing business processes within the company. The organization must also consider deployment issues such as training and support and deal with other issues as detailed in Chapter 3.

Some new ERP products allow business customers to directly place orders and access related information in a secure, reliable way from a single vendor. Other products allow business partners to improve their relationships by providing ad hoc access to information and self-service ordering transactions. Organizations must account for a trading partner's preferences for transaction processing and seamlessly link all information repositories across the supply chain. Oracle's ERP application suite is built to the standards in Oracle's Network Computing Architecture. It was built specifically for Web access and provides support for real-world transaction processing, scalability, integration with existing applications, and a secure shopping experience for the business-to-consumer market.

SAP is also Web-enabling its applications. R/3 Internet Application Components link the Internet to business processes. For example, after business partners fill a virtual shopping basket with articles, they can then request an individual quotation. They can also check whether all the items are available and when they can be delivered. All this information is available from the operative R/3 System via an interface to the R/3 database. R/3's other modules can receive transactions over the Web as well.

BUILDING AN E-COMMERCE PROGRAM

Successfully completing an e-commerce initiative requires organizations to rethink their approach to developing information technology (IT) systems. In traditional systems development, organizations simply developed their systems in accordance with the requirements specified by organizational staff. Now they must work with external parties as well. Building an IT infrastructure to meet e-commerce challenges also involves looking outward to Internet hardware and software standards. And the process of constructing an e-commerce system is different with regard to programming, testing, and implementation.

The Web-Based Approach to Building Information Systems

When organizations move from IT development processes that look strictly at internal requirements to a process that has to account for business partners and customers, an organization has to adopt a much more collaborative approach. It can't just work in an isolated fashion. Most current system development methodologies look at only one set of requirements. In a Web-based environment, the organization must reconcile internal requirements with those of their business partners and customers.

The design of the new system must also account for the needs of business partners and customers. Design specifications should be reviewed by as many people as is reasonable to ensure that the new specifications meet the requirements of all involved. Getting multiple parties to agree to the requirements and the design specifications can be a time-consuming process. Organizations must build time into project plans for collaborative activities. Systems analysts must recognize requirements that have an impact on people beyond the walls of the organization. Project managers must develop project plans that include activities for testing and implementation across organizations.

Building and Integrating the Infrastructure

Building an electronic commerce infrastructure also requires collaborative activities and planning. Organizations and other business partners must agree to the hardware, software, and data transmission standards they will use to process transactions. An organization's business partners must be kept current on the configuration and status of the organization's IT infrastructure. In the business-to-consumer market, organizations must make decisions regarding content management tools, how often to update content, and what kind of security to use.

Organizations also face unique technical challenges when building an electronic commerce infrastructure. Processor, storage, and bandwidth capacity must often be added quickly to meet steep Web site activity growth curves. Reliability is also a major issue. Organizations must decide whether to host their own Web site and content, use an Internet service provider, or use a Web hosting provider. Obviously, security is a major issue as well. Organizations must decide how to implement security, where to implement security, and the policy they will use to enforce security. Hardware and software upgrades must be planned around the activity of the Web site. In some cases, notifying concerned parties may be necessary months ahead of time when doing upgrades.

The Construction Process

The process of constructing and testing sites and electronic commerce initiatives is different from traditional systems development. Besides the collaborative nature of electronic commerce initiatives, a tremendous number of potential failure points exist in an electronic commerce system. Multiple computers, complex transmission lines, and dozens of pieces of software must all work together to make electronic commerce happen. E-commerce developers must have an in-depth understanding of all of the pieces of technology. E-commerce project teams must work closely together to ensure that nothing is missed when building these systems.

Testing these systems is just as complicated as developing them. All the various failure points must be tested individually and as a group before the system can be placed into production. Business partners and, in some cases, customers must also be involved the testing process. Multiple test cycles will likely be necessary to ensure that the system is functioning properly. Business partners must also test equipment to make sure that all processing and communication points work seamlessly. Customers may need to be involved in usability studies to ensure that Web sites are easy to use and accomplish their stated goal.

WRAP UP

■ **A Web server returns information in the form of Web pages when client software issues page requests.** A Web server may consistent of both hardware and software, including a network operating system and Web site content. If a Web server is used internally only, it is known as an intranet server.

■   **A transaction server processes business transactions sent to it by the Web server.** The transaction server accesses the database through the database server. Business transactions include purchase orders, inventory accounting activity, and order entry activity. These transactions are used to update the database in real-time.

■   **The Internet is composed of many interconnected networks.** These networks are connected over various types of communication lines, typically supplied by telephone companies. Routers, switches, gateways, hubs, and bridges are examples of communication devices that are used to transmit data over the Internet via communication lines.

■   **A browser is the software that acts as an interface between the user and the World Wide Web.** A browser resides on a client PC and accesses the World Wide Web via Internet technology. Graphical browsers allow users to point and click their way around the World Wide Web.

■   **Firewalls, routers, and SSL software provide security for Internet-based business.** Firewalls may be combinations of both hardware and software, which are designed to prevent unauthorized penetration of the system. Public Web servers are usually outside the firewall, where as internal transaction processing systems are usually inside the firewall.

■   **External service providers offer Internet access, content hosting, and application hosting.** Internet service providers (ISPs) help individuals and organizations obtain Web addresses, create Internet content, and set up Web servers. Application and content hosting organizations allow individuals and businesses to outsource their business processing and Web content access and hosting functions.

■   **Electronic commerce initiatives require that Web interfaces be built between Web servers and back-end legacy and Enterprise Resource Planning (ERP) systems.** Organizations must be able to link all of their systems and make them accessible via the Web. Many interfaces must be built to allow customers and business partners to access data on internal systems from their browsers.

■   **Successfully completing an electronic commerce initiative means that all organizational staff must think in a collaborative nature and recognize that e-commerce project team members will exist outside the organization's walls.** Information technology teams have traditionally worked only within an organization and its business functions. E-commerce projects require that

IT teams work with customers and business partners in the supply chain to automate business functions both within and beyond an organization's walls.

Taking Stock

1.   Are your legacy and ERP systems Web enabled?

2.   Do you have multiple layers of security for your electronic commerce initiatives?

3.   Are you collaborating with your business partners and customers on the requirements of your electronic commerce initiatives?

4.   Does your IT staff think in a collaborative or isolationist manner?

5.   Does your IT staff have the technical depth and breadth to undertake and successfully complete an electronic commerce initiative?

6.   Is your communication infrastructure stable and reliable? Is there some kind of back up in case of a failure?

7.   Are you using a formal systems development methodology and can it handle Web-based projects?

ACTION PLAN

❏   Get your IT staff certified as Internet professionals via Web sites such as *www.gocertify.com.*

❏   Set up team-building meetings between your organization's IT staff and your business partners.

❏   Check your communication infrastructure to make sure that there are at least two paths for every electronic commerce transaction.

❏   Web-enable your legacy and ERP systems.

❏   Have your organization's system architect draw a complete, graphical diagram of your organization's electronic commerce infrastructure and post it on a wall where it is visible.

❏   Share that diagram with your business partners.

❏   If you don't already have one, consider purchasing a Web-ready systems development methodology.

Chapter 6

E-Commerce Site Essentials

To maintain good relationships with business partners and customers, organizations must create Web sites that download fast; present useful, timely, information; are easy to use; and look good. To help make this happen, decision makers should understand the basics of successful Web-site design.

Successful Web sites are designed for the purposes they serve. A business-to-business Web site should be designed differently from a business-to-consumer Web site. However, many Web sites are missing sales in both the business-to-business and business-to-consumer channels every day because they are poorly designed. In many cases, users get frustrated by waiting for big graphics to download, become confused with the navigational structure, or simply are put off because of poor presentation. The most frequently cited complaints are long download times, difficulty of use, and obsolete content. Some general design principles exist that all Web sites should utilize. How those principles are applied depends on the purpose of the Web site. Usability is key, and Web designers must keep user needs at the top of the design priority list.

YOUR OPENING LINE: THE HOME PAGE

Your home page is the first impression you make on your Web visitors. Whether your market is business-to-business or business-to-consumer, you should strive to present visitors with a visually appealing, easy-to-use page that gives them access to the information they need quickly.

Some Web sites use the three-deep rule: Visitors should never be more than three clicks away from what they want. Indices on the side of a page act as a table of contents that can be broken down into various levels of detail so that users can read your Web site like a book. Microsoft's home page offers content organized in a number of ways, including by type of visitor. Its home page allows visitors to see pages customized for business users, developers, home users, and others. This mass customization feature is useful for preventing visitors from having to wade through content they don't need.

All Web sites should have certain basic elements regardless of the type of visitors expected. These elements are generally accepted Web design standards, and this chapter discusses each element in some detail. These elements include:

- "What's New?" section
- Site search engine
- Site map
- Feedback and comment forms to survey visitors
- Security and privacy information
- Links to business partners

Other elements are important. An appealing color scheme, compelling graphics, up-to-date content, and clear navigation elements will help ensure that visitors find your site useful and worth coming back to. Web sites for business-to-business transactions on extranets face some unique challenges. Extranets provide a path for an organization's business partners into the organization's systems. Real-time inventory updates, customer service and problem resolution, order status, and other business information must be kept current to make business-to-business e-commerce sites worthwhile.

The Sprint PCS Web site provides help for both first-time users and regular customers. Besides offering the company's latest promotions, the home page offers links to an online brochure that includes products and service plans divided into home and business use. You can also shop, purchase Sprint PCS phones and accessories, and sign up for a service plan online. Current customers can access their accounts to get information about their service plans and account usage (for example, used and remaining time). Sprint follows the three-deep rule, and access to relevant information is easy.

What's New?

The rapid growth of the Internet has radically altered user expectations of their online experiences. Increasingly, when people visit Web sites, they expect new content, often even if they visit multiple times in a day. As a result, organizations must keep their content fresh and current to keep visitors coming back. The staff at Bivings Woodell, a Washington, D.C.-based Web-design firm, must often help clients understand that image management on the Web is as critical as managing the brick-and-mortar image of a physical location. Organizations constantly update their hard assets to keep pace with trends, yet their Web sites might languish for months with old, obsolete content.

According to Matthew Benson, Senior Director and Chief Information Architect, and Jake Levine, Production Director, both of Bivings Woodell, an effective e-commerce site always has a lot happening, just like a regular business. New products, new pricing specials, new customer service features, and background information are all important to visitors. Users want to know about these updates and they're not going to stumble across them unless your home page points them out. A good home page is like a newsletter that's updated at least weekly, daily, or even more often, depending on the volume of traffic to your site and the average frequency with which a typical user visits. The blurbs or stories in your newsletter can range from one or two simple words or phrases to several paragraphs that highlight, advertise, and promote the most important new site developments that deserve the most attention from your visitors.

WHAT'S NEW? ON SOME OF THE BEST WEB PAGES

■ TradeMatrix offers information about its newest business partners, solution providers, and site features.

■ The Meta Group has its "What's New?" section front and center. It provides blurbs on the latest research and reports, as well as new job opportunities.

■ The Giga Group's GigaFlash is a newsletter updated weekly, keeping the content fresh. It contains press releases, blurbs on research, and other news of the day.

(continued)

What's New? On Some of the Best Web Pages *continued*

- General Mills keeps its Web site current with news about its products, career opportunities, financial information, and press releases.

- Chemdex provides information on the latest site features, products offered for sale, and updated information on solutions for business partners.

- Yahoo! has a section devoted to the latest world news, new features, and product and service promotions. Yahoo!'s finance and stock page is updated in real time with the latest financial news.

- Amazon.com's hot book list is updated hourly. It also features various promotions that change daily.

- Monsanto's Web site not only features the latest news on the company but also presents information related to its industry and consumers.

- Chase Manhattan Bank and others include current price quotes for their stock.

- Wal-Mart Stores provides information on new products, seasonal promotions, and community-related human-interest stories.

Home page space is the most valuable real estate on your site. Use it to good effect by designing multiple, individual spaces for text and small images that can be changed and updated quickly. Filling the entire page with a single, large chunk of text or giant image will get old fast and be difficult to update as new site features and content become available. According to Bivings Woodell's Benson, the objective is to increase user satisfaction by reducing the number of clicks users need to make to get to the information or functions they're most interested in. Rather than offering a "What's New?" button, for example, why not list what's new in a few short blurbs right on the home page. Every click saved means time saved for the user, and saving time makes Web users happy.

Benson says that managing a well-designed home page in a way that provides frequent "What's New?" updates is actually easier than some might think. The real work is in creating the new content or the new features on the back end. With a little planning, merely reflecting those changes on the home page is a snap. Your organization must provide people with strong reasons for using your Web site. You must provide users with fresh current content and an easy way to find the products, services, and information they want. Your challenge is to compel your customers to visit your site.

Web Site Search Engines

No matter how effectively you promote new content and new features on your home page, there will always (you hope!) be more content on your site than users can reference and access directly from the home page. That's where a search engine comes in. According to Benson, a search engine is one of the most difficult functions to set up properly, but it also is the one that pays the biggest returns in user satisfaction and repeat visits. If users know they can find what they're looking for on a site, they come back. If they get pointed to dead ends or have to spend time wading through lengthy indexes or shoddy search results, they don't. It's often that simple.

Numerous off-the-shelf search engines can be installed on your site. You can use the same basic search engines as large portal sites like Excite, AltaVista, and HotBot, or you can use smaller, specialized search engine packages offered by dozens of smaller Web-development firms. Each has its own quirks and special characteristics, and each offers advantages and disadvantages compared to the others. (See the sidebar that follows, "Finding the Right Search Engine for Your Site," to help you make the best choice.)

A good search engine will return results that are closely relevant to the terms or topics the user is searching for. But it's also important that the search results be formatted in a way that the user can pick up clues about the pages that are returned as hits without actually clicking through to them. The results should include:

- Web page title
- Site address
- A brief summary of the page
- Percent accuracy
- Last update date

All these items are available through most common search engines. Engines such as Excite, Lycos, and others have licensing agreements wherein an organization can use the engine on its Web site. Contact the particular search engine's maker for more information.

FINDING THE RIGHT SEARCH ENGINE FOR YOUR SITE

Literally hundreds of search engines are available for you to use within your Web site. The issue is finding the one that your visitors (both business and consumers) will use and like. Ease of use and accuracy are critical; speed is secondary though important. Here is a list of some of the better-known search engines and a brief description.

- HotBot is one of the many services of HotWired. It will conduct your highly specific Web search for you. You can search for just audio or video files or general Web sites, depending on your need.

- Lycos is a companion search engine of HotBot and offers similar features, though it has a slightly different search algorithm.

- AltaVista is one of the easiest search engines to use. It offers both simple and complex, Boolean operator searches. The interface is intuitive, though the accuracy is not always as good as it should be.

- InfoSeek is a solid general search engine. InfoSeek searches by word association, so you're likely to always obtain a result. The syntax requires the user to learn a specific set of symbols, which may be somewhat cumbersome.

- Yahoo! is one of the better-known search sites on the Web. It offers a simple, easy-to-use search syntax, as well as advanced searches. (It's worth noting that Yahoo! is different from the other search sites listed here in that a Yahoo! search is limited to the pages listed in the Yahoo! directory of Web sites. However, the Yahoo! directory is quite expansive. It might usefully be likened to a free, Web-based yellow pages directtory. It's also worth noting that you should be sure that *your* Web site is listed in the Yahoo! directory.)

- Excite is similar to other search engines and offers similar features. One interesting feature is Excite's ability to search by topic or category.

Each organization must evaluate its own needs and let that evaluation drive the choice of search engine. You should keep the likely visitor in mind and tailor your choice of search engines to the needs and characteristics of the visitor.

The most important feature of any search engine is ease of use. Some search engines require users to have knowledge of how to use such symbols as + or − signs or to understand the different functions of single and double quotation marks. Make sure that your search engine supports simple, natural English commands. Users quickly become frustrated with bad search results and will abandon your Web site if they can't find what they want. Having a search engine tested by nontechnical users before you put the engine up on your site for public use can be helpful. Remember that the purpose of your site is to offer products and services and to provide information. Make it easy for visitors to find what they want.

Web Site Maps

Web sites should be easy to navigate. Visitors should not get lost looking for information or wonder how to access various sections of your site. The use of a site map is a great way to prevent this. A site map is a graphical or text-based tool that portrays the information on the site and allows visitors to click on and be connected to their areas of interest within a site. A site map depicts the hierarchical structure of the pages in your Web site. Graphical site maps provide visual clues to content as well as a short description. The downside to image maps is that they tend to be fairly large graphics and are slow to load, whereas text-based site maps load and display much quicker.

Experienced Web users who are therefore more familiar with conventional directory structures and the architecture of a typical Web site often find a site map even more useful than a search engine. A site map outlines on a single page all the content on a site and where it can be found in relation to other pages. A site map can be as simple as a text-only index or outline, just like the topic outline exercises you probably had to do in elementary school. Or a site map can be graphically based, like a road map or a subway map that visually displays the routes to get from point A to point B.

Bivings Woodell advises clients to create site maps that contain the elements of both a simple text outline and the visual cues that correspond with graphical elements and navigation tools that exist throughout the site. Frequently, e-commerce sites and other complex sites allow visitors to access content, features, and functions in many different ways and from many different entry points. A site map shouldn't try to represent all these different access routes because that would merely confuse matters. A site map should reflect the underlying structure of the site's true directories. Different pages may be accessible from many different places, but they all have a true, permanent location within the scheme of the larger site.

Omaha, Nebraska-based food manufacturer ConAgra's site map is static, which means it is created manually, posted to the site like any other page, and loads quickly. Static site maps tend to become obsolete faster than those generated from the site itself. Still, ConAgra's site map is easy to use and features useful descriptions of site contents. Book publisher IDG's Web site map is generated and documents are drawn and presented from a database. IDG's site map link is at the top of their page, which makes it easy to find, even though the text is rather small. IDG's site map is organized logically, though not by product or service. The listing of career opportunities near the top of the map reflects a priority for the organization. Site maps are good ways of guiding visitors to the areas you want them to see.

Finding Out What Visitors Think

The Internet is an interactive medium. Good e-commerce sites take advantage of this two-way street by making it easy for users to offer feedback and ask questions and for users to see results and obtain answers. Including a robust mechanism for gathering comments, questions, and feedback is a must. A successfully designed Web site comment form can provide an organization with invaluable suggestions and guidance from visitors.

To meet your customers' needs, you must fully understand them. What do your customers need and want? What aspects of your site do visitors like and dislike? What features would set your site apart and create extra customer loyalty? Don't assume that you know the answers. One of the best ways to obtain this information is to ask visitors. Create a prioritized list of things you want to know. Narrow the list to 10 or 15 specific questions that are important to your organization. If you have one specific question that is especially important to your organization, the best time to ask is when taking or confirming a customer's order. One question can be easily worked into the process, and the feedback can then route to the appropriate staff.

Try to think in terms of all the points of contact you have with visitors and what information you can unobtrusively obtain from them at each point. A survey is an effective tool for gathering information and can be used at several points on a Web site. Post-order is one point in time when visitors might be interested in discussing their experience. One drawback to a post-order survey, however, is that it filters out those whose input may be the least flattering but also the most valuable—those who bailed out early and never consummated a sale.

For support questions answered via the Web, a follow-up e-mail survey the day after a purchase can obtain feedback as well as catch any potential customer service problems before they result in a dissatisfied customer.

TOP 10 TIPS FOR FEEDBACK MECHANISMS

Dr. Kathryne A. Newton, Associate Professor at Purdue University, offers the following ten tips for designing online customer care surveys:

1. Make sure that survey items target the organization's major concerns and business objectives.

2. Ask for feedback only about elements that you would be willing to change. Nothing turns off visitors like seeing their feedback ignored.

3. Customize surveys to a particular type of visitor if possible.

4. Know your audience (that is, demographics, purchasing habits).

5. Put the survey deep enough into the Web site that a casual visitor wouldn't see it but a significant user would. Doing so helps raise validity, though it lowers response rates.

6. Make sure the survey isn't too long so that visitors don't grow bored and either quit or select middle or "no opinion" ratings that don't tell you anything.

7. Pilot test the survey in a controlled environment to check for potential misunderstandings and wording errors.

8. Consider using open-ended questions to avoid leading visitors to a specific conclusion.

9. If you perceive that visitors will not take time for "essay" questions, make objective questions as targeted as possible without being leading.

10. Offer rewards such as discounts on future purchases for filling out the survey.

The point is to follow the same best practices with Web surveys as you would with paper, telephone, or e-mail surveys. Valid comments are important, and these tips should help you avoid the noise.

Bivings Woodell creates feedback mechanisms that range in complexity. Feedback mechanisms can be as simple as a mail-to link, which is a clickable e-mail address that relies on the user's e-mail program to open a new messaging window and is pre-addressed to the site owner or Webmaster. More sophisticated feedback mechanisms include interactive Java applets that establish an interactive communications pipe between users and the site. Regardless of the specific mechanism chosen, making sure that users receive confirmation that their messages are appreciated is always important. Automated acknowledgement can be delivered immediately. A complete answer to a question or response to feedback should be delivered as soon as possible, certainly within 24–48 hours. The Internet operates in real time. If you don't move quickly enough, it's likely a competitor will.

The Hewlett Packard (HP) Web site provides a multilevel drill-down appropriate feedback forms. Because of the large number of divisions within the company, HP carefully directs its site visitors to the right place for assistance and feedback. IBM's comment form is found through a "Contact" link, which is another popular way of directing people to the right spot. IBM's comment and feedback form is fairly complete and the company's response time is typically less than 24 hours. Procter and Gamble provides a "FAQ" (Frequently Asked Questions) link near its feedback and comment form. This link helps answer questions and may prevent some visitors from having to wait on answers to questions already asked by other visitors.

Providing Security and Privacy Information

Both business partners and consumers are extremely concerned about security and privacy on the Internet. The potential for losses due to security breakdowns during large business-to-business transactions can seem enormous, though such losses are in fact very unlikely, as stated in Chapter 3. And the potential for abuse of individual and corporate privacy is a concern to many. With these issues in mind, it is recommended that on your site, you clearly and conspicuously state the security capabilities of your Web site, its transaction-processing capabilities, and the policies you use to enforce security and ensure privacy. Your security statement should discuss your approach to the protection and encryption of data transmitted during a business transaction on your site. Your privacy statement should discuss what information you gather on your site and how your organization uses the information acquired.

Security

Be honest about your security capabilities. Exaggerating your ability to prevent cyber crime will eventually catch up with you and you will lose the trust of your customers and business partners. Along these same lines, be sure to clearly define processes and procedures for changing and adding security information to your Web site. Also, continuously monitor and update policies and capabilities. Continually increasing and refining your security policies and capabilities will provide reassurance to site visitors. A common process used to create and control security policies includes the following steps:

1. Identify what you are trying to protect.

2. Determine what/who you are trying to protect it from.

3. Determine the likelihood of the threats.

4. Implement measures that will protect your assets in a cost-effective manner.

5. Review the process continuously and make improvements each time a weakness is found.

The real key to this process is Step 5. New threats such as viruses are created every day; new employees are hired every day. Your policies and capabilities must continue to evolve and improve. Ongoing risk analysis involves determining what you need to protect, what you need to protect it from, and how to protect it. It is a continuous process of examining all your risks and then ranking those risks by level of severity. This process involves making cost-effective decisions on what you want to protect, which will change as the organization changes over time. One of the most important reasons for creating a computer security policy is to ensure that efforts spent on security yield cost-effective benefits. Although this goal may seem obvious, it is possible to be misled about where the effort is needed. As an example, intruders on computers systems generate a great of publicity, yet most surveys of computer security show that the actual loss from insiders is much greater for most organizations.

According to William Boni of PricewaterhouseCoopers, providing information that is accurate is important both for customer service and legal reasons. Boni believes that it's a good idea to have lawyers involved in creating the language, particularly if your markets will span state or national borders. In addition, make sure that you adhere to your own policies. Numerous instances exist of organizations completely disregarding the policies they enforce concerning their customers and business partners. Because so much of electronic commerce depends on trust, your organization should adhere to tight, well-controlled security policies.

Most organizations that do business online offer specifics for their Web sites. The Amazon.com Safe Shopping Guarantee states that Amazon.com will protect you while you shop at its site so that you never have to worry about credit card safety. Amazon guarantees that every transaction at Amazon.com is 100% safe. This guarantee means that customers pay nothing if unauthorized charges are made to credit cards as a result of shopping at Amazon.com. Like most organizations, Amazon uses secure sockets layer (SSL) technology to protect electronic commerce transactions. This technology encrypts all personal information, including credit card number, name, and address so that the information cannot be read as the information travels over the Internet.

Posting the details of the Fair Credit Billing Act on your organization's site is useful. This act states that a bank cannot hold you liable for more than $50.00 of fraudulent charges. Amazon, however, takes this policy a step further and states that if a customer's bank does hold the customer liable for as much $50.00,

Amazon.com will cover that entire liability. Amazon.com will cover this liability only if the unauthorized use of a credit card resulted through no fault of the customer from purchases made at Amazon.com while using the secure server. Amazon's policy is one of the best-worded ones and provides information as well as reassurance for customers.

Privacy

Many organizations are understandably nervous about tracking and recording data that might be deemed private. Visitor observation tools track where Web surfers have been, who they are, their preferences and demographics, and sometimes even security-related data such as passwords. Both business and consumer visitors are becoming wary of sharing personal or organizational information over which they have no control. Advances in technology are making it increasingly easy to gather information without users even knowing about it. New computers are being built with the ability to transmit personal registration information that's captured when a user first turns on a computer. The computer may register the home or business user via the Internet with the hardware and software vendor. Some content management tools can read this information from the visitor's computer, which may upset the visitor and subject the organization to legal action.

Most legal experts strongly suggest that you post a privacy statement that clearly states your policies on gathering and using user information. These policies should undergo legal review, and you should enforce your own policies throughout your organization.

Links to Business Partners

Cooperation is a major element in the success of an electronic commerce initiative. Organizations should help their business partners continue to grow and prosper, because doing so will help the organization grow and prosper as well. Providing links to your business partners on your Web site is one way of directing business to them. These links also provide your customers with the resources they need to do business. Besides, even if the content you provide on your own site is complete and accurate, your business partners may well have something to add regarding the topic, product, or service.

Benson believes that linking to business partners provides many opportunities. If your site does a good job of directing users to supplemental resources by providing well-selected links to them, visitors will quickly learn to appreciate the effort and will show their satisfaction in the form of repeat visits and word-of-mouth endorsement. Providing a list of links related to your own site's content is a good place to start. The most effective link lists or indexes, however, also provide a short, two- or three-sentence description or review of what users can find at the link and why you've included it on your list. Also consider setting aside a separate section of your home page to list business partners. They will thank you and your customers will, too. Microsoft provides an entire section devoted to its partners and offers links that help visitors find service, resale, and consultant partners.

TIPS FOR BUSINESS PARTNER LINKS

1. Make sure your business partners know you're linking to them.

2. Be sure to get links to your Web site from your business partners.

3. Update the link targets frequently; obsolete links are lame and unprofessional.

4. Put topical links where they're relevant (for example, links to business partners in press releases).

5. Put general links in a section marked "Partners," or something similar.

Remember that you need to assess what your visitors are looking for and determine the best way to help them find it.

Bivings Woodell typically advises clients to offer business partner links not only as a compilation on a single Web page but also as individual links, provided wherever appropriate throughout you're an organization's site. If you are offering for sale a product that has been favorably reviewed in a consumer or trade publication, for example, you may want to offer a link to that review from the page where your own site lists the product specifications. Offering links in joint press releases with your business partners also is useful. You can link to the press release if it is stored online (and these days, it should be!). For example, Yahoo!'s finance and stock quote pages offer links to organization Web sites in the press releases they put online.

Remember that links are like currency on the Web: they can be traded and exchanged. If you are the owner of a well-trafficked Web site and you refer a portion of that traffic to someone else's Web site via a prominent link, you are creating real value for that other Web site. It is perfectly reasonable to request or even insist that the other Web site owner provide the same value to you in return by creating a link from his or her site back to yours. You should be generous in offering links to other, quality sites on the Web that your audience would find interesting. Links can be a way of increasing cooperation between business partners. Whatever you give will come back to you eventually, one way or another, whether in the form of higher scores in search engines, more reciprocal links from other Web sites, or better customer satisfaction.

SHOW SOME STYLE!

Style and design elements are extremely important and deserve extra attention during the development and management of your Web site. The Web is, after all, a visual medium. Style and design elements should always be judged by the answer to one simple question: Do they facilitate or impede visitors' efforts to navigate through and use the site? Design elements that rely on more advanced browser capabilities or greater bandwidth capacities, such as Java applets or video clips, will act as roadblocks for visitors who don't upgrade their browser every six months or those who use a slow modem connection. In short, less is more in Web design. Some general standards to use for designing Web sites, particularly concerning usability and aesthetics, are described in the following sections.

Graphics

Graphics portray the image of your organization and provide visual information about your product or service. However, overdoing the use of graphics always does more harm than good. Remember that the majority of your customers will be using 28.8 Kbps modems, or at least will not be connecting at the full-rated speed of the faster modems. If consumers leave your site because they grow tired of waiting, it doesn't matter how nice your graphics look. Internet access capabilities vary from user to user, whether customer or business. If you are a business-to-business Web site and cater to small businesses, access will likely take place via dial-up lines (although ADSL is growing quickly). Optimize your Web site's performance for your audience so users can move quickly and efficiently.

Large images take time to load. Try to limit the use of large images to only the necessary logos and product images. If you must display large product images, do so on a separate screen at the user's request. Icons usually load quickly but may take longer if loaded from a database. Animation should be used sparingly because animated images generally take too long to load. On a business Web site, animated images are usually not necessary. Also, you need to be sure to update controls and displays such as hyperlinks and icons to avoid broken links and obsolete images that don't reflect current content. Operational controls (buttons, gifs, drop-down lists, edit fields) that are loaded from databases may also take more time than users like to spend, so use these sparingly.

Navigation

Users should be able to move around your Web site easily. Provide users with meaningful menu labels. Don't use image maps that require users to wait for them to download. Use a consistent menu structure that does not change from page to page. Don't make users rely on browser-dependent navigational controls (for example, the Back button). If your site is large, provide users with a site map or index. Buttons and icons are useful, but only if the images they portray are intuitively obvious. Navigation aids should also be visible without scrolling. If you put a button below the frame of the screen, users won't see it and probably won't look for it, either.

Don't make users traverse your entire Web site to find a simple piece of information. Organize your Web site in an intuitive manner. Always group similar items together. Popular products or frequently used features should be so easy to find that users accidentally trip over them. Items that are similar should be grouped by topic, function, business partner, and so on. The sequence of content is also important. If your site has a store capability, the content should be organized in a way that facilitates the purchase process. Users who get frustrated trying to find what they want are unlikely to continue the buying process. Search engines can help, but only if the content is organized in a way that allows the user to search logically.

Layout and Usability

When people are shopping, they want to find what they are looking for quickly and they want to purchase the product in a way that makes them comfortable. Design with your customers in mind. Your site should provide information that your customers find valuable, not flashy commercials. Clutter is a big problem. Some sites continue to add content to their main pages until the average visitor is either overwhelmed and leaves, or ignores 90 percent of the content and just goes to the same spots each time. Wal-Mart's home page is organized in a logical sequence from left to right. Because most people go to its site for products, the products are first on the left. Special promotions are centered for high visibility, whereas corporate information is on the far right.

Convenience is also highly important. Delta and Northwest Airlines offer users the ability to find flights right on their home page; other airlines make visitors wade through two to five pages. Color and familiarity are important ways of helping users find their way. If you are a traditional business going online, use the same colors and layouts that your brick-and-mortar or paper versions (if you're in the publishing business) use. *Time Magazine's* online version uses a layout and color scheme similar to its print version. Kraft has its familiar logo at the top of its screen and uses a neutral color scheme with URLs in a traditional blue color. The key is to give users what they want quickly and in a visually pleasing way, or they'll find someone who will.

EXTRANETS FOR BUSINESS-TO-BUSINESS TRANSACTIONS

Business-to-business Web sites are slightly different than business-to-consumer Web sites, although the same features and design standards apply. Business-to-business Web sites must be designed in a way that allows organizations other business partners to quickly and accurately complete business transactions. The potential for industrial espionage means that security plays a big role in business-to-business electronic commerce. Extranets must operate as quickly as a normal transaction processing system. Reliability is also very important. If your business partners can't exchange information with you, you are effectively out of business for that period of time. Virtual private networks can help by providing fault-tolerant transaction processing over the Internet.

Sites such as Chemdex.com offer businesses a kind of central exchange for products and services. Chemdex offers a solution to life science organizations consisting of an online marketplace, purchasing functionality tailored to the business requirements of each customer, and service and support. Chemdex offers scientists a marketplace of hundreds of thousands of products. The company also helps users by offering streamlined creation of multi-supplier orders. It has a product search engine that provides detailed product information. It also provides real-time reviews of order status, which can be truly important if an organization is using just-in-time business processes. TradeMatrix is similar. It's a business portal offering value-added services that span multiple digital marketplaces. These value-added services are tailored for buyers, sellers, designers, and service providers.

CONTENT MANAGEMENT TOOLS

The number of pages on organizational Internet sites is growing at a blistering pace. Some studies show that large corporate Web sites will eventually average about 15,000 pages and several times that number in scripts, banners, applets and so on. This growth forces companies to effectively manage their Web sites and content in order to compete in the world of electronic commerce. Organizations risk their reputations if they don't monitor and control the content on both business-to-business and business-to-consumer Web sites. The ability to manage and monitor who sees what, when, where, and how is at the heart of content management.

Fast Fact: Features of a Good Content Management Tool

1. Coordinates the creation process
2. Manages access rights
3. Features workflow-enabled edit/approval processes
4. Includes security management capabilities, such as digital signatures and audits
5. Catalogs how and where content is stored, accessed, and retrieved
6. Provides easy-to-use backup, recovery, and mirror capabilities
7. Integrates documents/components with applications
8. Enables dynamic content assembly
9. Allows separate creation and management processes for static vs. dynamic content
10. Tracks visitor navigation using click-stream analysis

Content Management Process

The process of managing content for large organizations is complex and can be frustrating. Having a standard process helps eliminate confusion and provides a guide for new content developers. Any content management strategy uses four key steps:

1. Creation

2. Submission/assembly

3. Storage/management

4. Publishing

These four steps are performed on all Web content projects, though different organizations may name the steps differently. Employing checkpoints for each of these steps is imperative. The implications of having improper content on an organization's Web site reach beyond merely incorrect product information. False promises, bad privacy/security information, and bad financial data (for publicly held companies) can result in significant legal problems.

Content creation means creating Web pages using some kind of editor such as Microsoft FrontPage. Microsoft Word is also capable making documents Web ready when you use the Save As HTML/Web Page feature. Content submission/assembly is the process of assembling many Web pages into a single Web site, or bringing together Web content from several sources and creating a single, cohesive unit. You can create a workflow process with standard requirements to guide content creators through the submission and assembly process. Content storage/management involves managing the database of Web content in a structured, efficient manner. Content publishing is the act of making the content visible to the public, either internally or externally to the organization.

Controlling Content

In the recent past, most organizations built Web sites by appointing a Webmaster, who then created a few static HTML pages that people visited for information. Users depended on IT departments to create and manage site content. One or two people typically managed the small amount of content that existed. This situation is now completely different. With the introduction of tools such as Microsoft FrontPage, end users can now create complex Web pages. Instead of one or two programmers controlling an organization's Web content, hundreds or even thousands of employees now represent the organization globally in cyberspace. Unfortunately, this means that many organization executives have no idea of the content on their Web sites.

Content management tools must support a diverse group of content developers, ranging from nontechnical business people to highly skilled Web developers. Webmasters must have the tools to manage Web server usage and control what content is made visible to the public. Web project managers need a high-level view of Web projects and must be able to approve content prior to public publishing. Project teams must be able to quickly recover Web site content when a Web site breaks. Webmasters and site managers must have an efficient way to respond to Web site errors and usage events. Nontechnical team members need an easy way to contribute content to a site.

Content Management and Privacy

Some content management tool features are controversial. For example, content management tools exist that can read information from a visitor's computer without the visitor's knowledge. Obviously, if uncovered, this practice might upset visitors and subject the organization to legal action. As mentioned earlier in this chapter, many organizations are nervous about tracking and recording data that may be deemed private. Obtaining legal advice, posting a privacy policy, and enforcing that policy should reassure both your users and your organization's legal advisors regarding privacy issues.

Site Management Strategy

When implemented properly, content management tools can have a powerful impact on an organization's ability to manage and control its Internet image. Site managers face perpetual growth and are searching for tools that help them develop and maintain unified Internet strategies and architectures. A good site management strategy addresses organizational growth, visitor demographics, and the increasing number and types of business transactions executed on a Web site. It also forms the basis for understanding and agreement on standards, methods, tools, techniques, deliverables and the overall direction of Web-based systems development in an organization.

WRAP UP

- **Web site design should be simple, easy to navigate, and follow general Internet standards.** Users should typically not have to follow more than three links to find what they're looking for. Web designers should use standard frames and navigation devices such as buttons and colored links to help users get around quickly and easily.

- **Web site features such as site maps and search engines should be easy to find and use.** These features also should be accurate and helpful in aiding navigation. The site map should act as an index to the Web site, providing links to at least each key content area. Search engines should return results that are useful, easy to read, and sorted in any order that a user chooses.

- **Web site content should be continually updated to keep visitors coming back.** Site visitors get bored easily and want content that is fresh and reflects current trends. Front page links should be provided to any news that is important to a visitors or that is significant about the organization or the Web site.

- **Listening and responding to visitor feedback is critical.** If visitors have the same problem reading or navigating the site each time they visit, they will soon stop visiting. It's important to acknowledge receipt of feedback as well, which helps the visitor connect with the organization.

- **Colors and aesthetics are important.** Consider using neutral, low-key colors and keep images to a minimum to improve Web site performance and increase access speed. Large graphics slow response time significantly. Organizations must keep in mind that not all visitors of powerful PCs, and may be using slow telephone lines to connect to their Web site. Organizations should try to use the same color schemes online that they use in print media.

- **Links to business partners and other interesting sites can help make your Web site a vital resource to visitors.** Since the Web is really one big network, it's important to help visitors navigate that network. The more links that an organization's Web site provides, the more visitors will depend on it as a resource and visit more often.

Taking Stock

1. Do you like your organization's home page? Does it appeal to you?

2. How easily can you find what you need on your Web site?

3. Is your content updated frequently to maintain visitor interest?

4. Does your feedback form provide you with the information you need to know?

5. Do you listen and act on visitor feedback?

6. How accurate and helpful is your site's search engine?

7. Is the security information provided on your Web site accurate and current?

8. Are your business partner links current and relevant?

9. Do your business partners use your Web site and provide positive feedback?

10. Do you have a content-management tool to manage your site?

ACTION PLAN

❑   Visit your Web site often!

❑   Gather comments from business partners and visitors.

❑   Purchase a content management tool that helps your Web-masters do their job.

❑   Continually check your Web site for outdated/broken links.

❑   Make sure that the Web site's content reflects the organization's goals and current activities.

(continued)

Action Plan *continued*

- ❏ Look at visitor comments often and act on them whenever possible.

- ❏ Involve organizational attorneys in writing the security and privacy information provided on your Web site.

- ❏ Stay current on the laws regarding collecting, retaining, and using visitor data.

- ❏ Have your Web site reviewed by expert designers against common style standards.

- ❏ Visit your Web site often!

Chapter 7

E-Commerce Best Practices

*The Internet and e-commerce are evolving rapidly.
Organizations must therefore be agile and able to adapt their best
practices quickly. Successful organizations stay competitive by
learning from others and by improving on established concepts.*

Best practices for e-commerce initiatives change almost daily as the Internet continues to grow and change rapidly. On the business-to-consumer side, the emphasis is moving from presenting information from the organization's perspective to making the site usable by visitors and customizing the site to the visitor's needs. For business-to-business electronic commerce, the emphasis is moving from the simple exchange of business transaction information to the creation and management of knowledge as a resource for all members of the supply and value chains. In both cases, organizations must be very careful handling the data they capture and observe both written and implied privacy laws in their operating environments.

MANAGING THE VISITOR RELATIONSHIP: PROFILING AND PERSONALIZATION

Visitor relationship management (VRM) appears to be the next big thing for Web-based businesses and electronic commerce in general. Businesses ranging from high-tech startups to car dealers are trying to use the Web to better manage the relationship with their customers. To do so, businesses must handle large amounts of data effectively to make Web visitors feel comfortable and welcome online. To track customer habits and personalization data, businesses are turning to data warehouses and their high-volume data handling capabilities to customize online shopping experiences. Data warehouses allow organizations to use various tools and techniques to analyze their visitor data and create personalized experiences for both business-to-consumer and business-to-business Web sites.

Data warehouses can provide a tremendous boost to online businesses trying to improve their Web sites. The right data used properly can help businesses provide customers with choices they didn't know existed, if the businesses know enough about the customer. Studies frequently cite convenience as the most important reason customers (both business and consumer) shop online. Businesses can personalize a customer's shopping experience, which makes shopping easier for the customer. Online businesses can use data warehouses to help customers find what they need faster and more easily. Increased convenience can translate into customer loyalty over the long haul.

Profiling Customers

Creating a customer profile is the linchpin of the personalization process. If an organization understands what makes a customer tick, the visit can be tailored to a customer's individual style and tastes. Key data for online businesses to capture in a data warehouse include:

- Where a visitor browses on the site
- Where a visitor has been before coming to the site
- What a customer buys on the site
- A customer's purchase history on the site
- Any and all available demographics regarding the customer

Online businesses can use this data to personalize a customer's shopping experience. The business can use the data for targeted promotions, if a customer allows the business to provide occasional e-mails announcing sales that are relevant to customer tastes.

Businesses can also use purchase data for pricing analyses. Monitoring the effect of pricing on customer buying habits can be instructive. Large amounts of data stored in a warehouse provide marketing and pricing analysts with the ability to more easily maximize profits without sacrificing sales. Reactions to price variations can be analyzed by age, income, location, and other demographic segments. Demographic data can be used in many other ways. Businesses can use customer demographics to supply discounts one-to-one or based on broad demographic, or purchase-habit, segments. For example, suppose that teenagers typically buy more music CDs than most other market segments. Teenagers might receive discounts on CD purchases to keep them coming back to a particular site.

Amazon.com uses its data warehouse to personalize a customer's shopping experience and to manage its relationship with customers. For example, personalized recommendations appear as a menu option based on your past purchases. Amazon.com looks at other customers who have purchased the same products as you have and develops recommendations based on a combination of their buying patterns and yours. These recommendations include materials by author (or artist, in the case of music) as well as by subject, based on a customer's past purchases.

Amazon.com helps maintain the relationship between a business and its customers by providing order status online via the Your Account menu option, as well an 800 number for customer service. One minor issue is that a cookie needs to be kept on the customer's computer, otherwise information is lost and Amazon.com doesn't know where to start. Signing in through the Your Account menu option, using an e-mail address as an ID, and entering a password can remedy this. Amazon.com likes customers to think of its Web site as a discovery machine. Its data warehouse can be used to provide customers with links to titles based on their purchase history, even titles that customers might not think of on their own.

Personalizing Business-to-Business Electronic Commerce

Business-to-business electronic commerce methods are changing the face of the corporate world. The ability to work directly with business partners means faster, more accurate business transactions. Companies and individuals who trade electronically, whether exchanging tangible products or intangibles, such as digital content or information or services, are being supported by electronic trading systems. Personalization can help them to find the trading opportunities and the best conditions to arrive at a deal. Personalization for business-to-business electronic commerce can help organizations create sophisticated negotiation strategies that can deal with many variables in a global, multilingual, and multicultural environment.

By allowing organizations to customize your Web site to their needs, you enable them to find what they want faster and more easily, making them more likely to continue doing business with you. Companies such as SAP allow registered users to create a My SAP environment. Users can set up the SAP Web page so that they see information about only the modules they purchase. After businesses start using your Web site, you can capture and profile them just as you would profile a consumer. The same principles that apply to business-to-business electronic commerce apply to consumers as well. Profiles must be created from large amounts of data that include past purchases, information requests, and other aforementioned data.

MANAGING AND MAINTAINING VISITOR PRIVACY

Consumers are usually more concerned about data capture than businesses are, but it's critical that organizations disclose to both customers and business partners how their gathered information will be used. When organizations collect the type of data mentioned in the previous section, consumers, and even business partners, naturally wonder what the organization is going to do with that data. Public concerns are related to the violation of privacy guidelines and norms by a number of software applications, access providers and suppliers of information, and goods and services on the Internet. Several surveys provide evidence that consumers have little privacy protection on the Internet. A survey of more than 1,400 Web sites, conducted recently by the U.S. Federal Trade Commission (FTC), indicated that the "industry's efforts to encourage voluntary adoption of the most basic fair information practices have fallen short of what is needed to protect consumers." According to this survey, 92 percent of the 674 commercial Web sites examined collect personal information. But only 14 percent provide any notice with respect to their information practices. Only 2 percent have a comprehensive privacy policy. An even more disturbing picture is presented by the privacy policy related to Web sites directed toward attracting children. Almost 90 percent of the 212 surveyed children's Web sites collect personal information from children. But less than 2 percent of those sites tell children to seek parental permission before providing information to the site.

The FTC also claims that the leading proponents of self-regulation in the field of privacy have not been living up to their professed standards. A review of 100 of the most frequently visited Web sites concluded that none of them met basic standards for privacy protection. Other surveys indicate that efforts of business organizations, such as the U.S. Direct Marketing Association (DMA), to promote sufficient privacy practices are having little impact on its members. Businesses must improve in this area because various government agencies are considering regulatory practices. Most organizations would agree that industry self-regulation is far better than having political agencies step in.

Laws and Ethics

As companies benefit from the wealth of information available from data warehouses, they must also face some ethical and legal issues concerning the data itself. The biggest among these issues are questions of who owns the data and how it can be used. The U.S. legal system views the business entity that collects the data as the owner of that information in most cases, based on long-existing property laws. Much of this data is gathered as the result of consumers conducting their own daily personal business, such as making ATM withdrawals, paying with debit or credit cards, taking out loans, renting commodities, and using the Internet.

Internationally, the European Union's Consumer Data Directive was passed in 1998. This directive's standards are stricter than those in other parts of the world and could block some organizations from receiving information about European consumers. The European Union's laws follow the policies of the Organization for Economic Cooperation and Development (OECD), which are designed to establish worldwide standards (see the following sidebar). Canada's Personal Information Protection and Electronic Documents Act follows the OECD's policies and requires the consent of the individual for the collection, use, or disclosure of any personal information. This act directly impacts the way marketers conduct business. Canada is trying to stay in step with the strict European standards, and the bill corresponds to Europe's consumer data privacy laws as well.

OECD DATA PRIVACY PRINCIPLES

The OECD established some basic principles for data privacy and protection via a committee through the United Nations. The principles are as follows:

1. **Collection Limitation** Personal data should be obtained by lawful and fair means and with the knowledge or consent of the data subject.

(continued)

OECD Data Privacy Principles *continued*

2. **Data Quality** Personal data should be relevant to the purposes for which that data is to be used. To the extent necessary for those purposes, such data should be accurate, complete, and current.

3. **Purpose Specification** Prior to or at the time of collection of the data, the purpose of the data collection should be specified and the subsequent use of such data should be only for the stated purpose.

4. **Use Limitation** Personal data should not be disclosed or otherwise used for any purposes other than as set forth in the Purpose Specification except with the consent of the data subject or by the authority of law.

5. **Security Safeguards** Personal data should be protected with reasonable security measures to prevent unauthorized access, destruction, modification, or disclosure.

6. **Openness** The data controller should make available information concerning the existence, use, and nature of personal data.

7. **Individual Participation** An individual should have the right to ascertain from a data controller whether the data controller has personal data relating to that individual and to have the data corrected if the data is incorrect.

8. **Accountability** The data controller should be held accountable for complying with the foregoing principles.

Technologically developed countries generally agree to these principles. What's frequently debated is how these principles are implemented. Strong disagreements exist among nations, and agreement on one set of standards is still some time away.

Common Mistakes

According to Bill Boni, Director of the Dispute Analysis and Investigations department of the Financial Advisory Services Division of PricewaterhouseCoopers in Los Angeles, one common mistake that organizations make is failing to adhere to privacy standards. This failure includes lack of recognition or compliance with local standards in other countries. Boni says that organizations should ask themselves some basic questions:

■   Do we expect to acquire and retain private customer information?

- If so, where it will be stored?

- How do we expect to use it?

- Who will manage it and make decisions concerning new uses?

- Will it be resold or traded outside our organization, and is it legal and ethical to do so?

- Do we know the data privacy rules for all the areas and industries in which we operate or even plan to operate?

Customers and business partners expect organizations to address these questions locally, regardless of where either party is based. This expectation means that organizations must work with customers and business partners to create privacy policies that are customized both by industry and by operating location.

Larry Kanter, a partner in the Financial Advisory Services division of PricewaterhouseCoopers in Dallas, Texas, adds that organizations capture information that a consumer gives to an organization for use in a business transaction, and the business then sells that information. Kanter identifies some key problems that organizations encounter when capturing information:

- **Involuntary taking of information via cookies** Organizations may scan a PC and accidentally capture inappropriate or illegal information.

- **Tracking clickstreams** When an organization tracks the user's previous activities, it may capture information such as passwords, which is illegal in many countries.

- **Using hardware identifiers** Intel created a unique identifier on some of its Pentium chips that allows a person's PC to be identified wherever that user goes in cyberspace. Customers and privacy watch groups have expressed great concern about this.

- **Committing identity theft** Organization employees can use personal information captured on their databases to configure a new computer to use the name, address, and so on of another person.

Kanter says that some organizations' reaction to these problems has been to disclose privacy policies, though some don't or they aren't entirely honest about their policies. Also, many people don't read the policies.

Some very public flaps have resulted from bad data privacy practices. Major legal problems resulted for Minneapolis-based U.S. Bank when it resold customer account information without telling its customers. Tandy Corporation's Radio Shack stores have long been a point of contention with some customers, both retail and online. Many Radio Shack stores ask for name, address, and so on when customers make purchases. Customers aren't told that the information is voluntary and some become quite upset. Organizations must be honest, open, and clear about how they use data captured doing e-business.

MAKE YOUR SITE EASY TO USE

In both business-to-consumer and business-to-business e-commerce, ease of use is critical. The Web design tips provided in Chapter 6 are good guides for both types of sites. Business-to-business sites, however, require a slightly different approach. Organizations need to make it highly efficient for business partners to get around on their Web sites. In many cases, business people don't have as much time to browse as consumers do. Make your Web site's feature list easy to find. Provide interactive tours for new business partners and those who are using new features. Also, keep the pizzazz to a minimum. Most business people aren't impressed with flashy graphics that take hours to load. Make the Web site functional and fast.

The technology functions of business-to-business electronic commerce should be simple as well. Make it easy for business partners to connect with you—don't make them memorize your entire architecture. Give them the information they need to transmit and receive data, but don't overwhelm them. A simple handshake protocol should be sufficient. Use standard data layouts (such as ANSI EDI or UN/EDIFACT) to transfer data so that organizations can get up and running with you quickly and with a minimum number of questions. Provide your business partners with the necessary technology architecture diagrams early on so that they understand how you operate. The point is to make interacting with your organization as simple as possible so that consumers keep coming back and business partners continue to work with you.

Tradematrix.com provides a simple interface at its home page. The page displays a table of contents on the left side, with an expandable/collapsible index. The main frame on the page contains links for each type of visitor, including buyers, sellers, designers, and even potential business partners. Chemdex has a similar setup and includes a login screen at the home page. A list of new suppliers is set to the left side as well, so a business partner can check out the new wares available. Both of these sites provide simple, easy-to-use interfaces that make getting business done quick and efficient. HomeSource uses a customized interface for each business partner. HomeSource provides data in the format that each of its business partners needs. Each business partner supplies data layouts and requirements so that HomeSource can transmit data in the format that its business partners need, when they need it.

MANAGING VISITOR PERCEPTIONS

It has been said that your perception is your reality. Assuming that this is true, organizations must set realistic expectations and carefully manage the perceptions of their visitors. Realistic expectations on the part of customers and business partners help ensure the success of your e-commerce initiatives. You should strive to maintain a balance of perceptions about your Web site. As your organization designs the site, keep in mind that the process is a team effort. Your design team should work with all departments in your organization, with business partners, and with consumers via focus groups and other methods, if you are in a direct-to-consumer business. When your Web site goes live, it's critical to manage and improve the perceptions of all visitors over time. These goals are accomplished by listening to and responding to comments, continually reading about industry best practices, and having your site reviewed by experts.

Business-to-Consumer Sites

The home page of a Web site serves much the same function as the table of contents of a magazine or the front page of a newspaper. The home page helps Web site visitors understand how to get to the information they're seeking and provides links to stories that are important to the visitor. This page can take the form of a descriptive list or it can be something more. For example, General Mills' home page introduces the visitor, in a playful, imaginative way, to the products that General Mills produces. A simplified table of contents sits on the left of the page and describes broad categories of subpages, which are then broken down into more detail when the visitor clicks a specific link. Accordingly, all elements of the site share a clear organizational structure, and the information resources work together to create a perceptual world that gives a sense of warmth to the site. Visitors see familiar brands and items such as Betty Crocker and Cheerios, which helps them relate the Web site to the real shopping world. As such, this Web site operates in a manner consistent with its promotional purpose: increasing awareness of the brand and its related products, and offering devices such as recipes and coupons that promote product use.

Computer-mediated communication does intrinsically lack warmth, and consumers want Web sites that present product information in an interesting, entertaining manner. Presenting product information in a way that entices the visitor both captures the interest of the audience and presents the product in an environment that relates the product to the new age of technology and Internet-based advertising. The factors that result in effective communication on the Web involve both what you say and how you say it. It is not enough just to present information; you must do so in a way that helps visitors experience that information in a positive manner. Visitors are attracted to information that adds value in both form and substance and reaches them in a time period commensurate with the perceived value of the information.

Business-to-Business E-Commerce

It's just as important for organizations to manage their business partner's perceptions as it is to manage customer perceptions. Your business partners expect a certain level of accuracy, speed, and professionalism from your Web site. According to Steve Diorio, President of IMT Strategies, a Stamford-based sales and marketing advisory firm, the most important feature of a business-to-business Web site is easy access to support and products. It's also useful to create communities where business partners and potential business partners can communicate. Discussion boards can facilitate this process. Communities provide organizations with unedited feedback from business partners and allow business partners to exchange important information. This type of Web site also helps the host organization become a central meeting point for its business partners, building loyalty and trust.

Organizations must also innovate constantly to keep themselves and their business partners competitive. Organizations can spur innovation by feedback and collaborative activities with business partners in the development of the Web site or through automated links. Business partners have more buy-in when they're part of the development process. Organizations should also optimize their Web site for their business partners, not for their own convenience. Try to "walk a mile in the visitor's shoes" to see what might be improved. Using personalization services can be as beneficial for business partners as it can be for consumers. For example, if you buy wood and nails from your business partners, you can customize one page for wood vendors and another for nail vendors. If you do business internationally, be sure to account for language and culture differences. Business partners are part of your value chain—treat them well and your chances of success increase!

GIVE 'EM WHAT THEY WANT AND DON'T INSULT THEIR INTELLIGENCE

Balancing simplicity with sophistication is sometimes difficult. Web sites should be kept simple but should have sufficient features to make them useful. Yet you don't want to overwhelm visitors with an extremely busy home page. If they can't find what they want in about a minute, most visitors will leave.

As you design your Web site, consider the overall layout. For example, as the amount of content grows, you will probably want to either shrink the font size or encourage users to scroll to find information. Identifying what content goes where on a Web site is one of the keys to making your site sticky (a site on which visitors linger) as well as a driving force in generating return visits.

Think Like a Visitor

One way to generate longer visits and more return visits is to shift the focus of your Web site from the organization to the visitor. This means that your content creators and designers need to think like the visitor. They need to create content that the visitor can use immediately. The content should be created in the context of a structure that the visitor can understand. Your organization can get help from visitors through surveys and feedback forms on the Web site, and your content will continue to evolve as visitors' needs and tastes change. Your organization must be willing to roll with these changes, and your Web site must evolve with those changes.

A common method of achieving visitor-oriented content is to use outside reviewers. These reviewers can be consultants or visitors. The visitors' job is to provide structured feedback that helps the organization change its content to meet the visitor needs. The organization should design surveys that provide structured feedback. The survey should contain specific questions that reflect the organization's goals and the information that the organization wants to communicate to visitors. Keep in mind that the content should reflect the business goals of the organization but at the same time must serve a purpose for visitors. This balancing act can be quite difficult, and organizations frequently use consultants who are experts in Web design and content creation.

Anticipate Visitors' Needs

Working closely with customers and business partners, sometimes an organization can actually anticipate visitors' needs. To do this, the organization must truly understand their visitors, which requires sophisticated profiling tools. Organizations moving from the brick-and-mortar position to an online presence often have years of customer and vendor data. This data can be used to create tools and information that will be useful to visitors. Of course, customers expect something different from an online presence than they do from a facility. Therefore, a Web site is likely to be somewhat different than what an organization might expect after analyzing old customer data. However, an organization can generate the initial Web site from what the organization already knows about its customers and business partners.

A Web Site of Their Own

Personalization software allows visitors to dictate how they will use your Web site. In business-to-consumer electronic commerce, the focus is on attracting and retaining visitors and extending the organization's market share. In the business-to-business market, the goal is to make your business partners' experience as pleasant and efficient as possible. In both cases, the site design must be simple and flexible, with an emphasis on informing visitors and guiding them to where they want to go. The system must respond appropriately to a wide range of visitor actions and customize itself in response to those actions. The system's response may include a range of sales and information strategies. The system should be able to act in the context of the customer's value to the organization.

Yahoo!'s My Yahoo! service allows visitors to customize what they want to see in the order they want to see it on the screen. It provides local weather by reading information on a visitors' PC that lets Yahoo! know where the visitor is located. Of course, a major issue with personalization services such as My Yahoo! is the retrieval of personal data from visitor PCs, as mentioned earlier in the privacy section of this chapter. Amazon.com provides a somewhat customized interface, but it also sends e-mails to frequent buyers if special deals occur on items in which the customer has indicated an interest. Amazon.com provides customers with the ability to turn personalization on or off, which reduces the likelihood of customers giving away information involuntarily.

SITE CONSISTENCY

Another important best practice in designing and maintaining a Web site is consistency. Both within one Web site and across multiple Web sites (when an organization has more than one), the design, navigation, and overall look and feel of a successful site typically is consistent. So, if your home page contains standard frames that are sectioned into three pieces, you should probably continue that structure throughout your site. You might have the left side of the frame as the table of contents. The top of the frame might contain advertising and header information about your site. The main window of the frame would then typically contain the primary content to be viewed. Because in this type of design the table of contents and header information hold steady while the content frame changes, visitors are able to see where they are and can find their way to other parts of the site easily. Some Web sites scroll the table of contents with the content in the main window, whereas others provide independent scrolling for all three windows. Whatever approach you take, it might make sense to be consistent across your entire site.

One of the best examples of a consistent look and feel for a Web site is Yahoo!. Whether visitors are viewing Yahoo!'s home page, going through its stock quotes, or perusing its personal ads, they find Yahoo!'s interface exactly the same. The sign-in screen is always the same, regardless of the activity in which the user is engaging. A table of contents is always on the left, with promotional banners on top. Yahoo! also provides a list of its other resources in the bottom-left corner of the screen. A standard header at the very top of the screen provides users with an easy way to get to other Yahoo! Web pages that are relevant to the users' current activities.

Microsoft's Web site also works the same regardless of where the user is within the site. An expandable table of contents is always on the left side; the Microsoft header with other Web pages is always at the top. The content stays neatly within the main frame and is easily viewable with some scrolling. Microsoft also provides a guide to common resources such as contact information, special events, and newsletters.

MANAGING BUSINESS KNOWLEDGE USING E-COMMERCE

E-commerce allows organizations to capture enormous amounts of knowledge. The real issue for organizations today is how to use this knowledge to beat competitors. Organizations must learn how to gather and share intelligence. A good knowledge-management process integrates people and technology with collaborative processes to create a smarter and more competitive organization. It allows employees to use knowledge enterprise wide, not just what knowledge is found in their department. By extending its digital nervous system to their business partners, an organization can share the knowledge they capture with other parts of the supply chain. Providing business partners with the information they need to be more efficient lowers their costs and prices, which ultimately benefits everyone in the supply and value chains.

There are two core types of knowledge: quantitative and qualitative. Quantitative knowledge includes any numerical data, such as financial figures, order quantities, and customer information, such as age and income. Qualitative data includes best practices and non-numerical customer data, such as product comments by customers. A good knowledge management system provides the ability to mine and manipulate both types of data discretely and together. As described in Chapter 6, good Web site feedback mechanisms provide organizations with the ability to capture both types of data.

THE ROAD TO ENLIGHTENMENT

Capturing knowledge from electronic commerce transactions is easy. Deciding what knowledge to capture and using it properly to benefit the organization and its business partners are the tough parts. The first step in the process is for a knowledge analyst to gather and model knowledge requirements. Remember to consult your business partners, because they will want to know of any information that relates to them. The analyst works with business users in the organization to understand what users know now and what they need to know to do their jobs better, faster, and cheaper. This is different from the traditional systems-analyst role. A knowledge analyst can't simply supply decision-support capabilities (like tools such as Cognos' PowerPlay) and a bunch of data. The data sent to users must enable them to go beyond day-to-day job duties. The effective knowledge analyst should provide data that allows users to discover things that they wouldn't otherwise know without the data.

The knowledge analyst must also supply data from other departments and business units across the enterprise. This effort can produce political struggles within the organization but represents the heart of the knowledge management idea. Most organizations have people who are walking encyclopedias of corporate knowledge. Those people have been in the organization for a long time and possess valuable tips and tricks for getting things done more quickly and efficiently. This is the type of knowledge that everyone else in the organization should possess and use. However, cross-functional knowledge bases are often difficult to create because of turf battles between department and/or business unit managers.

The technology available today allows organizations to easily share the knowledge they create with their business partners. Web-enabled data warehouses and high-speed transmission capabilities allow organizations to transfer knowledge bases to their business partners in real-time. Databases are generated from the knowledge model and are populated as data flows from the Web site or transactions. Figure 7-1 shows a common architecture that HomeSource used for this process.

Data comes in by consumers entering data on the Web site or calling an 800 operator. If consumers come through the call center, their data is transferred to HomeSource. The data in the transaction database is converted to information that is meaningful to HomeSource and its business partners and is stored in the data warehouse. Information that is meaningful to its business partners is transferred to them in their own format for maximum efficiency. This architecture is simple, elegant, and effective.

Potential Problems

The real benefit that organizations derive from knowledge management systems is the ability to share knowledge among departments, business units, and business partners. This exchange allows everyone in the supply and value chains to benefit from everyone else's knowledge. Convincing management that

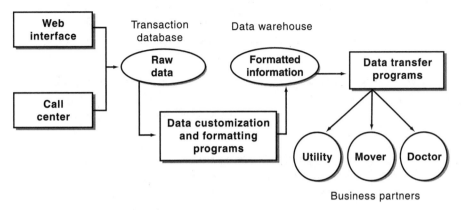

Figure 7-1. *HomeSource data transfer architecture*

everyone in an organization needs to be connected is often difficult, however. Also, cost/benefit and ROI calculations are tough to do for knowledge management programs. You might intuitively know that more information helps you do your job better, but quantifying the cash value of that information can be next to impossible.

Cultural issues and politics kill more projects than any technical glitch ever could. The major problem with knowledge management is that organizational politicos typically bristle at the idea of sharing information because many organization employees still think that withholding knowledge creates power for those doing the withholding. Wrong! The sharing of knowledge is where the real power is. If you do your job better because you obtained good information from someone in another division, you still look good. If you supply knowledge to someone who does a great job, that person will remember you, and you look good as well. Organizations must learn to share information not only internally but with their external business partners as well.

WRAP UP

- **E-commerce best practices are changing rapidly as Internet business models evolve.** Organizations must continue to change and adapt to new practices as e-commerce business models evolve and are refined by industry leaders.

- **Profiling and personalization services can help make visitors feel welcome.** Organizations can capture data that will help them personalize the visitor's experience for business-to-consumer transactions

actions. Personalization services can also help business-to-business transactions become more efficient because business partners will spend less time finding what they need on your Web site.

- **Like the business models, privacy practices are evolving.** Organizations need to stay current on legal and ethical issues regarding data privacy and disclosure laws. Organizations must account for the laws and culture in all their operating environments.

- **In electronic commerce, simplicity is elegance.** Both business partners and consumers should be able to traverse your Web site easily. Standard technology should be used wherever possible to make communication between you and your business partners easy.

- **Managing perceptions is just as important online as it is for brick-and-mortar organizations.** Maintaining a professional, effective, efficient Web site will help gain new visitors and keep current visitors coming back. Technology should be used to make the Web site fast and easy to use for both consumers and business partners.

- **Make sure that your Web site doesn't waste a visitors' time.** An organization should provide meaningful content that visitors can use immediately. Try to avoid too much flash advertising, especially on business-to-business sites. Thinking like a visitor can help you anticipate the visitor's needs, which improves your site's image.

- **Make your site(s) consistent.** The general look and feel of all parts of your Web site should be about the same. Navigation, color scheme, and links should match other parts of the Web site to avoid visitor confusion.

- **E-commerce can help organizations extend their digital nervous systems beyond organizational walls.** Sharing knowledge empowers both the organization and all its business partners in the supply chain to compete more effectively. Organizational management must get over the concept that knowledge withheld is power and warm to the idea that sharing knowledge is how real power is generated.

Taking Stock

1. How much does your organization really know about its customers, business partners, and other site visitors?

2. Do you make it easy for business partners to find what they need and traverse your site?

3. Do you know the data privacy rules for all areas and industries in which you operate or plan to operate?

4. Has your company developed a written privacy policy or set of privacy principles? Are pertinent parts of the policy or principles accessible to your Web site visitors?

5. Does the company clearly disclose the purposes for personal data collection and use?

6. Is your Web site easy to use? Can *you* get around on it easily?

7. Is your site's content customized to the type of visitor?

8. Does your site have a consistent look and feel?

9. Do you capture meaningful and useful knowledge from your e-commerce efforts?

10. Do you now share knowledge with your business partners, or do you plan to do so in the future?

ACTION PLAN

❑ Create a list of profile items (things you want to know) about customers and business partners.

❑ Find out what you already know about your customers and business partners and compare it against your knowledge requirements.

❑ Make sure that your corporate attorneys know the privacy laws in all your operating environments, and make sure that your e-commerce initiatives follow those laws.

❑ Write your site privacy statements in both the language and terms of your operating environment. This action includes providing native-language support.

❑ Solicit feedback from customers and business partners about your Web site.

❑ Prepare an action plan to make your Web site easier to use and more complete.

❑ Visit and use your Web site frequently!

Chapter 8

Brand Management Strategies

The Internet business model is changing brand management strategies. Brand managers must learn how to leverage their real-world brand recognition on the Web and to continually innovate to stay ahead of smaller, more agile upstarts.

Branding on the Internet is a relatively new and evolving process. Organizations recognize that operating in cyberspace is different from doing so in the real world, but they must find ways to leverage their real world brand equity and build on it in new and innovative ways. Brands on the Internet often grow by word of mouth via the Internet grapevine. Organizations should be careful when moving from the brick-and-mortar world to cyberspace, and they should learn to use the grapevine to imbue their brands with positive images. Organizations should also carefully monitor trends and continually update their brands to stay current with the latest new thing on the Web. Organizations must also protect their brands to avoid dilution—or even destruction—of the trust they've earned with real-world brands.

Passing from the Brick-and-Mortar to the Virtual World

When an organization goes online, its staff needs to recognize that they must create brand management strategies for passing from the world of brick and mortar to cyberspace. They must create a cyberbrand that attracts the same or better levels of customer loyalty. Depending on the organization's products and services, it may face significant transferability challenges. Meeting those challenges means using the organization's real-world brand to earn trust and respect for its cyberbrand.

Many organizations find the move from real-world brand management to cyberbrand management frustrating. Levels of customer loyalty in cyberspace tend to be much lower than in the real world. Customer turnover can be very high, sometimes driven by nothing more than a new face on the block and the hype surrounding the new entry, which drives customer curiosity. Businesses that operate in small, local areas face the largest potential losses from e-tailers who can build a presence with little effort and can offer lower prices and larger varieties than local businesses. Even the business-to-business channel isn't immune. If you supply widgets to several manufacturers and a new player goes online, it's quite possible that your customers will take a look and decide to switch. Because entry barriers can be quite low for online business (meaning that almost anyone can put up a Web site and get started), customer retention costs are much higher in cyberspace. Customer acquisition costs, on the other hand, are lower in cyberspace, which is good for smaller organizations looking to build brand equity, but bad for larger, more established organizations trying to fend off new players.

As organizations move from the real world to cyberspace, they must realize that the basic elements of brand management remain the same, but how those elements are applied or adjusted can vary greatly. According to Steve Diorio, President of IMT Strategies, a Stamford, Connecticut-based sales and marketing advisory firm, the four basic elements of brand management that are affected in cyberspace are the following:

- Branding investment mix
- Strategy
- Value
- ROI (discussed in detail in Chapter 4, "Measuring Success")

The branding investment mix varies by company and includes public relations, marketing, and promotions such as television and radio. An organization's brand management strategy dictates how those elements will be applied, which demographics will be targeted, and what steps are taken to apply those elements. Each organization has different expectations of what value is brought by their investments in branding. Some organizations spend money to build traffic (for example, in stores for inbound telemarketing order lines); others use it to change the demographics of that traffic; and still others use it to increase the purchasing of current traffic.

Branding Investment Mixes Change

Diorio believes that the branding investment mix will almost certainly change. Some organizations that are strictly Web based might do only Web-based advertising. Organizations that have current real-world brands might continue ads on television, radio, and so on, but will also likely invest in cooperative advertising (such as banner ads) in cyberspace. And many organizations will invest in brand building in both realms. Yahoo! advertises across the Web but also uses billboards, television ads, and other forms of advertising. Barnes and Noble's Web-based sister barnesandnoble.com spent millions of dollars on real-world advertising to build its cyberbrand. It had to compete with Amazon.com, which was taking away business from Barnes and Noble's brick-and-mortar stores at an alarming rate. Microsoft also advertises in both the real world and cyberspace. The famous Intel bunny-suit television ads drove up Intel's Web site activity significantly.

Strategies Change

The strategies or applications used by organizations for their cyberbrand typically are similar, though certainly different than traditional brand management. IMT and The Meta Group have divided strategies into three types:

- Business
- Process
- Technology

The business strategy defines the role of branding in a virtual supply chain and in community-based markets. Organizations must decide how to position their brands relative to customer expectations as well as to competitors. Organizations that successfully create e-brand equity and cross-POI branding strategies will dominate their markets. Organizations must redefine branding strategies to generate loyalty in electronic communities and across multiple channels. Investment in traditional branding activities must be balanced with new alternative sources of loyalty, switching costs.

The process strategy is a full life cycle, e-based customer care for retention, penetration, and growth. Organizations must decide how to actually execute the plan to meet its goals and objectives. The process for managing cyberbrands is different in several ways. First, written and graphic communication are more important. In many real-world situations, verbal communication drives the ad or promotion, with graphics backing up the words. Cyberbrands require written communication (though sound cards may eventually make this statement obsolete). Thus organizations may need to hire more writers and fewer actors. Organizations must also decide how they will execute customer care processes. For example, how many e-mail exchanges will take place before the customer or organization initiates personal contact via phone? It's easy to lose customers because switching costs are so low on the Web, so customer care will be a differentiating factor for many organizations.

The technology strategy determines the infrastructure for driving consumer, client, and end-user expectations for enhanced services. Speed and ease of use are the two big aspects of business-to-consumer electronic commerce that technology can assist. Adding processor and storage capacity is a fairly easy (though not necessarily inexpensive) way to keep customers happy. Most complaints about Web-based business-to-consumer sites involve slow response time and sites that are difficult to use. New Web-based software development tools provide developers with the ability to generate robust, user-friendly systems that will keep customers coming back.

Value Expectations Change

Organizations must ask themselves where the real value of their cyberbrand lies. A business-to-consumer organization probably wants to build customer loyalty, recognition, and of course, sales. A business-to-business organization may also want similar benefits, though it's more likely to sign up a partner via phone or other personal means before transacting business. Some organizations, such as Intel, simply use their cyberbrand for recognition. This use has an indirect but tangible dollar benefit. If Intel builds loyalty with consumers (end buyers), they will demand the Intel Inside label, which benefits both Intel and its business partners. As Intel enters new markets, such as Web hosting, its cyberbrand provides a foundation on which to build more direct services.

ROI Measurements Change

As mentioned in Chapter 4, ROI calculations for cyberbranding are different from those in the real world. What an organization expects from its brand in cyberspace may be completely different from its expectations in the real world. New measures of integrated media ROI and overall Sales, General & Administrative (SG&A)

effectiveness are needed to determine how technology, marketing, advertising, and other organizational functions contribute to brand value. Hybrid media measurements of interactive media are needed that capture measurements of brand enhancement and lead generation. And to reiterate from the previous section, ROI calculations must evolve as value is redefined.

Advertising Changes

In broadcast and print media, the role of advertising is to communicate a product's competitive advantage to a predefined target audience. According to Lester Wanninger, a professor at the University of Minnesota's Carlson School of Management, the competitive advantage is expressed in terms of the target customer's motivations, benefits, and rewards. Broadcast advertising strategy is based on the idea that exposure to a message is separated in time and place from the opportunity to respond. Advertisers work hard to increase *reach*, the percentage of unduplicated audience members who are exposed to a message. Messages are intended to influence future purchase decisions and to build overall brand awareness and image. However, often these messages wash over many consumers because those consumers are not current prospects for the product or service being offered.

Wanninger says that advertising in a digital and interactive medium, however, involves a different set of assumptions and strategies. One primary difference is consumers' ability to interact with a message and respond in one time and place. Closing the gap between exposure and response fundamentally changes advertising's role in the sales process. In the electronic service landscape, the principles of advertising are integrated with customer service, relationship marketing, and sales. Thinking of advertising as removed from immediate inter-action with the product or company is not effective. Advertising can be viewed as a process of bringing consumers as close to a real-time purchase as possible. That is, advertising functions to facilitate quality interaction. Thus advertising, brand management, and customer relationship management are all tightly integrated.

Leveraging Real World Brand Strength

Although cyberbranding is different from real-word brand recognition, organizations can still leverage their real-world brand strength. A well-recognized brand or mascot such as the Pillsbury Doughboy provides organizations with a foundation or starting point for building their e-brand. Advertising in the real world serves to build awareness along with brand equity and traffic. In the virtual world, it can actually generate leads and business (for direct-to-consumer) through click-streams generated by banner ads and direct e-mail. Spokespeople for IMT and The Meta Group note that different opportunities on the Web actually enable some organizations to spread their brand awareness. These include:

- Expanded customer touch points or points of interaction (POI) such as e-mail, fax, kiosk, Web, phone, and Web business partners

- Hybrid distribution channels with independently managed selling channels, marketing automation programs, and disintegrated e-care deployment

- Outsourcing of brick-and-mortar infrastructure and nonessential infrastructure

E-business, customer interaction centers, and increased customer access to information are altering the role and value of traditional brand equity. Established organizations must also eventually partner with channel innovators, such as Yahoo!, AOL, and Excite, that dominate channel branding and distribution. Portals such as Yahoo! can offer lots of exposure in a fairly quick time frame. Markets and consumers seem to recognize this, as announcements of cooperation with AOL or Yahoo! can often send a small Internet start-up's stock flying.

Increasing Customer Intimacy

Building virtual brand equity requires changes to branding investment mix and value measures. Branding is redefined to be a more intimate, experiential, and interactive situation. When a television commercial is broadcast, few consumers believe that the ad is talking to them individually. However, when consumers (and even business partners) interact with a Web site, they're looking for a personalized experience (see Chapter 7, "E-Commerce Best Practices," for more on personalization). The jury is out as to whether simply throwing money at electronic commerce projects just to build a presence works. It is yet to be determined whether transition players (from bricks and mortar to cyberspace), such as barnesandnoble.com, can make a significant dent in e-tailers, such as Amazon.com, simply by spending their way into electronic commerce.

Most organizations are investing most heavily in e-customer technology, realizing that they have little to lose and everything to gain. Customizing Web sites of new ventures to specific demographics is one effective way to succeed. Chapter 7 provides insight into personalization and profiling, which help organizations track customer characteristics. Carrying those concept one step further, some organizations may want to customize large parts of their Web pages, or even create separate sites, each targeted at a specific demographic.

I VILLAGE REDEFINES COMMUNITY

*i*Village.com provides women with many of the same features available on other Web sites. The key to *i*Village.com's success is a customized approach. *i*Village.com's brand builds equity because the site is tightly monitored and carefully designed to make women feel comfortable. That means that the content is customized in a way its designers believe resonates with women. *i*Village.com advertises via traditional media (such as television and radio) as well as via Web portals and business partners. Its brand is carefully managed to protect its image, because statistics show that women are moving to the Internet in significant numbers.

*i*Village.com provides relevant and targeted information and tools to women. *i*Village.com is an online women's network providing practical solutions and everyday support for women between the ages of 25 and 54. The site is organized into branded communities that focus on issues of most relevance to women, providing interactive services, peer support, and online access to experts through 15 channels and several shopping areas. Content channels include Parent Soup, allHealth, Money Life, Career, Work from Home, and Click!: Where Computers Make Sense. Commerce channels, such as iBaby, iMaternity, and Shopping Central, complement the content channels. Established in 1995 and headquartered in New York City, *i*Village, Inc. is a new media company that develops sponsorship and commerce relationships to match the desire of marketers to reach women with the needs of *i*Village.com members for information and services.

*i*Village.com achieves continuous growth by providing content that matches women's needs without being condescending or stereotypical. The site provides information ranging from hair and hygiene to health, money, and politics. *i*Village.com attracts many political candidates who want to get their message out to women. Overall, the content mix is light in some ways and more serious in others. This delicate balance has served *i*Village.com well. *i*Village.com recently became the Internet's #1 women's network, according to the New York-based Internet watch firm Media Metrix.

Transferability Issues

Established organizations moving to the Web face a number of transferability challenges. Many marketing departments and brand managers lack the experience and expertise to manage electronic commerce projects. In most cases, when suppliers launch new e-business strategies, their marketing and positioning efforts concentrate on tangible product functionality and site design, not the process or the inherent benefits of purchasing online. After spending months or years on product development, and pouring hundreds of thousands or millions of dollars into the development of an e-commerce site, the typical supplier becomes convinced that the functional merits of the product and the appearance of the site are so compelling that the market will find it far superior to any competitor. Often, little thought is given to how that information will be communicated in a way that works in cyberspace.

WHAT'S REALLY IMPORTANT?
SUPPLIERS AND CUSTOMERS ARE MILES APART

Traditional organizations that go online seem to be way behind in how they perceive cyberbranding and how customers describe what's really important in a cyberbrand. Most organizations seem to think that tangible product functionality and site design are important. Customers, however, have some specific things on their mind, including (in no particular order):

- Product reliability
- Security (of transactions)
- Organizational responsiveness and accessibility
- How the organization communicates with its customers
- Convenience of product or service purchases
- Product's cost competitiveness
- Product's capability to add value to a business or home
- The organization's competence (as perceived by the customer)
- The organization's fulfillment of its commitment to customers

Before organizations can really profit from cyberbranding, they must understand what the customer wants. The organization's perspective and focus must change from an internal view to an external view, focused on the customer.

Source: IMT and The Meta Group

According to research from The Meta Group (and supported by work from others), the broad e-buyer community in this age of abundant options is finding it increasingly difficult to differentiate competitive products. Therefore, e-buyers are relying more heavily on intangibles (such as reliability, credibility, business support, and responsiveness) and branding. Although the combination of e-commerce sites and commerce bots will enable rapid price evaluations and comparisons, the ability to lower the buyer's cost to buy (reduce cycle times, automate redundant or repetitive tasks, simplify inventory management, improve control assets, and so on) is just as important to business-to-business e-buyers.

It's critically important for traditional, established organizations that are transferring their brand to cyberspace to keep the trust they've earned over time. Factors such as controlling where the brand is seen, who has permission to use it, and how the brand image (for example, the Doughboy) is portrayed are all necessary to protect the brand and its reputation (legal issues are discussed later in this chapter). Partnering in cyberspace (also mentioned later in this chapter) can be beneficial, but organizations must pick their business partners carefully. An online service that doesn't protect your interest or handle your advertising correctly can do more damage than no online presence at all. Don't let another party damage or destroy the trust you've earned with your brand.

USING THE INTERNET GRAPEVINE

The Internet relies more than any other media on word-of-mouth advertising. Whereas the effectiveness of banner ads has not been demonstrated, studies show that the grapevine has a significant impact (either positive or negative) on an organization's ability to grow a brand in cyberspace. The content of a Web site determines whether visitors stay and what their overall impressions are. Nothing in cyberspace is worse than a site that promises much and delivers little. Word soon gets out on the Internet grapevine (and in a sense, the Internet is all grapevine) that the pages in question are not worth visiting; as a result, the site languishes. On the other hand, if an organization provides good value for the time and/or money, visitors tell their friends, who tell their friends, and so on—and traffic soars.

Managing Visitor Perceptions

As mentioned in Chapters 6 and 7, there are standard approaches to Web site design that address specific issues. Relative to visitor perceptions, three or the most important aspects of Web site content are the following (in no particular order):

- It needs to be appropriate to its intended audience.

- It must add or create value (as perceived by the visitor).

- It must constantly change.

You must have a clear idea of what kind of visitor you want to attract (generally, this will be the same as your typical online customer profile), just as you would with conventional marketing. Online content must be more highly targeted than conventional marketing so that visitors can tell at a glance (which is all the time you'll get) whether lingering and exploring further is worthwhile. Assuming that visitors find your pages to be of genuine interest, you need to ensure that there is at least one element that changes on a regular basis in order to draw people back. So much competition exists online that Web sites must fight for their audiences every day. As visitors become more excited about your content, they'll very often share that information with others, thereby increasing traffic.

As visitors find the site interesting and worth returning to, and as they spread the word to their friends, relatives, and so on, the site becomes a powerful online marketing tool. The more time people spend on your site, the more they absorb messages about your brand. Amazon.com, Yahoo!, and other major online organizations grew initially through word of mouth as much as through advertising. In fact, Yahoo!'s discussion boards are one of the best known Internet grapevines. Particularly useful are the stock talk discussion boards. If an organization wants to develop public awareness of its brand, especially if it isn't a direct-to-consumer organization, the stock boards are one way of reaching a large number of people quickly at a zero cost. An organization can monitor the boards to see what its customers think, or even post messages in the form of press releases to promote the brand.

Reshaping the Message

Unfortunately, few organizations—even relatively large, established brands—really use the Internet well when it comes to brand management (see "Managing E-Brand Risk" later in this chapter). Effective brand management entails developing a strong relationship with the customer, and that relationship is often shaped on the Internet. The Internet is the most explosive communication phenomenon today. Customers are turning to the World Wide Web and the Usenet discussion groups to learn about your products and to shop. Disgruntled customers air their grievances (often on the stock talk sites), and competitors can reposition your brands without your even realizing it. The media has arrived on the Web, too, launching hundreds of electronic newspapers and magazines to editorialize, review, and report on you. Organizations must reshape their approach to brand messaging to address misperceptions and to capitalize on market opportunities in cyberspace.

Reshaping the approach to brand messaging can be done in a number of ways. The first way is to increase the organization's response speed to negative press. Most organizations ignore negative press in the real world, particularly if it's not true. In the real world, negative rumors can spread, but not nearly as quickly as in cyberspace. Consider how long it would take one person to reach 25 people by phone. Next, think about how long that same task takes via e-mail. Now, think about how many people can be reached via discussion boards with one paragraph of rumor or innuendo. If that discussion board is read by only 1,000 people (a tiny number for a popular discussion board), the organization's name can be smeared to several thousand people in less than 24 hours.

Another alteration to traditional brand management approaches is the recognition of the changing competitive landscape. Organizations can use the Web to monitor competitor Web sites and respond to their brand messages quickly. Barnesandnoble.com came about because Amazon.com was draining business from the brick-and-mortar Barnes and Noble stores. Now, the management at barnesandnoble.com can monitor the competition and quickly respond to competitive moves by Amazon.com and others.

Even business-to-business organizations can benefit from this change. The organization's competitive strategists can easily gather information for their brand management teams. They can capture the rumors about new products, strategic relationships, and corporate crises. You can gauge your image and position relative to the competition. Focus groups and expensive marketing research studies aren't necessary. Direct contact with your customers, competitors, suppliers, and distributors helps you get straight, unedited information for competitive analysis. You can even view your business partners' Web sites to see how they're positioning themselves and their relationship with you. It's pure, unadulterated intelligence from the people shaping your organization's future.

MANAGING E-BRAND RISK

Perhaps the biggest brand management problem posed by electronic commerce is gaining and retaining trust in a brand. Most commerce has previously occurred face to face, primarily among people who know each other or are in physical proximity. Infomercials and telemarketing are some of the exceptions, but even that type of marketing gave an organization control over the message in the form of how, when, and where it was delivered. Today, however, consumer products are increasingly sold in markets hundreds or even thousands of miles away, where no personal contact between the buyer and seller is possible.

Controlling the Message

Most direct-to-consumer electronic commerce organizations really have little control over who sees their Web sites and to whom their message is delivered. This lack of control produces a problem of trust. The Internet can't necessarily be relied on to maintain consistent standards in the way products are packaged, promoted, and serviced, and inconsistency leads to customer dissatisfaction and distrust. Several solutions to this problem can be applied. Forming partnerships (discussed earlier in this chapter) is one possible solution. Organizations can establish partnerships vertically downstream with their independent distribution channels so that they can impose quality controls. Large organizations can also use their financial resources to use traditional media advertising to provide the certainty and familiarity that customers have grown to expect from the organization.

An extension of the branding process for all services and products that can be exchanged over digital networks is needed as electronic commerce reaches globally over the Internet. Organizations must assess the competence, reliability, and reputation of the product or service, as well as the distribution channels through which those products and services are delivered. Separated by even greater distances and cultural barriers, customers and business partners need the reassurance of brands. Providing the trust that holds electronic supply and value chains together is a new and highly important value-added service, one that is critical to realizing the full potential of electronic commerce.

Managing Trust on the Internet

The Internet can remedy much of the trust problem if used properly. It can connect businesses and consumers to a large variety of potential products and services well beyond the scope of the yellow pages or friends. However, because the Internet offers such a vast array of options, a problem of trust arises. Even when customers can talk to merchants and service providers in person, they often do not have enough information to make an informed decision. Trying to make major purchasing decisions over the Web is even more difficult. That's why established organizations need to leverage their brands on the Internet. If consumers already trust a particular product or service from an established brand, they're more likely to purchase it via the Web.

One of the real opportunities created by digital commerce is the potential for creating new intermediaries (middlemen) into the process of branding.

The solution lies in using branding as the surrogate for face-to-face relationships. A new product or service is more difficult to sell than a product the consumer already trusts and simply purchases via the Web rather than a retail store. However, smaller firms do not necessarily have to establish their own reputations for quality and reliability when branding can be provided by third parties. Larger, more established firms can act as intermediaries and connect consumers and smaller e-tailers. The key to building trust on the Web for both business-to-consumer and business-to-business organizations is to learn to use the Internet to relay information about reputation, competence, quality, and reliability.

PARTNERING WITH EVERYONE

The Internet is about working together—even with competitors (known as *coopetition*). Organizations must continuously develop strategic alliances to provide a complete set of solutions that help business partners and customers meet their challenges. An organization's business partners must be carefully selected around the globe and exhibit the principles of relationship building, caring, and providing exceptional value to customers. To build a long-term relationship with each customer, organizations must continue to grow with both customers and business partners and commit to providing exceptional value via electronic commerce. Alliances are motivated by a variety of factors:

- The cost of research and development
- Marketing and distribution growth requirements
- The risks of entering new geographic and technological markets
- The desire for diversification
- Time to market where product cycles are getting shorter

Alliances can take a variety of forms, including licensing arrangements, marketing agreements, and R&D cost sharing. For smaller firms wanting to go global, partnering with local firms in their target market is a quick, relatively inexpensive way for an organization to gain a foothold in new geographic areas.

Combining Forces with Business Partners

As mentioned in Chapter 1, combinatorial innovation allows organizations to outsource various pieces of a project, coordinate those pieces, and bring them together in single solution that would have been otherwise impossible with a single firm's resources. According to IMT's Diorio, partnering and using combinatorial innovation can help your brand because consumers want organizations to deliver solutions, and one particular organization may not have everything they need. This represents a fundamental shift from competition to cooperation. It's possible that your business partners hold the key piece of the puzzle that your customers want. In such a case, an organization can buy the business partner, work with the partner, innovate internally, or lose the customer. It's a tough decision and is one that must often be made quickly to keep the customer happy.

Web-Based Communities

Brands should generate a feeling of belonging. Traditional brand companies must work with Web-based intermediaries, sometimes adjusting or adapting their brand management strategies to work with the rules of the community run by the intermediary. Communities are being built on the Web, and the community expects multiple brands to coexist. That's a tough concept for traditional organizations to swallow because brands have to move from a perspective of self-interest to a broader sense of what would be for the good of the community. One of the earliest examples of a commercial online community is the Cambridge Information Network (CIN). CIN is a division of Cambridge Technology Partners, a Cambridge, Massachusetts-based analyst and consulting firm. CIN is a professional online network of senior information technology (IT) executives providing the first Internet-based research, advisory, and consulting service specifically designed for Chief Information Officers (CIOs) and other senior IT staff.

CIN's members from around the globe collaborate in a secure online environment to share experiences, solve common problems, and exchange benchmarking data and other information. Their sponsors gain brand awareness and credibility with a hand-screened audience of CIOs worldwide. CIN also provides online (and traditional) awareness programs that help their business partners improve the exposure and perception of their brands. By delivering information to its community members, CIN does the job of both an advertising firm and a brand-management group. Even business partners that are inexperienced or new to the Web benefit from CIN's ability to market their products and services to its audience in an appropriate, Web-enabled manner.

PROTECTING YOUR BRAND

Brands seem to face many challenges on the Web. Once viewed as the road to commercial success for established brands, new cyberbrands are eroding established brand loyalty, and the new Web-based brands are gaining a power that poses a real threat to older, more traditional brands. Another serious threat posed to brands is adverse publicity. The negative effects of intense adverse publicity are severely detrimental in the short term and may make rebuilding brands difficult even over a longer period of time. Widely distributed negative publicity on Usenet forums can be archived and dredged up for years. Whereas print and/or broadcast media negativity can go away in a short time, it is not that way in cyberspace. Every time a drug maker or restaurant or soda bottler experiences a tampering problem, the public gets upset, sometimes for a long time. Remember the Tylenol scare?

Crisis Management

The news media unfortunately play a huge role in brand management, and they all have Web sites. Thus, having a good public relations staff that is intimately involved in your cyberbranding strategies is critical. Remember that a rumor can spread faster via the Web than via any other medium. Whether rumors spread via the Web have long-term effects depends on several variables, including:

- The organization's reaction
- Current public trust in the brand
- Current awareness of the brand (the less well known, the less damage)
- The size of the organization

Crisis situations vary in terms of how the public perceives the cause, to whom the cause is attributed, and how broad the effect is likely to be. The two key items are the current brand trust and the organization's reaction. If the public trusts the organization, and it reacts responsibly, little damage is likely to occur. The organization must post any relevant information on its Web site as soon as possible. Doing so will help those who use the organization's Web site to get the truth, not the information as filtered by a media bent on sensationalism at all costs.

Legal Issues

Laws in various nations cover most legal issues related to brand management. The bigger issue is trans-border protection. Many U.S. companies have had trouble protecting their brands abroad, and the Internet simply multiplies that problem exponentially. Luckily, court decisions on brand confusion related to domain names have gone to the established brand. For example, a smaller Internet company can simply capitalize on the potential misspelling of an established brand name. Most large, established brands reserve various combinations of their corporate brands to prevent the unscrupulous exploitation of brand-related Web domain names. Still, it's a good idea to register all the names that could be derived from your organization's name, including misspellings.

The other good news is that court decisions on squatters' rights for domain names have consistently gone against the squatter. Trademark laws prevent unauthorized parties from using or benefiting from well-known brands. Early in the domain name registration game, squatters reserved popular names such as Pepsi, Coke, and others and then sold those names to the actual company for exorbitant prices. Eventually the courts ruled that the Internet is just another medium and the trademark registration was good for Web sites as well as newspaper, television, and so on. One particular issue is international reservations. A good example is the Giga Group, a Cambridge, Massachusetts-based analyst firm. The domain names "Giga.com" and "Gigagroup.com" were both registered to organizations outside the United States, so the Giga Group had to use "Gigaweb.com." Domain name registration issues will continue until an international standard is created. In the meantime, organizations should watch for bad imitations, brand rip-offs, and the like on the Web.

INNOVATING CONSTANTLY TO BEAT COMPETITORS

The Internet business model changes rapidly, making innovation mandatory. First, portals, such as Yahoo!, were big. Next, e-tailing (such as Amazon.com) became big. The newest trend now seems to be auctions, such as eBay. What will the next big thing be? It's impossible to tell, but new ideas and innovation drive the Web. The Internet public has a truly short attention span and craves new content all the time. Thus, organizations must continue to figure out what hasn't been done and try to do it before anyone else does. Interestingly, the odder the idea, the more the Internet public seems to like it. Reverse auctions such as Priceline.com are just one example.

Sometimes it's not the idea but rather how the idea is implemented that is new. New concepts such as customer self-service, Web media, and online trading are emerging quickly, although they're really just variations on old themes. Customer self-service facilities allow customers to check the status of their order online rather than call a customer service center. As a result, organizations now have automated customer service 24/7/365. Web media allows Internet surfers to watch sports events or movies, or listen to music over the Web, delivered in real time. Technologies such as Microsoft Windows Media Player, RealAudio, and RealVideo allow surfers to listen to radio as though it were broadcast over the airways.

Online trading is probably one of the best-known (and somewhat infamous) Internet innovations. Online trading was originally seen as a way for investors to save money on commissions and for brokerage firms to increase sales. Online trading, however, quickly gave way to *day trading*, in which online investors try to make money on small moves by buying large numbers of shares. However, day trading quickly became a fiasco because many small investors were trying it at home with little or no understanding of the market. Many day traders lost some or all of their savings, and in one case, a Georgia man's response to his own heavy losses allegedly was to murder several people in a day trading center and then commit suicide. Many online brokerages had to do serious damage control to avoid losing large numbers of clients as a result of this incident. The moral here is to communicate clearly to customers as to just what your capabilities are and to take whatever cautions are necessary to cover the organization's backside.

ACQUIRING AND RETAINING CUSTOMERS

Acquiring customers via the Web is easy; retaining them is ridiculously difficult. As discussed throughout this chapter, brand loyalty in some markets, both business-to-business and business-to-consumer, is nearly nonexistent. Thus, organizations must find new and innovative ways to attract and retain customers. Business partners can certainly help an organization create integrated solutions. Portals such as AOL, Yahoo!, and Excite serve as one way of providing a total solution to Web surfers. Another possibility is to survey and find holes in product or service lines and then fill those holes with unique solutions. Such a strategy requires nearly constant innovation and an extremely creative staff. The key here is to find a need, fill the need, and provide real value for each second that a surfer spends on your site.

Even if you attract visitors, caring for them (which leads to retention) presents a challenge. Today, suppliers provide few alternatives to their customers for call center, technical, or help-desk support. When alternatives are presented, it's the customer who determines where to begin the search for answers. Therefore, the fact that they choose the most interpersonal (and costly) alternatives— phone or direct support—is not surprising. Suppliers, facing intense customer demands for superb service, are therefore compelled to build and maintain costly support infrastructures. To achieve the inherent economic benefits of the e-market, new customer-care strategies must simultaneously squeeze out inefficiencies and boost client satisfaction. The Internet enables mass customization, access to greatly improved knowledgebases, and just-in-time direct interaction. The result is a more effective distribution of resources, more quickly addressed customer problems, and greater brand value.

Organizations can use advanced Web-based scripts, FAQ (frequently asked questions) repositories, and Internet chat and push technologies as a front end to existing support and call center activities. In this way, suppliers can control the flow of information and support, rapidly direct clients to the information they need, and, most important, maintain an interpersonal dialog. Customers retain all the benefits of working with a live support staff and receive the benefit of speed, a richer support information repository, as well as solutions and support that can be pushed to them over the Web. Clients get what they demand (better, more directed, and faster service) while the supplier can use the least expensive methods possible. This scenario is a win-win situation that helps both customer and supplier exploit the benefits of electronic commerce.

WRAP UP

- **The Internet changes almost everything about brand management.** Organizations must find the optimal mix of investments in Internet ads, television, and other media. Organizations must also create new strategies to keep up with a rapidly changing competitive environment. Advertising strategies change, as do the expected returns on investments in various advertising mixes.

- **Established organizations must leverage their real-world brand strength in their cyberbranding mix.** Using the trust already established by widely recognized brands can help smooth an organization's transition to cyberbranding. Many issues must be resolved, however, when an organization transfers a brand to the Internet. These issues include demographics and exposure to international cultures and scrutiny.

- **Organizations can leverage current brands and build new ones using the Internet grapevine.** As with any other grapevine, any information that is released must be carefully controlled and monitored. Good Web sites communicate information in a way that makes visitors tell their friends good things about the site.

- **Managing and protecting cyberbrands presents a whole new set of challenges.** Because the Internet is by nature international and widespread, organizations may encounter situations in which their brand is co-opted, outright stolen, or suffers negative exposure.

International laws remain vague, so the best defense for this situation is a strong, well-planned offense.

- **Innovation in many forms is required to manage cyberbrands.** Whether dealing with a whole new thing, a variation on an existing idea, or simply a change of tone within the content, organizations must continue to monitor (or, better yet, set) trends to stay ahead of the competition.

- **Acquiring customers on the Web is easy. Retaining them is nearly impossible.** Innovative customer care strategies will go a long way to building brand loyalty and help feed the Internet grapevine with positive talk.

Taking Stock

1. Does your organization know enough about cyberbranding to ease the transition of your established brands to the Web?

2. Are your established brands up-to-date or hip enough to make the transition, or must new brands be created for cyberspace?

3. Does your brand management staff possess the skills to create and transfer brands on the Web?

4. Do your brands receive high marks for customer loyalty and trust in the real world so that they'll be trusted in cyberspace?

5. Does your organization know how to protect your brands in cyberspace?

6. Does your organization constantly find new ways to leverage your current brands and create new ones?

7. Do you monitor electronic commerce trends and your competitors?

8. Do you and your business partners work together to create solutions, or do each of you deliver disparate pieces?

9. Does your legal team know the ins and outs of protecting your brand in cyberspace?

ACTION PLAN

- Look at your current brands. Make sure that they resonate with the demographics you're likely to find on the Web.

- Listen to Web-site visitors and people in other Internet venues, such as newsgroups. Find out what the grapevine says about your organization.

- Make sure that the members of your brand management staff understand cyberbranding. If not, hire some who do.

- Carefully monitor your brand's recognition and awareness levels on the Web.

- Innovate constantly. Try to find unfilled needs or opportunities. If possible, leapfrog the competition often.

- Make sure that your customer care surpasses all others in your industry.

- Make sure that your legal team knows how to protect your brand in cyberspace.

- Work with business partners to find total solutions to customer problems.

- Visit your Web site.

Part III

The Microsoft Total E-Commerce Solution

Chapter 9

Microsoft's E-Commerce Strategy

Microsoft has designed a complete and sophisticated e-commerce strategy that organizations can depend on to help them achieve success online. Organizational leaders can benefit from learning about Microsoft's e-commerce products and services, which are designed to create a powerful, integrated, and stable software environment to help companies establish stronger ties with customers and business partners.

Microsoft's e-commerce strategy continues to evolve with the ever-changing world of both business-to-consumer and business-to-business electronic commerce. Microsoft's products and services form an integrated electronic commerce platform and include alliances with key industry players to ensure a comprehensive, open set of products for linking organizations to their business partners and customers. The BizTalk Framework, Microsoft's industry consortium, provides a set of standards and an open community for discussing ways to utilize extensible markup language (XML) for enhanced e-commerce performance. Microsoft's other product categories, including knowledge management and business management, are evolving to a more Web-like look and feel. Microsoft believes that Web technologies will eventually set the standard for the way things get done: Web-based interfaces are the future for both business-to-business and business-to-consumer electronic commerce.

STRATEGY STATEMENTS

Electronic commerce should eventually become the mechanism by which organizations communicate with business partners and customers. Microsoft platforms and strategies are all moving toward Web-based technologies. Microsoft's Business Internet strategy is to help organizations create an information technology (IT) environment in which all systems work via Web technology. The desktop and utilities such as Windows Explorer are all becoming increasingly Web oriented. The interfaces on these programs will eventually resemble a Web browser, such as Internet Explorer. Microsoft's Digital Nervous System and Business Internet strategies are designed to create an environment in which all business operations are performed using Web-based technologies. To accomplish this goal will take many vendors creating many types of hardware and software. Recognizing that no company can do everything, Microsoft has organized the Microsoft E-Commerce Alliance.

Microsoft works with E-Commerce Alliance members to create and co-market offerings that combine the products and services of multiple members into one-stop e-commerce solutions that build on the Microsoft e-commerce platform. These offerings cover a broad range of e-commerce categories, including corporate purchasing, value-chain trading and direct marketing, selling, and service. One-stop e-commerce solutions, including software, services, and support, are specified, integrated, and tested through a collaborative process between Microsoft and E-Commerce Alliance members. Deployment and ongoing support of these solutions is provided to customers through a single point of contact in the E-Commerce Alliance. Together, Microsoft and its partners are assisting organizations in moving all internal and external business operations to Web-based technologies.

Business-to-Consumer Strategies

Microsoft's e-commerce strategy aims to help organizations establish stronger ties with customers and business partners by developing solutions using its e-commerce platform, its partners, and the services of its Internet portal, MSN: The Microsoft Network. Microsoft's business-to-consumer strategies involve assisting organizations in meeting the rapidly changing needs of the electronic commerce environment. These strategies also focus on helping organizations acquire and retain customers more efficiently. Microsoft's products (see Chapter 10, "Microsoft's E-Commerce Platform") provide a strong platform on which to build e-commerce Web sites. Microsoft provides its business partners with opportunities to acquire and retain customers through the use of its products and services. Information gathered through Microsoft's customer surveys and ongoing contact with consumers through MSN *(www.msn.com)* is used to drive product development. Microsoft can also drive traffic to business-to-consumer Web sites through MSN advertising.

The Microsoft e-commerce platform and products

Microsoft's e-commerce platform is the set of software technologies and products that implement and support e-commerce. Microsoft strives to offer the best technology platform for e-commerce solutions. The platform starts with Microsoft Windows 2000 serving as a universal access point to provide consumer and business users with secure access to online e-commerce services. Windows 2000 has built-in support for standard Internet security protocols to enable secure, convenient online payment. Front-end tools such as BizTalk Server 2000, Commerce Server 2000, Microsoft FrontPage, and Visual Basic provide the tools that developers need to create robust electronic commerce sites. Back-end products such as Microsoft BackOffice and Microsoft SQL Server provide the core transaction-processing systems that help front-end products perform well.

Microsoft Wallet, Microsoft Windows 2000 Security, and other products described in Chapter 10 provide organizations with the ability to improve their relationships with business partners and customers. These products enable organizations to rapidly deploy high-quality electronic commerce solutions. Microsoft's bCentral Web site (*www.bcentral.com*) provides emerging enterprises with the ability to drive business to their sites via links to their sites and to receive free or highly discounted advertising. MSN LinkExchange provides these enterprises with the ability to quickly create advertising, increase online traffic, and improve revenues. Using LinkExchange, organizations can increase their exposure to both consumers and other businesses quickly and easily.

Managing the customer relationship

Microsoft can also help organizations with brand development, direct selling, and customer service for business-to-consumer relationships. Microsoft's products enable organizations to accomplish the following:

- Create site visibility
- Target offers at specific consumers
- Generate sales leads (through LinkExchange)
- Provide fast, effective customer service and support

As online purchasing continues to grow exponentially, businesses must handle increasingly large volumes of customer transactions and data in order to tailor the online shopping experience to the customer's needs and desires. Microsoft's products provide front- and back-end data-handling capabilities for storing and using customer information to improve the relationship between online businesses and their customers.

Even if organizations don't rely extensively on the Internet for marketing, sales, and service, they and their customers may benefit considerably from online billing and payment. Studies have shown that the average person receives 12 bills a month by mail from retailers, credit card companies, and utilities. The MSN Money Central Bill Paying service (see Chapter 11, "Web Portals") provides the benefits of sending bills over the Web.

Business-to-Business Strategies

The direction of Microsoft's business-to-business e-commerce strategy is to move all business operations to Web-based technology. This includes both internal value-chain activities, such as marketing, inventory control, and accounting, and externally focused business operations, such as purchasing and billing. Microsoft products such as AppCenter Server provide organizations with the ability to quickly scale up their internal Web and application servers, enabling them to create a digital nervous system using an intranet rather than paper-based internal communications. Products such as BizTalk Server provide organizations with the ability to communicate electronically with their industrial customers and business partners, thereby increasing the speed and accuracy of business transactions. For more information on these products, see Chapter 10.

Optimizing the value chain with a digital nervous system

Microsoft's business e-commerce strategies and products enable the activities of an organization's internal value-chain, as well as other activities, to move to the Web, increasing the speed and accuracy of business transaction processing. An organization's digital nervous system enables the organization to quickly and easily share information among all the departments involved in the value chain. Figure 9-1 shows how a digital nervous system provides organizational departments with the ability to feed information up and down the value chain to continually improve products and customer service.

Microsoft's Business Internet strategy provides organizations with a clear vision of how to extend their digital nervous system to their business partners and customers.

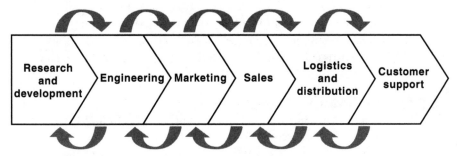

Figure 9-1. *Digital nervous system-enabled value chain*

Enabling the digital nervous system with Microsoft Windows DNA

Microsoft Windows Distributed interNet Applications Architecture (Windows DNA) is the new application development model for the Windows platform. DNA provides organizations with the ability to implement a digital nervous system using specific best practices culled from Microsoft's experience. Windows DNA specifies how to do the following:

- Develop scalable, distributed applications using the Windows platform

- Extend Internet reach to existing data and external applications

- Support a wide range of client device types, maximizing the reach of the application

Because Windows DNA relies on a comprehensive and integrated set of services provided by the Windows platform, developers are free from the burden of building or assembling the required infrastructure for distributed applications and can focus on delivering business solutions.

Windows DNA addresses requirements at all tiers of modern distributed and Web-based applications (both intranet and Internet):

- Presentation

- Business logic

- Data

Like most n-tier client/server and Web-based development models, Windows DNA enables developers to build tightly integrated applications by accessing application services in the Windows platform using a wide range of familiar tools. These services are exposed in a unified way through the Component Object Model (COM). Windows DNA provides customers with a road map for creating successful solutions that build on their existing computing investments and will take them into the future. Using Windows DNA, developers can build or extend existing applications to combine the power of Web technology, both within and beyond the walls of the organization.

Automating the supply chain

Microsoft's Business Internet strategy and its involvement with the BizTalk Framework (see the section "The BizTalk Framework," later in this chapter) as well as Microsoft's BizTalk Server (see Chapter 10) help organizations and their business partners and customers to move more accurate data more quickly up and down the supply chain. The goal of the Business Internet strategy is to make the Internet more useful with a combination of software, services, and partners that enable companies of all sizes to process business transactions on the Web, move manual processes online, understand and respond to their customers better, and connect to their suppliers and partners. The Business Internet is the realization of the vision of a digital nervous system in which information flows quickly through an organization and is delivered to employees and business partners who need it, helping them to respond effectively, take advantage of new opportunities quickly, and fix problems as soon as they arise.

The Business Internet uses an organization's digital nervous system as its plumbing to enable an organization to use the Internet and Web-based technologies to communicate both internally and with business partners. In the business world, it is difficult to bring large enterprises, small businesses, and consumers together simultaneously. Organizations simulate it with distribution networks or affiliate networks. The Internet not only provides a way to conduct traditional business-to-business buying but also enables distributors, consumers, and businesses to come together in new and different ways. Doing so benefits the people who set up these relationships and can profit by them. Figure 9-2 shows how an organization's network might look when it uses a Business Internet strategy to extend its digital nervous system to customers and business partners.

Organizations have entered a new era in which accessing and managing information efficiently throughout the extended enterprise (including business partners and customers) is the key to competitive success, even survival. The traditional linear manufacturing process—from raw materials to supplier to engineer to producer to distributor to end customer—is fast being replaced by an interactive, dynamic, customer-driven business model that demands real-time access to all the information needed for concurrent decision making at every level in the virtual organization. Organizations must use IT systems that support the integration of applications, information flow, and communication to the fullest possible extent.

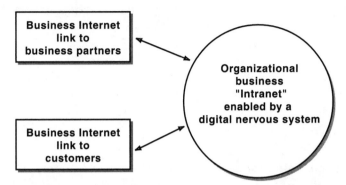

Figure 9-2. *Extending the digital nervous system using a Business Internet strategy.*

Furthermore, communication must provide a view of the entire manufacturing process to customers and partners so that they can interact with greater certainty. Known as *transparency*, this type of communication allows customers to obtain answers to questions—such as availability and price—without being slowed down by human intervention. A supply chain that offers this kind of transparency provides the benefit of forward visibility. With great forward visibility, the supply chain is fully aligned to variations in demand by the end customer and demand uncertainties are managed in near real time.

MICROSOFT AND THE FUTURE OF E-COMMERCE

Microsoft constantly researches electronic commerce trends and works with nearly every research analyst group to remain at the crest of coming technology waves. Microsoft is also fortunate to have a large base of computer users to listens to for new ideas and demands regarding e-commerce computing. Microsoft's ongoing contact with its customers frequently leads to new products, changes to current products, strategy ideas, and even new services. Microsoft's own experience with business-to-business electronic commerce inside its company also drives its software and services offerings. Microsoft's MSN site and LinkExchange provide direct business-to-business and business-to-consumer electronic commerce experiences that the company uses to better formulate strategies and products for its customers and business partners.

Microsoft helps its customers prepare for the future by providing them with tools for planning and implementing electronic commerce initiatives that are the result of Microsoft's own experiences. Some of the key issues that Microsoft helps customers face are the following:

- **Developing user profiles** Organizations must monitor the frequency of user interaction with the site, such as how many times users access an organization's home page and over what span of time, or how many catalog searches users make each time they visit an organization's site.

- **Creating and maintaining site profiles** The size of databases and Web pages, the number of unique pages included in the site, and how many users are contained in the profile database are all important when planning site capacity, whether internally on an intranet or externally for business partners and customers.

- **Assessing technology expenditures** As mentioned in Chapter 4, developing a budget for the hardware, software, and services that an electronic commerce initiative will require can be difficult. Microsoft provides its customers with planning tools and budgeting guides that help organizations make better, more accurate budget estimates.

- **Setting performance targets** Organizations must decide on desired server response times for returning the bulk of the Web pages, including any throughput goals, based on similar sites or those of competitors. , or other benchmarks.

- **Creating a service-to-service architecture** Site architecture plans should include both network diagrams to describe the bandwidth necessary to support the planned throughput and event-sequence charts to map the flow of requests through the various systems so that planners can view potential bottlenecks. Generating these diagrams in the earliest planning phase can highlight difficult-to-envision problems and bottlenecks.

All these issues can be resolved using the planning and implementation tools that Microsoft provides to its customers. Microsoft will continue to work with its customers to help them be successful and will provide significant assistance to them to ensure high-quality, cost-effective implementations of an organization's electronic commerce initiatives.

The Future of the Digital Nervous System and Business Internet

Both the Business Internet concept and the digital nervous system plumbing will continue to evolve with the rapidly changing world of electronic commerce. Microsoft will continue to upgrade its products and services to match the changing needs of its customers. Microsoft is moving its Digital Nervous System concept to a deeper level of integration with current IT and business processes. This push is designed to embed an organization's digital nervous system into all its business operations and make using a digital nervous system and the Business Internet as ordinary as talking on the phone. Microsoft business software is designed with the needs of the Business Internet in mind and will continue to change and evolve. The idea is to give organizations a choice of devices, networks, services, and business partners to develop solutions that meet the unique needs of each organization.

Many of the tools, services, and solution providers that are needed to build a Business Internet (and the underlying digital nervous system) already exist. Microsoft products are interoperable—so that they work with an organization's existing systems—and scalable—so that solutions can evolve and adapt to meet changing business conditions. This interoperability and scalability prevent companies from having to start from scratch and throw away the significant investments they have already made in hardware, software, and knowledge. The Business Internet is not a rigid approach. By providing interoperability through the digital nervous system plumbing layer, the Business Internet provides flexibility so that organizations of all sizes can build sophisticated, customized solutions quickly. Microsoft's goal is to use technology, services, and partners to deliver solutions that best meet the particular needs of each business and that deliver a longer lifespan, better value, and greater total return on investment.

The Future of the Microsoft E-Commerce Strategy

Microsoft's goal is to help customers understand the evolving world of e-commerce and to continue to help them meet the needs of their organization's e-commerce initiatives. Microsoft spends more than $5 billion in research and development annually to keep up with rapidly changing e-commerce technology. With the help of Web technology, Microsoft has dedicated itself to helping customers realize the complete integration of all business products and processes with both customers and business partners. Extensibility and scalability are key to Microsoft's product line as it continues to evolve with customer needs. Microsoft Windows DNA provides a flexible platform that easily adapts to the peculiarities of an organization's electronic commerce needs.

Microsoft continues to survey its customers to determine their needs as the electronic commerce world changes. Customer feedback on products and services is used to drive changes to both product lines and strategies. Microsoft's size and resources allow it to back its bets on the future, which ensures continued support for its customers. Microsoft also eats its own dog food—that is, uses its own products and strategies within its organization. The lessons that staff learn from this use help drive Microsoft's strategy. Microsoft builds future strategies into its products, which makes those products flexible enough to change with the inevitable evolutions of Microsoft strategies.

Combining E-Commerce, Knowledge Management, and Optimized Business Operations

The key to realizing the value of the Microsoft e-commerce solution is to use the knowledge that an organization possesses in a way that optimizes the operation of the organization. This knowledge must be applied to the conducting of commerce using electronic means to increase the accuracy and speed of business transactions. Microsoft's products allow organizations to process business transactions more quickly and accurately and to share the transaction information with business partners and customers. The new Microsoft suite of products for both business-to-business and business-to-consumer electronic commerce are built on the Microsoft DNA concept. The Microsoft DNA solution core products (detailed in Chapter 10) are as follows:

- **Microsoft Windows 2000** The core Windows DNA application services, including the Web server, Active Server Pages, transactions, messaging, data access, clustering, and IP load balancing services are now integrated into the operating system for greater consistency, easier management, and faster performance.

- **Microsoft Visual Studio** This package contains the world's most popular set of development tools, spanning multiple languages. Now including the Windows 2000 Readiness Kit.

- **Microsoft Host Integration Server 2000** This product provides network, data, and application integration with a variety of legacy hosts.

- **Microsoft Application Center 2000** This new product simplifies the deployment and management of Windows DNA applications within farms of servers. Application Center 2000 makes it easy to configure and manage high-availability server arrays.

- **Microsoft BizTalk Server 2000** A new XML-based business-to-business commerce solution, BizTalk Server 2000 provides business-process integration within the enterprise and with trading partners across the Internet through the exchange of XML-formatted business documents.

- **Microsoft Commerce Server 2000** The next generation of the industry's leading packaged business-to-consumer commerce software provides deeper personalization, customizing the site visitors' experience to their needs.

- **Microsoft SQL Server 2000** The next generation of the popular SQL Server 7.0 adds native XML support, enhanced data-mining capabilities, and integration with Windows 2000 for even greater scalability and availability.

These products provide services that enable organizations to move toward a completely Web-based model of doing business, both internally and externally. Figure 9-3 shows one way in which the products might be situated in an organization.

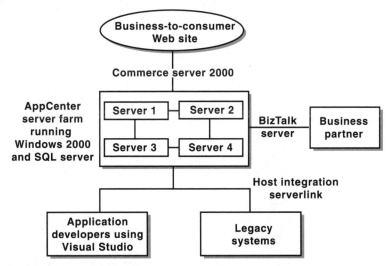

Figure 9-3. *Microsoft product configuration scenario*

Microsoft's products are created to work together as one cohesive unit, facilitating the exchange of accurate information more quickly and efficiently between organizational business units and business partners. The common platform of Windows 2000 means that the products will communicate through common interfaces, making support and upgrades easier. This suite of products provides organizations with the ability to optimize their business operations by sharing the knowledge they possess with both customers and business partners. Along with Microsoft Exchange, these products provide a collaborative platform that organizations can use to manage their intellectual capital to gain a competitive advantage. These products also provide organizations with the ability to communicate seamlessly with their business partners through the BizTalk XML standard.

THE BIZTALK FRAMEWORK

BizTalk is an industry initiative started by Microsoft and supported by a wide range of organizations, from technology vendors such as SAP and CommerceOne to technology users such as Boeing and BP/Amoco. BizTalk is not a standards body. It is actually a community of standards users, with the goal of pushing the adoption of XML to enable electronic commerce and application integration. The BizTalk Framework is a set of guidelines on how to publish schemas in XML and how to use XML messages to easily integrate software programs in order to build e-commerce solutions. The framework is designed to help organizations leverage what they have today—existing data models, solutions, and application infrastructure—and adapt it for electronic commerce through the use of XML.

The BizTalk Framework is designed to address the challenges associated with enabling efficient and automated interactions between applications across business boundaries in a cost-effective manner. The framework should provide organizations with the ability to transact business across organizational boundaries as easily as if it were within an enterprise or departmental boundary. New challenges in the areas of security and reliability should be addressed in order to communicate with other organizations. These challenges to interaction across business boundaries include but are not limited to the following:

- Lack of a flexible and universal language to specify, package, publish, and exchange both structured and unstructured information across application or business boundaries

- Lack of a flexible and universal language to execute transformation rules to convert information from one format to the other as application and business boundaries are crossed

- Lack of middleware-neutral application-level communication protocols to enable automated interactions across application or business boundaries

The BizTalk Framework, using XML, meets these challenges. XML and XML-based schema languages provide a strong set of technologies with a low barrier to entry. These languages enable organizations to describe and exchange structured information between collaborating applications or business partners in a platform- and middleware-neutral manner. As a result, domain-specific standards bodies and industry initiatives have started to adopt XML and XML-based schema languages to specify both their vocabularies and content models. These schemas are becoming widely published and implemented to facilitate communication between both applications and businesses.

The application communicates with other applications by sending business documents back and forth through BizTalk servers. These documents are implemented according to the implementation defined in the transport-specific message schema and the supporting BizTalk Document schema. Communication is facilitated by a BizTalk server, which provides a defined set of services to the application. Multiple BizTalk servers communicate with one another over a variety of data communication protocols, such as HTTP or MSMQ. The BizTalk Framework does not prescribe what these data communication protocols are and is independent of the implementation details of each. Figure 9-4 diagrams how the BizTalk standard is used to move data from one organization to another, though this method could just as easily be used within an organization between business units.

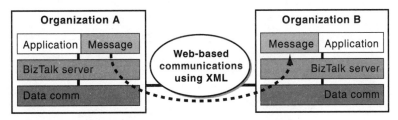

Figure 9-4. *Schematic of the BizTalk communication method*

The application is responsible for formatting BizTalk documents and submitting them to the BizTalk server. The server processes the documents and constructs BizTalk messages as appropriate for the transport protocol. The BizTalk server uses information contained in the optional BizTags to determine the correct transport-specific destination address(es). The server then hands the message to the data communications layer for transmission to the destination BizTalk server(s). The interfaces between the application, BizTalk server, and Data Communications layer are implementation specific.

USING KNOWLEDGE MANAGEMENT TO IMPROVE E-COMMERCE SUCCESS

Organizations possess enormous amounts of knowledge that is stored in their employees' brains, on paper, and in computers. The question is, how can a company gather and share this intelligence in order to create a business advantage? A good knowledge-management process integrates people and technology with collaborative processes to create a smarter and more competitive organization. It also lets employees use knowledge from the enterprise as a whole, not just the information found in their department. There are two core types of knowledge: quantitative and qualitative. Quantitative knowledge includes any numerical data, such as financial figures, order quantities, and customer information (age and income, for example). Qualitative data includes best practices and nonnumerical customer data, such as product feedback by customers. A good knowledge-management system lets users mine and manipulate both types of data both discretely and together. Quantitative knowledge can be stored in various Microsoft products, including Excel, SQL Server, and Access. Qualitative knowledge can be stored and shared using Exchange Server.

Most organizations must create and use some kind of knowledge management function in order to survive. Organizations today need to be able to continuously evolve and grow with their customer base and few can afford to waste precious human or financial resources. Personalization means more than just providing a customer with a customized Web page. It means knowing your customers well enough to send them targeted marketing information and using data about your customers' buying patterns to detect product and pricing trends. Knowledge management also lets a company decide which vendors to use and which to drop. Microsoft's Internet Information Server, BizTalk Server, and Commerce Server 2000 can help organizations share knowledge internally and with their business partners.

Data Warehousing for E-Commerce

Businesses ranging from high-tech startups to car dealerships are trying to use the knowledge they have to better manage their relationship with their customers and business partners. Accordingly, businesses must handle large amounts of data effectively to make customers feel comfortable and welcome online and to provide business partners with the information they need. To track visitor habits and personalization data, businesses are turning to data warehouses and their high-volume data handling capabilities to customize online shopping experiences. Well-designed data warehouse systems are efficient at handling large volumes of data and at facilitating the accurate and timely query and manipulation of that data. Microsoft's SQL Server provides organizations with the ability to store data, and tools such as Excel and the SQL Server Programmer Kit provide organizations with the ability to analyze the data. Microsoft also partners with other companies that supply decision-support and data-analysis tools, thereby providing Microsoft's customers with a variety of choices.

Internal users, such as marketing staff, have historically used data warehouses to slice, dice, and monitor trends in customer buying habits, complaints, and product or service requests. Web-based businesses now use that same data in real time to provide customers with a shopping experience tailored to their personal needs and desires. Web-enabled data warehouses connect the shopping program with the data in the warehouse through various types of interfaces, depending on the database management system, programming language, and operating system.

Setting prices

Businesses can use purchase data for pricing analysis. It's often important to monitor the effect of pricing on customer buying habits. Large amounts of data stored in a warehouse provide marketing and pricing analysts with the ability to more easily maximize profits without sacrificing sales. Reactions to price variations can be analyzed by age, income, location, and other demographic segments. Demographic data can be used in many other ways. Businesses can use customer demographics to supply discounts one-to-one or based on broad demographic or purchase-habit segments. For example, suppose that teenagers typically buy more music CDs than most other market segments. Customers who identify themselves as teenagers might receive discounts on CD purchases to keep them coming back.

Getting personal

Data analysis can also prevent businesses from discounting infrequent customers and help them reward frequent shoppers. Very detailed analysis can also provide insight as to what items might be good loss leaders. *Loss leaders* are items that a business sells at a loss to gain customers or reward frequent shoppers. Data warehouses can provide a tremendous boost to online businesses trying to improve their customer relationship management (CRM) systems. The right data used properly can help businesses provide a customer with choices they didn't know existed, if the businesses know enough about the customer. Studies frequently cite convenience as the most important reason that customers shop online. Businesses can personalize a shopping experience, making shopping easier for customers. Online businesses can use data warehouses to help customers find what they need faster and more easily. Increased convenience can translate into customer loyalty over the long haul.

Leveraging Knowledge Assets for Global Competition

Organizations that use a standard platform across all business units at all locations will find it easier to manage information resources because of simplified data sharing and communication methods. Microsoft's products provide a complete platform for sharing information among all business units of a global entity. Microsoft's wide variety of products allows organizations to simplify the communication of data between departments because of the way that Microsoft products are built around common data interfaces. By using Microsoft's suite of products across an international organization, the organization realizes benefits from:

- A standard platform with common Microsoft Windows 2000 Server interfaces

- Standardized data design using common Microsoft SQL Server databases

- Collaborative tools such as Microsoft Exchange

- Standard document formats in Microsoft Office

Windows 2000 provides the standard interface for all Microsoft's products. This common platform allows organizations to quickly and easily hook their information systems together, which in turn enables organizations to more easily share information and leverage the knowledge that they possess for a competitive advantage. Standardized, distributed databases mean that organizations can easily exchange data between their departments and business units globally. Collaborative tools provide organizations with the ability to share qualitative knowledge and best practices across global entities. Standard document formats make exchanging important business documents simple and fast.

ADAPTING BUSINESS OPERATIONS TO IMPROVE E-COMMERCE SUCCESS

Microsoft's products allow organizations to become faster and more efficient at completing business transactions, which ultimately optimizes the use of financial and human resources organization. In general, automated information systems are more accurate and faster, and Microsoft's products help organizations automate the processing of business transactions. By using Windows 2000 as a standard platform, organizations may avoid the need to build interfaces between competing products that can result in inaccurate data and slow transaction processing. The fewer variables introduced into a business operating environment, the faster and more efficient the business can operate. Using Microsoft's product line to automate and optimize business operations increases the efficiency of internal value chains and both internal and external supply chains. Organizations must reorganize their business operations to take advantage of the new Web technology available.

Changing the Value and Supply Chains for the Future

Microsoft's standard platform (Windows 2000 Server) provides organizations with the ability to apply both Microsoft's products and those of their partners to the task of increasing the efficiency of information flow both within the organization and beyond its walls. Internal value chains can be made more efficient by automating manual tasks using Microsoft's standard suite of products. These products enable better information to flow more quickly within the organization, which means that decisions can be made faster and more accurately. Using products such as Microsoft Exchange allows an organization to store best practices that can be used by all participants in the value chain. Shared databases using Microsoft SQL Server provide decision makers with the information they need to guide the organization through the evolving e-world.

Supply chains are quickly moving toward a completely automated model. Microsoft's suite of e-products, including BizTalk Server, Application Center 2000, Commerce Server 2000, and Host Integration Server, provides organizations with the ability to link their supply chain partners together electronically. By reducing the number of touch points, or how often data is touched by human hands, Microsoft's products increase the accuracy and speed with which the organization and its business partners can exchange information. Increasing the efficiency of the supply chain with better data allows organizations to move products more quickly, develop better relationships with business partners, and provide better and more efficient service to customers. Microsoft's products enable organizations and their business partners to link themselves together to form a seamless flow of products, services, and information.

Re-Engineering for E-Commerce

Organizations are changing their business models to take advantage of the new Internet economy. Organizations such as barnesandnoble.com have moved from the traditional retail-logistics model of buy-store-sell to the Internet model of sell-source-deliver. This means organizations emphasize product selection and customer service rather than inventory tracking and accounting. This new business model requires an organization to react much more quickly to competitive pressures and their business operating environment than in the past. Because so many organizations are trying to become virtual, some are trying to avoid carrying inventory at all. This caused problems in the 1999 Christmas season when companies such as Toysrus.com couldn't deliver by their published deadlines and offered $100 gift certificates to customers who did not receive their items on time.

Microsoft's products enable organizations to process orders and exchange information with business partners at the speed of light. This means that inventory availability is known at all times to all participants in the supply chain. Retailers and e-tailers can get real-time availability from wholesalers and distribution organizations. Wholesalers, in turn, can advise manufacturers of inventory needs and receive information on inventory availability from manufacturers in real time. Using Microsoft's products such as BizTalk Server to link all supply-chain participants results in reduced inventory outages, increased efficiencies, and, ultimately, higher customer satisfaction, all of which translate into better organizational performance.

WRAP UP

- **Microsoft believes that eventually all business will be conducted electronically.** Organizations will continue to move toward a Web-based technology model, and business transactions will follow. Whether within an organization on an intranet or between business partners and customers over the Internet, business transaction processing will continue to migrate to Web technology.

- **Microsoft wants to help organizations strengthen their ties with customers and business partners through better data communication.** Microsoft's products and strategies are directed at helping organizations improve their relationships with supply-chain members from end to end. Increased accuracy and efficiency benefit organizations, their business partners, and their customers.

- **Microsoft's products can help organizations improve the efficiency of the value and supply chains.** Microsoft's E-Commerce product line is designed to automate all the functions normally performed when moving product from raw material to consumer. Microsoft's Digital Nervous System concept and Business Internet implementation provide organizations with the ability to process data without boundaries. Microsoft's DNA architecture presents the blueprint for those implementations.

■ **Microsoft will continue to invest in research and development to stay ahead of the rapidly evolving e-world.** Microsoft listens— to its customers, to its business partners, and to consumers. By using the customer data at its disposal, Microsoft can react to technology trends before they overtake Microsoft's customers. Microsoft's Digital Nervous System and Business Internet concepts will continue to evolve and be updated as necessary to keep Microsoft's customers at the forefront of e-commerce technology.

■ **The BizTalk Framework is a platform-neutral e-commerce framework that makes it easy for businesses to integrate applications and conduct business over the Internet with trading partners and customers.** The BizTalk Framework is based on extensible markup language (XML) schemas and industry standards that enable integration across industries and between business systems, regardless of platform, operating system, or underlying technology.

■ **Microsoft's products and strategies enable organizations to leverage their knowledge assets and realize a competitive advantage.** Organizations must link suppliers, manufacturers, wholesalers, and retailers to speed the flow of information and product through the supply chain. Microsoft's strategy is to enable all supply-chain participants to share and use the knowledge possessed by each participant to improve their competitive position.

Taking Stock

1. Does your IT infrastructure allow you to communicate with and serve your customers quickly and easily?

2. Can you and your business partners exchange data seamlessly with little or no translation?

3. Is your supply chain e-commerce ready?

4. Can your IT infrastructure support an automated supply chain?

5. Is your IT infrastructure embedded in the day-to-day processing of business transactions?

6. Can you leverage not only the knowledge that your organization possesses but also that of your business partners ?

7. Are your data warehouses accurate, complete, and easily accessible?

8. Can your IT infrastructure support a sense of boundarylessness for your organization or is your staff still internally focused?

9. Are all your business processes and systems Web enabled?

10. Do your current software vendors have a firm direction for the future? Do they understand e-commerce well enough to present a cohesive strategy?

ACTION PLAN

❑ Find out what your customers and business partners are saying about your ability to share information with them.

❑ Develop a baseline architecture diagram of current systems and sketch out a vision of the perfect architecture. Visit Microsoft's Web site to see how Microsoft's products can help you realize that vision.

❑ Find out how your business partners are getting ready for e-commerce. Find out what their standard platforms are.

❑ Develop a vision of a digital nervous system for your organization. Look for opportunities to automate currently manual tasks.

❑ Examine the BizTalk Framework to see how the XML standard can assist your organization in communicating with business partners.

❑ Check your data warehouses to see whether all data warehouses at all business units have similar data structures and can share information easily.

❑ Determine whether your organization uses the information it possesses appropriately, and whether it can share that data with others outside the organization's walls.

Chapter 10

Microsoft's E-Commerce Platform

*Microsoft's e-commerce products provide a significant boost to an
organization's e-commerce efforts. Organizational leaders can
rely on Microsoft's products for high-quality, cost-effective,
efficient electronic commerce implementations.*

To link themselves to other organizations and to enable the flow of information electronically within and beyond their walls, organizations must utilize information technology that works together efficiently and effectively. Microsoft's products are built on a common platform with the common Business Internet strategy in mind. These products work together to provide organizations the ability to leverage information. Microsoft's products communicate with each other and build on each other's strengths. Microsoft's goal is to make Web technology the everyday approach to business. All Microsoft's products are aimed at helping organizations realize this goal as easily as possible. Microsoft's products enable organizations to work collaboratively and to link their digital nervous systems, using Web technology to create a seamless flow of information between business partners and customers. Microsoft's platform products enable organizations to build the foundation on which all their applications can run reliably.

Note

At the time of this writing, some of the products discussed are still undergoing initial development. Features and functionality of the final products might differ from those described here. Check the Microsoft Web site at *www.microsoft.com* for the latest product information.

DOING BUSINESS ON THE INTERNET THROUGH COLLABORATION

Organizations must share information in a timely, efficient manner. Microsoft Outlook 2000, Microsoft Exchange 2000 Server, and Microsoft NetMeeting enable collaborative capabilities. Outlook 2000 contains the leading implementation of Internet messaging and collaboration standards and protocols. Outlook 2000 integrates tightly with the Web and becomes a great e-mail application regardless of the Internet service provider or browser. Microsoft Exchange 2000 Server provides organizations with the ability to share information in a reliable groupware environment. Exchange 2000 Server represents the next generation of high-speed, highly organized collaborative computing. NetMeeting delivers a complete Internet conferencing solution for all Windows users with multipoint data conferencing, text chat, whiteboard, and file transfer, as well as point-to-point audio and video. NetMeeting provides organizations with the ability to communicate with their business partners and customers in real time, increasing the speed and accuracy of business. These tools provide organizations with the ability to work as though business partners and customers are simply part of the business process—and they are.

Microsoft Outlook 2000

The Microsoft Outlook 2000 messaging and collaboration client helps users organize, view, and share information—all in one place, using a consistent interface. As Microsoft's premier e-mail application, Outlook 2000 combines support for Internet standards–based e-mail with integrated calendar, contact, and task management features. Outlook 2000 supports all current Internet communication protocols, including Simple Mail Transport Protocol and Post Office Protocol 3 (SMTP/POP3), Internet Message Access Protocol 4 (IMAP4), Message Disposition Notifications (Read Receipts), Lightweight Directory Access Protocol (LDAP), Dynamic HTML, Secure/Multipurpose Internet Mail Extensions

(S/MIME), Network News Transfer Protocol (NNTP), vCard, vCalendar, and iCalendar.

Outlook 2000 allows users to take advantage of the Internet for more than just Web pages and electronic mail. It enables new ways to collaborate and share information. For workgroups and enterprises, Outlook 2000, combined with Microsoft Exchange 2000 Server, is a comprehensive solution for developing and deploying a wide variety of collaborative applications—from contact management solutions for workgroups to enterprise-wide workflow and tracking applications. Organizations can also use Outlook's remote features to coordinate and communicate with business partners and customers to ensure a seamless flow of information up and down the supply chain. This coordination capability is critical as organizations move to just-in-time models of electronic commerce.

Microsoft Exchange 2000 Server

Microsoft Exchange 2000 Server provides organizations with the ability to share information both within and beyond organizational boundaries. Exchange 2000 Server incorporates two years of customer and partner feedback and addresses many key issues. Customers and partners outlined three broad requirements that they wanted to see in the next generation of their messaging and collaboration infrastructure:

- Increased reliability, scalability, and performance of the enterprise messaging and collaboration platform; further utilization of the capabilities of the operating system to reduce the cost of system ownership

- New forms of collaboration for knowledge workers, integration of Web and workflow application design, and a single infrastructure and user model for working with messages, documents, and applications to increase productivity

- A communications infrastructure that provides access to information at any time and from anywhere through emerging technologies such as wireless communication, unified messaging, hand-held devices, and teleconferencing

Based on these customer requirements, Exchange 2000 Server has been designed to be a solid, fast, efficient platform for messaging and collaboration. Exchange 2000 Server's security and open architecture make it a high-quality solution that is easily integrated into any organization.

Scalability

Microsoft Exchange 2000 Server provides greater reliability and system availability than previous versions of Exchange Server through advances in messaging database technology and clustering. System clustering provides organizations with the ability to create groups of Exchange servers that work together in a highly reliable, redundant configuration. Exchange 2000 Server also fully utilizes Microsoft Windows 2000 Active Directory, providing a unified infrastructure for users, messaging, and network resource administration. Exchange 2000 Server takes advantage of the full power of Windows 2000 Active Directory, enabling system administrators to create a single, unified enterprise directory for administration of all users, groups, permissions, configuration data, network login, file and Web shares, and more. Active Directory services provide a single point of administration for e-mail and network resources that can lower the cost of ownership of a typical messaging and collaboration infrastructure.

Exchange Server 5.5 offered an unlimited database size, and Exchange 2000 Server takes this architecture to the next step, enabling administrators to split a single logical database across multiple physical databases. This feature reduces the time required to restore data while also increasing reliability, resulting in fewer lost user hours in the event of system failure. To increase the already high levels of Exchange Server reliability, the combination of Exchange 2000 Server with Windows 2000 Server enhances clustering to include Active/Active (multi-master) clustering. Multi-master clustering provides the ability to maintain multiple master copies that are available to all users. Each copy is mirrored and constantly updated to maintain currency. Windows 2000 Advanced Server will support two-way clustering, whereas Windows 2000 Datacenter Server will support four-way clustering. By combining unlimited database capabilities and multipoint clustering, Exchange 2000 Server can grow with the needs of any organization.

Distributed reliability and performance

Distributed configuration architecture enables services to be partitioned across multiple servers. This architecture provides scalability to hosted services that can potentially serve millions of users. Exchange 2000 Server provides high-performance routing of e-mail messages between servers using advanced algorithms and SMTP as a peer-connection to X.400-based routing, for a high level of system-wide reliability, despite multiple network or machine failures. Exchange 2000 Server significantly increases the performance of Internet e-mail while maintaining compatibility with existing Mail Application Programming Interface (MAPI) messaging clients by enabling e-mail clients to store and retrieve MIME content directly from Exchange 2000 Server with on-demand format conversion.

Administration and security

Administration of Exchange 2000 Server becomes easier through integration with the familiar, single-seat management interface of Microsoft Management Console (MMC) in Windows 2000. A single console for managing all Microsoft servers, including Windows 2000 itself, means that administrators can take training once and reuse their expertise across management tasks. Exchange 2000 Server uses Windows 2000 to ensure messaging and collaboration security, including native use of Windows 2000 security descriptors (access control lists) for setting permissions on all Exchange resources. System administrators can create and manage all user groups and permissions once for all network and messaging and collaboration scenarios.

Access to information

Information stored in a central repository called the Web Store, such as e-mail messages, documents, Web content, and applications, can be accessed through a variety of client software, including Microsoft Outlook, Microsoft Windows Explorer, a Web browser, Windows 32-bit applications, Microsoft FrontPage 2000, and the MS-DOS prompt. Microsoft Office 2000 users can store and retrieve Office documents directly to and from the Web Store using the standard File menu commands Save As and Open. This feature provides a consistent model and set of tools for managing e-mail and documents together.

The built-in content indexing of the Web Store enables high speed and accurate full-text searches across a diverse set of information types, such as e-mail messages, e-mail attachments, Web content, and documents. Indexing and searches enable knowledge workers to find content using familiar search tools such as those found in Outlook 2000. All data stored in the Web Store can be accessed through a Web browser, enabling easy access to information. The Web Store allows user-defined and application-defined custom properties (such as document author, workflow recipient, or description) to be stored with each item in the database, providing powerful opportunities for rich viewing and searching of information.

Microsoft Windows NetMeeting

Microsoft Windows NetMeeting provides a conferencing solution for the Internet and corporate intranet. NetMeeting's features let you communicate with both audio and video, collaborate on virtually any Windows-based application, exchange graphics using your computer as an electronic whiteboard, transfer files, use the text-based chat program, and much more. Using your PC and the Internet, you can now hold face-to-face conversations with friends and family around the world and it won't cost a fortune to do so. Because NetMeeting works with any video capture card or camera that supports Video for Windows, you can choose from a wide range of video equipment.

NetMeeting's multipoint data conferencing allows users to share any Windows-based application or folder with several other participants using standards-based T.120 data conferencing. NetMeeting also has an electronic whiteboard for text-based chat, as well as file transfer capabilities. With a sound card, microphone, and speakers, NetMeeting lets you place standards-based H.323 audio calls over the Internet or a corporate intranet. You can also add a video camera for face-to-face communication. Complete Internet conferencing allows users to share data with audio/video to conference with colleagues in real time! Support for industry standards ensures that you can call, connect, and communicate with compatible conferencing products. NetMeeting is included in Windows 2000.

CREATING AND MANAGING INTERNET CONTENT

For any organization involved in electronic commerce, the first step is to create a Web site that is easy to use and access (see Chapters 6 and 7 for discussions of usability and Web design). Microsoft's products enable organizations to get started quickly in creating both business-to-consumer and business-to-business Web sites. Microsoft Office 2000 provides simple, easy-to-use Web content creation capabilities with Microsoft Word 2000 and Microsoft FrontPage 2000. Microsoft Visual Studio provides organizations with the ability to develop advanced Web applications for e-commerce ventures. Microsoft Visual Studio ties into tools such as Visual InterDev, Visual C++, and others. Microsoft Commerce Server 2000 provides organizations with a fast, reliable platform on which to build electronic commerce applications using the Windows DNA architecture.

Microsoft Office 2000

Microsoft Office 2000 has been integrated with Web technology. Besides Microsoft Outlook, (see the previous section on collaboration), Microsoft Word and, of course, Microsoft FrontPage are geared toward creating documents and Web content. Microsoft continues to keep the goal of designing for the Web in mind when adding features and function sets to Microsoft Office.

Microsoft Word 2000

Microsoft Word 2000 provides support for HTML as a companion file format to its native document format. Users have access to the full power of Word whether they are working in the Word file format or in HTML. With this kind of access, users can create documents in Word 2000, save them as HTML, open them again in Word, and still find all the rich editing features of Word available. Word 2000 also provides a set of Web page themes and templates. These themes provide consistent backgrounds, picture bullets, fonts, and other formatting features to documents.

Frames provide a simple way to make Web sites easier to navigate but can be quite difficult to create by hand. As a full HTML editor, Word 2000 provides powerful tools to create and view the "what you see is what you get" (WYSIWYG) frame pages. With Word 2000, it is now possible to preview published documents in the default Web browser from within Word. On the main command bar, the Print Preview button has been expanded to support Web Preview. The File menu also includes this command. Web Preview makes it easy to see the final result just the way others will see it. Word 2000 also offers an improved hyperlink interface to help users have an easier time managing hyperlinks in documents. Users can create different kinds of links, such as jumps or e-mail triggers, without having to know the necessary HTML programming code. Users can easily specify the text displayed in hyperlinks and create links to new files as well as to multiple files from the same source. When users save documents, Word 2000 checks the links and repairs those that aren't working because of moved files or other conditions. This feature prevents broken links from appearing to visitors.

Microsoft FrontPage 2000

Microsoft FrontPage 2000 lets organizations create rich Web sites with improved ease of use and productivity for all users. FrontPage 2000 gives users control of their Web sites. They can position elements exactly where they want them on the page, give their Web site a professional and consistent look across all its pages, import and edit HTML just as they like, and use the latest in Web technology. FrontPage 2000 allows users to create engaging Web sites that look and work exactly the way they want them. FrontPage includes the ability to lay out pages with exacting care and design the pages with color-coordinating elements and cutting-edge features such as Dynamic HTML and Cascading Style Sheets, adding style, movement, and interest to pages.

Editing Features

FrontPage 2000 combines the easiest to use WYSIWYG editor with HTML source preservation and new HTML editing productivity tools. FrontPage 2000 allows users who author in a text editor and know HTML to create code faster that is formatted just the way they want. This is a breakthrough for HTML authors who want to preserve their formatting and authoring preferences and for those who want to switch back and forth between multiple HTML editors without unnecessary formatting changes. FrontPage 2000 also has the ability to take database queries and easily incorporate them into FrontPage-based Web pages. Organizations can create Web sites with pages in which the data is updated when the user enters the page or refreshes it. This updating feature provides the user with the latest information at all times and saves the Webmaster from having to keep re-posting fresh snapshots of the database.

Site building

FrontPage 2000 allows organizations to create Web sites that take advantage of the latest Web functionality by using the prebuilt Web components that FrontPage ships with, buying third-party add-ons, or using its new programmability features, such as Visual Basic for Applications, to easily create add-ons of their own. FrontPage 2000 allows users to see a complete view of all the elements that make up their sites. Users can make sure that the site is operating at top performance and is arranged for easy navigation. FrontPage 2000 also allows users to work together easily in workgroups or teams. Teams can update their Web sites quickly with new management reports that summarize the status of the site at a glance, including reports on the total number and size of files, slow pages, unlinked (unused files), broken hyperlinks, and publication status for all files in the Web.

Collaboration features

FrontPage 2000 includes several improvements in the process of collaborative publishing of Web pages and files to Web servers that make updating sites even easier. New page-level control over publishing enables more flexibility in publishing Web sites to an Hypertext Transfer Protocol (HTTP) server (whether or not it is running the FrontPage Server Extensions). Building on the remote and multi-user authoring capabilities that FrontPage has had since version 1.0, FrontPage 2000 adds robust collaboration tools to enable teams to easily update their Web site with multiple levels of security. New tools such as built-in support for page level check-in and check-out help teams work together better than ever. The check-in and check-out-process at the page level means that team members can change a single page without changing the rest of the site. This process also provides more control over who makes what changes to which pages. Moreover, FrontPage's open site management allows any user to easily update a FrontPage Web site with new content, even if the user is not using FrontPage.

FrontPage 2000 was designed to make creating and maintaining Web sites as easy and worry free as possible. It helps automate routine tasks such as fixing hyperlinks to pages or files when they are renamed or moved and even inserting links to all Web documents in a specific category. It automates these tasks for both local and global sites. FrontPage 2000 allows users to incorporate advanced functionality that works on the browser and server platform that they want to target.

FrontPage 2000 is complementary to many of the products that customers already own. For example, it uses the same management console used by

Microsoft Windows NT Server, Microsoft Internet Information Services, and other BackOffice applications, and it ships with Windows NT Server, Microsoft Site Server, and Microsoft Visual InterDev. This commonality allows administrators to manage and create FrontPage-based Webs in an environment that is as familiar to them as Microsoft Office.

Microsoft Visual Studio 6.0

Microsoft Visual Studio 6.0 Professional Edition includes the complete set of development tools for building reusable applications in Microsoft Visual Basic 6.0, Microsoft Visual C++ 6.0, Microsoft Visual J++ 6.0, or Microsoft Visual FoxPro 6.0. Microsoft Visual InterDev 6.0 provides easy integration with the Internet and a full Web page authoring environment. These tools are based on the Windows DNA architecture. Visual Studio 6.0 addresses all aspects of Windows DNA application development, including integrated tools for multitier application design, user interface development, middle-tier component development and assembly, database programming and design, performance analysis, and team-based development support. Visual Studio allows developers to choose the programming language they already know (including C++, Basic, Java, or FoxPro) and to choose a language that best suits the technical requirements of a specific component of the application. In addition, because all tools in the suite support the Component Object Model (COM), a component created in any language can be reused by any other tool in the suite.

Visual Studio supports logical application design based on the Unified Modeling Language (UML) via the Visual Studio Modeler, which was jointly developed by Microsoft and Rational Software. UML is becoming the industry standard for developing object-oriented software. UML has been certified by the international certifying organization Object Management Group (OMG), whose Web page is at *www.omg.org*. UML is evolving into the standard world-wide notation for presenting object-oriented modeling and design. In addition, Visual Studio 6.0 includes Web site diagramming/design for Internet Information Server and database design tools supporting both Microsoft SQL Server and Oracle databases. All the Visual Studio 6.0 development tools share productivity features. The tools share a common look and feel, allowing developers to capitalize on their knowledge base from tool to tool. All tools support component development and assembly based on COM. The Microsoft Repository and the Visual Component Manager manage components written in any language in the suite. Developers can use the Visual Component Manager to publish, catalog, and search for components, designs, specifications, and other elements of a project to or from the Repository. In addition, Visual Studio 6.0 offers complete integration with Visual SourceSafe 6.0 for source code version control and file locking in team-based development scenarios. Of course, all Microsoft's Web development products are now geared toward team-based Web development and technologies.

Microsoft Commerce Server 2000

The next generation of Microsoft Site Server 3.0, Commerce Edition, Microsoft Commerce Server 2000 greatly simplifies the process of building sophisticated, customer-centric Internet and extranet selling sites. Commerce Server 2000 will help make it easier for business managers to more effectively control and manage their online business by giving them the tools to know their customers, understand how customers interface with the site, and realize how to best reach existing customers as well as attract new customers. The closed-loop merchandising capabilities of Commerce Server 2000 will make the site more relevant to users over time, building loyalty in the customer base. Closed-loop merchandising provides organizations with the ability to track products from customer order to customer receipt. This capability increases customer satisfaction and the ability of the organization to learn about its customers, as well as to continuously improve its products and services.

Business managers will benefit from the real-time marketing capabilities of Commerce Server 2000, including a higher-performance personalization and targeting system, advanced catalog management, and sophisticated business analysis with online analytical processing (OLAP) services. For the information technology (IT) manager, Commerce Server 2000 provides a more scalable and robust e-commerce foundation using the Windows 2000 Active Directory services and tight integration with Microsoft SQL Server 7.0.

For integration with legacy environments within the organization and for application integration across the value chain, Commerce Server 2000 provides seamless integration with both BizTalk Server 2000 and Microsoft Host Integration Server 2000. Businesses will be able to leverage the ubiquitous applicability of XML-based BizTalk schema easily from online promotions on Web marketplaces to backend interchange with customers and partners. Commerce Server 2000 will also make it easy to take advantage of the rich promotional services of The Microsoft Network (MSN), including bCentral's LinkExchange, to help build the online customer base more rapidly.

More than 100 industry-leading independent software vendors are working with Microsoft to build solutions that integrate with Commerce Server 2000. These experts know their markets and particular industries and are building and delivering horizontal and vertical industry-specific applications that provide special functionality (such as international tax calculations, product configuration, or shipping rates) or assist with integration (such as interfaces with popular enterprise resource planning (ERP) packages). The range of these solutions is extensive and includes payment, tax, shipping, logistics, procurement, accounting, customer management, , and electronic data interchange (EDI). This partner-centric approach to providing e-commerce solutions offers customers the best-of-breed choice of solutions that best meet their unique needs. Commerce Server 2000 provides the best set of tools and services to rapidly deploy custom, extensible e-commerce solutions based on Windows DNA 2000.

E-COMMERCE PLATFORM FOUNDATION

A strong platform foundation is important to any application, whether for use within an organization or across organizational boundaries with business partners and customers. Applications, like houses, must be built on a solid foundation to ensure the reliability of the system. Microsoft's operating system and connectivity software products are made to ensure simple, easy operation of information-technology systems. Microsoft's products share common interfaces and operating controls, making them easy to use together. Microsoft's support and ongoing maintenance of their products ensures that organizations will be able to continually upgrade to keep pace with the rapidly changing electronic commerce landscape.

Microsoft Windows 2000 Server

The Windows 2000 Server Family builds on the strengths of Windows NT technology, integrating standards-based directory, Web, application, communications, and file and print services with high reliability, efficient management, and support for the latest advances in networking hardware to provide a strong foundation for integrating your business with the Internet. Windows 2000 Server is the solution for running more reliable and manageable file, print, intranet, communications, and infrastructure servers.

Enables e-commerce

The Windows 2000 Server operating system provides all the features and benefits of Windows NT Server. It also includes additional functionality to enhance availability and scalability of e-commerce and line-of-business applications. It offers a platform for rich Web-based solutions, and its integrated Web services enable users to easily host and manage Web sites to share information, create Web-based business applications, and extend file, print, media and communication services to the Web. Windows 2000 Server supports Active Server Pages (ASP), consistently rated the easiest, highest performance Web server-scripting environment available. Windows 2000 Server also allows users to create applications that enable the Web server to exchange XML-formatted data with both Microsoft Internet Explorer and any server capable of parsing XML.

Compared with Windows NT Server, Windows 2000 Server enables more scalable ASP processing, improved ASP flow control, and ASP Fast Path for scriptless ASP files. Internet Information Server (IIS) 5.0 allows you to host more Web sites per server with high performance than was possible in previous versions. Windows 2000 Server also allows users to limit the amount of CPU time that a Web application or site can use; it does so to ensure that processor time—and therefore better performance—is available to other Web sites or to non-Web applications. With support for up to 1 gigabyte (GB) networks, Windows 2000 Server delivers high-performance processing on high-performance networks. Increased throughput increases performance without the need for increased network bandwidth.

Windows 2000 Server also offers support for Web Distributed Authoring and Versioning (WebDAV). WebDAV is an Internet standard that lets multiple people collaborate on a document using an Internet-based shared file system. It addresses issues such as file access permissions, offline editing, file integrity, and conflict resolution when competing changes are made to a document. WebDAV expands an organization's infrastructure by using the Internet as the central location for storing shared files.

Supports industry-leading models

Windows 2000 Server supports the Windows Distributed interNet Applications Architecture (Windows 2000 DNA)—the application development model for the Windows platform. You can build secure, reliable, highly scalable solutions that ease the integration of heterogeneous systems and applications. Windows 2000 Server also supports COM+, which builds on the integrated services and features of COM to make it easier for developers to create and use software components in any language, using any tool. COM+ includes Transaction Services and Message Queuing Services for reliable distributed applications.

Security features

Windows 2000 Server allows users to build secure intranet, extranet, and Internet sites using the latest standards, including: 56-bit and 128-bit SSL/TLS; IPSec; Server Gated Cryptography; Digest Authentication; Kerberos v5 authentication; and Fortezza. Active Directory integration with the underlying security infrastructure provides a focal point for security management of users, computers, and devices, making Windows 2000 easier to manage. Full support for the Kerberos version 5 protocol provides fast, single sign-on to Windows resources as well as to other environments that support this protocol. The Certificate Server is a critical part of a public key infrastructure that allows customers to issue their own X.509 certificates to their users for public key infrastructure (PKI) functionality such as certificate-based authentication, IPSec, and secure e-mail. Integration with Active Directory simplifies user enrollment for security on networks.

Windows 2000 Server supports out-of-the-box logon via Smart cards for strong authentication and tight access management to sensitive resources. You can secure network end-to-end encrypted communications across your company network using the IPSec standard.

Reliability

The Job Object API, with its ability to set up processor affinity, establish time limits, control process priorities, and limit memory utilization for a group of related processes, allows an application to manage and control dependent system resources. With this additional level of control, the Job Object API can prevent an application from having a negative impact on overall system scalability. Applications certified to run on Windows 2000 Server are tested by Microsoft to ensure high quality and reliability. Windows 2000 Server protects DLLs installed by applications from conflicts that can cause application failure. Active Directory uses multimaster replication to ensure high scalability and availability in distributed network configurations. *Multimaster* means that each directory replica in the network is a peer of all other replicas; changes can be made to any replica and will be reflected across all of them.

There are literally hundreds of other features that make Windows 2000 Server the product for the next generation of Web-based technologies and applications. For more information, go to *www.microsoft.com*.

Microsoft Windows 2000 Advanced Server

Scale up your network by utilizing Windows 2000 Advanced Server with the latest 8-way SMP servers for more processing power. (Windows 2000 Server delivers support for up to 4-way SMP servers.) Windows 2000 Advanced Server also allows you to take advantage of larger amounts of memory to improve performance and handle the most demanding applications, with support for up to 8 GB of random access memory (RAM) with Intel's Physical Address Extension (PAE). (Windows 2000 Server delivers support for up to 4 GB of RAM.)

Windows 2000 Advanced Server allows users to scale up quickly and easily by distributing incoming Internet Protocol (IP) traffic across a farm of load-balanced servers. You can incrementally expand capacity by adding additional servers to the farm using Network Load Balancing (NLB). You can run Windows-based applications on the server and access them from a remote PC, Windows-based terminal, or non-Windows device over Local Area Networks (LAN)s, Wide Area Networks (WANs), or low-bandwidth connections using terminal emulation software. In Windows 2000 Advanced Server, terminal services are up to 20 percent more scalable than those in Windows NT Server and have dramatically improved performance for both high- and low-bandwidth connections.

Microsoft Application Center 2000

Microsoft Application Center 2000 complements the Windows DNA Architecture now integrated into Windows 2000, which includes Internet Information Server 5.0 (IIS), Active Server Pages (ASP), COM+, and Microsoft Message Queue Services 2.0 (MSMQ). AppCenter 2000 enables users to take a Web application built using these Windows DNA features and easily deploy it to PC server farms (also called *Web farms* or *Web clusters*), combining the low-cost advantage of PC computing with the power and reach of high-end servers.

The combination of Windows 2000, the Visual Studio development system, and AppCenter 2000 provide a best-of-breed Web application server solution for quickly building, deploying, and managing high-volume, high-availability Web applications. AppCenter 2000 provides the following benefits:

- **Manageability** AppCenter 2000 includes a centralized management console to enable administrators to manage and monitor Web applications running in multiserver farms.

- **Scalability** AppCenter 2000 makes it simpler to achieve virtually unlimited scalability using farms of off-the-shelf PC servers.

- **Reliability** For maximum up time, AppCenter 2000 provides a self-healing, fault-tolerant environment with no single point of failure.

AppCenter 2000 enables customers to harness the power of the PC architecture to build Web applications that provide mainframe-caliber performance, scalability, and availability. AppCenter 2000 makes managing server farms as simple as managing a single machine. AppCenter 2000 includes several new tools and features to make running Web applications on Windows 2000 Server-based Web farms simpler:

- Single Application Image provides a central console to manage Web applications deployed across multiple servers.

- Application Replication automatically replicates files, components, and configuration settings across multiple servers.

- Real-time performance and health monitoring provides an integrated view of application performance, rolling up performance and event and log data from multiple servers into a common view.

- Fault tolerance provides a self-monitoring, self-healing environment that isolates point failures of hardware, network, and applications without interrupting application service.

■ Dynamic load balancing automatically balances Component Object Model (COM)+ component execution across multiple servers.

■ Load testing and capacity analysis tools enable users to test applications under real-world conditions, isolate performance bottlenecks, and plan hardware requirements to accommodate future planned usage.

AppCenter 2000 fills the gap that has existed for organizations that want to manage "Wintel-based" Web server farms effectively and efficiently. By improving and easing the management of these server farms, organizations can feel comfortable that their electronic commerce applications will run reliably and serve the needs of their business partners and customers.

Microsoft Host Integration Server 2000

Microsoft Host Integration Server 2000 solves the problem of integrating the Windows platform with other non-Windows enterprise systems running on platforms such as IBM mainframes, AS400, and UNIX. By using the powerful and comprehensive bidirectional integration services of Host Integration Server 2000, developers are freed from platform boundaries and can build highly scalable distributed applications that incorporate existing processes and data without requiring any recoding or wrapping of existing code. New Host Integration Server 2000 capabilities allows businesses to quickly build new business-critical Windows DNA 2000 applications while preserving investment in best-of-breed and custom in-house developed solutions.

Several integration services are provided with Host Integration Server 2000. Network and Security Integration services are one piece. Built on Microsoft's SNA Server technology, such services include extensive support for SNA and LAN protocols. Also included are APIs and integrated security that supports password synchronization and single sign-on. These services are scalable up to 30,000 concurrent sessions and support the load balancing and hot backup of these sessions. Host Integration Server 2000 also includes support for Active Directory services. Host Integration Server 2000 provides several data integration components that enable access, transformation, and replication of data in heterogeneous database environments regardless of the platform. Host Integration Server 2000 includes the following data integration services:

■ **Heterogeneous replication services** Provides bidirectional replication (merge, snapshot, and incremental) between Microsoft SQL Server, IBM DB2, and Oracle.

- **ODBC and OLEDB providers** Provides access to enterprise relational and nonrelational databases and file systems, including DB2, VSAM, AS400 file system, Oracle, and Sybase.

- **Host-initiated data access** Allows DB2 developers to transparently access SQL Server as a peer DB2 data source.

Host Integration Server 2000 also includes comprehensive application-integration services and supports both the traditional asynchronous (such as messaging) or synchronous (such as COM/DCOM) communication. Host Integration Server 2000 also supports the increasingly popular XML standards. One of the key features, Application Integration Services, enables developers to incorporate existing transactions and business logic into new, distributed applications. Four primary Host Integration Server 2000 components enable application integration:

- **COM Transaction Integrator (COMTI)** COMTI enables CICS and IMS transaction programs to be accessed as Microsoft Transaction Server (MTS) or COM+ components. These components are fully transactional and provide support for two-phase commit. As COM+ components, these objects are available and re-usable by a number of COM-compliant development tools. COMTI also provides the ability for CICS transactions to initiate MTS transactions.

- **XML Transaction Integrator (XMLTI)** XMLTI provides an XML interface to COMTI components. This interface allows XML-formatted documents and messages, including BizTalk-compatible schema and BizTalk Server 2000-routed messages, to initiate transactions. This feature is extremely useful for enabling existing business processes to be e-commerce ready.

- **Both COMTI and XMLTI use the COMTI Component Builder** The COMTI Component Builder provides developers with a graphical, drag-and-drop environment for encapsulating existing business logic and automatically generates the appropriate COM+-enabled component and XML interfaces.

- **MSMQ to MQ Series Bridge** Provides seamless messaging exchange between MQ Series (from IBM) and MSMQ Messaging (from Microsoft) formats.

Host Integration Server 2000 also ships with a software development kit (SDK) that allows software vendors and Microsoft's customers to build value-added components for the server. This SDK allows Host Integration Server 2000 to be extended to access platforms, applications, and data sources that are not currently supported in the product. In addition, the SDK can be used to enhance support for existing Host Integration Server 2000 features, such as adding additional business logic to COMTI-enabled transactions.

Active Directory

Active Directory technology both leverages and enables the rest of the Windows 2000 infrastructure. In short, Active Directory services play a key role in the Microsoft product line architecture. Active Directory technology enables general-purpose directory functionality at the network operating system level or sometimes at the enterprise level, through the following features:

- Serves as the base network operating system (NOS) directory enabling users to log on and obtain Windows 2000 file and print services

- Provides a secure single logon to multiple applications hosted on Windows 2000 servers

- Provides high availability with multimaster replication capabilities and partitioning of the database across multiple domains

- Publishes a Global Catalog view of subset information from multiple domain directories, including universal groups that can be referenced in access controls for multiple domains

- Unifies support for DNS and LDAP as well as other standard directory protocols and name formats; unifies public key infrastructure (PKI) and Kerberos support; in many cases, these standards enable Active Directory services to serve multivendor client and server products in a heterogeneous network, working with what is already available

- Provides directory services for electronic messaging users of Microsoft Exchange 2000 Server and Microsoft Outlook 2000

- Offers easy graphical administration with the possibility to delegate administrative responsibility for managing user and resource information through a hierarchical domain and organizational unit structure

- Exposes Active Directory Service Interfaces (ADSI) and object extensibility for the system programmer and the scripting language developer

- Enables remote control and configuration of desktop behavior through a Group Policy Editor (GPE) tool that can set defaults for domains, organizational units, or sites

- Enables the automated, self-healing, cost-reduction features of Windows Installer

- Enables distributed deployment of COM or COM+ software executable objects that customers can invoke remotely with minimal configuration on the desktop

- Provides backward compatibility with previous versions of the Microsoft Windows NT operating system

Active directory services provide organizations with the ability to manage directories across servers, departments, and even organizations via Web technology. This directory management is critical to organizations that are moving to a heavily distributed Web-based model of transacting business.

Microsoft Management Console

MMC is an extensible, common presentation service for management applications. MMC is included in the Windows 2000 operating system and also runs on the Windows NT 4.0, Windows 95, and Windows 98 family of operating systems. MMC provides a common host environment for snap-ins provided by Microsoft and third-party software vendors. Snap-ins provide the actual management behavior; MMC itself does not provide any management functionality. MMC provides the framework in which the snap-ins operate in a seamless manner.

Administrators and other users can create custom management tools from snap-ins provided by various vendors. Administrators can then save the tools they have created for later use or for sharing with other administrators and users. This model provides the administrator with efficient tool customization and the ability to create multiple tools of varying levels of complexity for task delegation, among other benefits. The goal for the MMC is to support simplified administration through integration, delegation, task orientation, and overall interface simplification—all key customer requirements.

MMC is a Windows-based multiple document interface (MDI) application that heavily uses Internet technologies. The console can be extended by writing MMC snap-ins, which perform specialized management tasks. The MMC programmatic interfaces permit the snap-ins to integrate with the console. These interfaces deal only with user interface extensions; how each snap-in actually performs tasks depends entirely on the design of the snap-in. The relationship of the snap-in to the console consists of sharing a common hosting environment and cross-application integration. The console itself offers no management behavior. Snap-ins always reside in a console; they do not run by themselves. Both Microsoft and third-party software vendors develop management tools to run in MMC and write applications to be managed by MMC administrative tools. MMC is part of the Microsoft Platform Software Development Kit (SDK) and is available for general use.

PROCESSING E-COMMERCE TRANSACTIONS

The processing of e-commerce transactions is at the core of e-business. As mentioned in Chapter 9, the BizTalk framework specifies a way for organizations to communicate business information with their business partners. Microsoft's business transaction processing products such as BizTalk Server provide organizations with the ability to process data effectively and efficiently. Microsoft SQL Server provides organizations with the ability to store and share data between internal departments and external business partners and customers. Microsoft OLAP services give organizations the ability to analyze the data they gather while processing business transactions. Microsoft BackOffice Server provides basic services for building, managing, and deploying single-server solutions in large businesses at the branch and department level, and in mid-sized businesses at the branch and central IT level.

Microsoft BizTalk Server

Microsoft BizTalk Server provides the tools and infrastructure that enable business process integration. Companies currently conducting traditional business-to-business e-commerce like EDI will find that BizTalk Server has all the required product components, such as trading partner management, document mapping and translation, reliable document routing and delivery, data extraction and storage for analysis and business process automation, to carry their legacy processes forward. BizTalk Server also extends the feature set of traditional e-commerce and EDI products to include extensive support for XML and Internet transport technologies, such as SMTP, HTTP, FTP, encryption, and certificate exchange.

BizTalk Server makes business process integration easier and provides a clean migration for companies to integrate XML into their business processes. In addition to solving platform issues, BizTalk Server also offers organizations:

- Document interchange services via XML translators
- Support for existing industry data formats
- Support for existing industry data communication protocols
- Security by means of digital signature and encryption

The core component of BizTalk Server is the document/data exchange mechanism. For HTTP, the SendHTTP component provides transport of documents over an HTTP connection. The ReceiveHTTP service uses Active Server Pages (ASP) to receive a document and submit it to BizTalk Server. For HTTP/S, the SendHTTP/S component provides transport of documents over an HTTP connection that uses a Secure Sockets Layer (SSL). The ReceiveHTTP/S service uses an ASP page to receive a document, which is secured with an SSL certificate, and submit it to BizTalk Server.

BizTalk Server uses Microsoft Windows 2000 security features, including full support for public-key infrastructure and Windows 2000 Microsoft Transaction Services (MTS). Public-key certificate management includes requesting certificates, processing certificates in a certificate-request response, and exchanging certificates with trading partners. These certificates are available for both digital signature and encryption.

For Simple Mail Transfer Protocol (SMTP), the SendSMTP component creates an SMTP-based e-mail message, which contains the document in the body of the message or as an attachment. The e-mail message is then sent to the target e-mail address that is configured as a property of the SendSMTP component. The ReceiveSMTP service uses an e-mail message to receive a document and then calls BizTalk Server to submit the document.

BizTalk Server supports the Windows 2000 Microsoft Message Queue Services (MSMQ) 2.0. The SendMSMQ transport provides transport of documents over MSMQ 2.0. The transport reads a configurable key on the transport dictionary and transports that data as an MSMQ message. The destination queue, which can also be thought of as the recipient address, can be configured on the component property page. The ReceiveMSMQ service checks the queue on a periodic basis and when a message arrives, it passes the message by calling BizTalk Server. Upon completion of that task, it dequeues the documents (MSMQ messages).

BizTalk Server also supports the File Transfer Protocol (FTP). The SendFTP component sends the document in the configurable key on the transport dictionary to a destination FTP server, which saves the document as a file. The component does this through an FTP PUT command, putting the file on the trading partner's server. Alternatively, the SendFTP component can pick up a file from the file system and do an FTP PUT of that file. The ReceiveFTP service does an FTP GET of a file from the trading partner's FTP server and then calls BizTalk Server. This component periodically checks for the file on the trading partner's FTP server. When it finds a file or files, the ReceiveFTP service creates a transport dictionary, places the contents of the file in the RecievedData key, and calls BizTalk Server.

Microsoft SQL Server 2000

SQL Server 2000 is an integral part of Windows DNA 2000, a comprehensive, integrated platform for building and operating state-of-the-art distributed Web applications as well as the next wave of Internet-based Web services. Windows 2000 is the cornerstone of Windows DNA 2000. SQL Server 2000, Enterprise Edition offers scalability and availability up to the highest levels of the enterprise by taking full advantage of up to 64 GB of RAM, up to 32 processors, and 4-node failover clustering supported out of the box with Windows 2000 Data Center. This means that processors can be clustered for automatic redundancy and recovery.

For improved enterprise manageability, SQL Server 2000 uses Active Directory services in Windows 2000 as a single, unified repository for configuration, location, and maintenance information. Integration of Active Directory gives database applications location independence, allows developers to build distributed applications more easily, and helps database administrators work more efficiently. Applications may connect to a database by looking up registered information in Active Directory, allowing administrators to change the name or location of a database without having to update the application. Database administrators may use Active Directory to identify when people have installed new servers on the corporate network, when users have created new databases or OLAP cubes, or even when database software has been updated. OLAP cubes are multidimensional databases that provide decision support capabilities. Database administrators (DBAs) may even search in Active Directory to find what data is available for replication and can do so without knowing the names or locations of any database servers. This integration offers enormous benefits by making it easier for DBAs and users to find, manage, and share their important data assets.

Microsoft OLAP Services

OLAP is an acronym that stands for online analytical processing, a key technology for e-commerce applications. Microsoft does not sell any unbundled OLAP products but does include OLAP components in two of its mainstream products. The widespread use of these products means that tens of millions of users will soon have access to OLAP technologies for the first time, though most will not appreciate just how much they can do with them. SQL Server 2000 includes OLAP Services, a hybrid OLAP server. This server can handle large (consisting of hundreds of gigabytes) multidimensional databases, which can be stored as various types of data structures providing flexible decision support and reporting capabilities. It can connect not only to SQL Server tables but also to other relational databases such as Oracle, regardless of whether they are running on

Microsoft Windows NT. This new OLAP server provides exceptional ad hoc calculation, filtering, and ranking functionality, which can be invoked through client tools that exploit the OLE DB for OLAP API and the rich new MDX multidimensional query language that the server includes. However, many general-purpose or older client tools and applications do not yet take much (or, in some cases, any) advantage of these powerful new capabilities.

OLAP Services also includes a client side component (PivotTable Service) that provides an automatic caching capability as well as a full local calculation engine. These features combine to deliver a fast response to many queries and to spread the total processing load over many machines in parallel, thus greatly improving the user scalability and performance of the system. This local multidimensional engine can also create and use smaller off-line cubes.

Office 2000 continues to be able to act as a basic relational report writer and query tool, but it can now also act as an entry-level OLAP client without needing add-ins. Its enhanced PivotTables can now work as a desktop OLAP and as a client to Microsoft OLAP Services and some other OLAP servers, both in Microsoft Excel and in Microsoft Internet Explorer. PivotTables now take account of hierarchies in dimensions, and data volumes are no longer limited to Excel's own capacity. Live OLAP data that is surfaced in Office applications, whether by using Microsoft's own PivotTables or third-party add-ins, can then be used in all the many ways that the Office applications provide for analyzing, presenting, sharing, and distributing information. This capability becomes relevant if multidimensional analysis is only a small part of a much larger business application.

Microsoft BackOffice Server

BackOffice Server delivers a series of unique value-added features not found in the individually sold component products. These features provide an even higher level of integration, ease of use, and manageability. BackOffice Server includes components such as Windows 2000 Server, Exchange Server, SQL Server, and Microsoft Systems Management Server. As the new suite of e-commerce tools evolves, the BackOffice package will also be modified to provide a tightly integrated set of tools that provide organizations with the ability to implement e-commerce transaction processing out of the box.

Included with BackOffice Server is a ready-to-use intranet site with seven Web-based starter applications that can be used as is or combined and customized to meet specific needs. Applications include a group directory, a document library, discussions, expense tracking, event calendar, news engine, and Helpdesk. Each application illustrates how multiple BackOffice components, such as Microsoft SQL Server, Microsoft Exchange Server, and Microsoft Site Server 3.0, can be integrated into a single application. This site is created automatically when the intranet publishing or collaboration options are selected during setup. The Latest Microsoft Development Tools BackOffice Server also includes the Microsoft FrontPage 2000 Web site creation and management tool and the Microsoft Visual InterDev 6.0 Web development system (both with single-user licenses) to help organizations start building powerful Web sites and Web applications.

By combining Microsoft Office and BackOffice applications, users have familiar tools with which to analyze, publish, and share a wide range of information in many formats. In tandem, for example, Microsoft Outlook 2000 and Microsoft Exchange Server create a rich environment for managing e-mail, tasks, scheduling, and contacts and for distributing knowledge anywhere in the organization. Working in Microsoft Access 2000, for instance, users can produce databases compatible with Microsoft SQL Server right from the start. The OLAP capabilities of SQL Server also let users perform data analysis using familiar Microsoft Excel features. Built to work together, BackOffice and Office 2000 can help make information processing faster and more productive.

MICROSOFT E-COMMERCE SECURITY INITIATIVES

Businesses that sell goods and services online face many security issues, including protecting their customers' transaction data. Products such as Microsoft Windows 2000 Server, Commerce Server 2000, and Internet Explorer 5.0 use standard protocols to guarantee secure transactions. The Secure Sockets Layer (SSL) protects a customer entering an order on the Web; the browser and server encrypt personal data. The Microsoft Wallet browser component (available for both Internet Explorer and Netscape Navigator) encrypts and stores payment information on the user's computer. The user can later send the data to an e-commerce site by typing a password. The emerging Secure Electronic Transaction (SET) standard allows electronic payment from accounts at participating banks, savings and loans, and so forth, during e-commerce transactions.

Windows 2000 incorporates a number of enhancements that provide improved security and protection for critical information. One of the most significant is the use of the Kerberos technology, developed at M.I.T. as a cryptographic environment and the availability of digital certificates for authentication and other purposes. In addition, an erase-upon-delete feature overwrites disk or media space that previously contained files. The password-protection feature for individual documents has also been substantially improved, making unauthorized access to protected documents on servers or desktop systems much more difficult.

The other key security features included in Microsoft's products are detailed in the following sections.

Proxy Servers

As the name implies, these are computer systems that take the place of another computer or application system. Proxy servers are widely used as a fundamental component of firewalls and other network servers to buffer the primary system against abuse or overload.

Passwords

Passwords are the simplest yet most fundamental of security control measures for information systems. The password, in combination with a user name or user account, serves as the basic method of associating a single, specific person with the activities and privileges of a user account and of fixing accountability for the activities of that user account. Generally, good passwords (those that are more resistant to guessing or cracking) are alphanumeric combinations, not dictionary words, and are no fewer than six characters in length. An example of a good password might be %tR*m9; a poor password, doggie. All fixed passwords are susceptible to discovery through the use of password-cracking software. Dictionary words or phrases associated with an individual's family, hobbies, professional responsibility, or position make the task easier.

Authentication

Authentication refers to the process of ensuring that the entity (which may include an individual user, computer system or application that is requesting access to the system, service, or information content) is in fact who or what they represent themselves to be. In the absence of strong authentication mechanisms, an unauthorized entity can assume the identity of an authorized user along with all the privileges associated with that identity.

Firewalls

A firewall is a computer system, which may be hardware and or software based, that is used to control traffic between networks. Firewalls are considered one of the basic protection measures for establishing and safeguarding the perimeter of a commercial organization. Properly implemented, a firewall significantly impedes the ability of external intruders to gain unauthorized access to the digital assets of an organization and may also enable secure communications through the Internet to other organizational locations by creating secure tunnels through the use of encryption.

Encryption

Encryption is one of the most powerful protection technologies available in computer and network security. Encryption relies on mathematical algorithms to convert human-readable clear text to unreadable ciphertext. Encryption is designed to prevent the use of intercepted messages and access to protected resources. Typically, encryption is only as strong as the mathematical formulas (algorithms) that perform the transformation to ciphertext and the implementation of these in the operations, applications, computer systems, and network environments.

One of the most popular and effective encryption implementations is that of the public key. Public key systems rely on a combination of a secret key known only to a user and a public key available to all users to create messages, documents, and access controls that are strongly protected against unauthorized access.

Certificates

Within public key encryption systems, a certificate allows a listed set of valid users to perform authorized tasks. Every individual user of the public key encryption system must be issued a certificate, usually by certification authority, or CA. The CAs determines valid users and their roles within the system and then issues the necessary keys and certificates to facilitate the activities it has approved.

Virtual Private Networks (VPNs)

Many firewall systems allow organizations to securely link remote locations via the global Internet through the application of encryption between compatible firewalls at entry points to the local network presence. These connections allow organizations to utilize Internet bandwidth to replace costly dedicated telecommunication lines and circuits, resulting in significant cost savings and increased flexibility to adapt to rapid changes in business requirements.

Extranets

Although no standard definition of an extranet exists, it is generally described as extended network connectivity between the key strategic business partners, customers, suppliers, and vendors of an organization. These collaborative relationships enable rapid response and superior adaptability in business-to-business transactions via network-enabled applications. The extranet may use VPN technologies to establish and maintain the communications links. Extranets are generally seen as the future of e-commerce because of their ability to link organizations in the supply chain.

WRAP UP

- **Collaboration, both within and beyond an organization's walls, is critical to the success of e-commerce initiatives.** Microsoft Outlook 2000, Exchange 2000 Server, and NetMeeting products allow organizational staff to communicate in real time and to create discussions that enable internal value chains. These pro- ducts also enable organizations to communicate with business partners and customers in the supply chain to smooth the flow of information.

- **Microsoft's products enable organizations to quickly and easily build Web sites for intranets as well as business-to-consumer and business-to-business e-commerce.** Microsoft Office, Visual Studio, and Commerce Server 2000 provide organi- zations with the ability to create simple Web sites and to program more complex systems in a short amount of time. Commerce Server 2000 also provides organizations with a quick-start capability in building business-to-consumer Web applications.

- **E-commerce applications must be built on a solid platform.** Microsoft's platform is based on the Windows 2000 Server product and includes Application Center Server 2000, Host Integration Server 2000, Active Directory Services, and Microsoft Management Console. These products form a complete, reliable, scalable toolkit for deploying and implementing E-Commerce applications

- **Microsoft provides organizations with end-to-end e-commerce transaction processing capabilities.** BizTalk Server, SQL Server, Microsoft OLAP services, and BackOffice form the core of Microsoft's e-commerce transaction processing and analysis capabilities. These products enable organizations to exchange information with business partners and customers in a business-to-business environment, process business-to-consumer transaction data effectively and efficiently, and use the transaction data from both to improve decision making.

■ **Fundamental information security is a key enabler of electronic commerce as it creates and sustains confidence in the safety of transactions performed in this environment.** Organizations must implement security programs that control and monitor e-commerce assets and allow individuals to do their work unfettered. Various features in Microsoft's product line enable this balancing act.

Taking Stock

1. Can your staff easily communicate with business partners and customers electronically? Can internal staff collaborate and share information in a way that enhances the organization's ability to compete in its marketplace?

2. Can your organization quickly create and easily maintain robust Web applications for both business-to-consumer and business-to-business electronic commerce?

3. Is your IT infrastructure platform solid and reliable? Do applications run fast and efficiently without crashing for long periods of time?

4. Can your organization process electronic commerce transactions quickly and accurately in accordance with industry standards?

5. Does your staff know what assets exist in the e-commerce system and how those assets will be used?

6. Does your staff understand the risks and vulnerabilities associated with those assets?

7. If you are an e-commerce product user, do your e-commerce products have the best security features?

8. If you are an e-commerce product maker, does your staff follow best practices when designing security features into your products?

ACTION PLAN

❑   Ask how easily internal staff can share information needed to operate the business. Discover how Microsoft's products can facilitate the flow of information both internally and beyond the organization's walls.

❑   Visit your Web site. Find out how much time was required to create that site and how much difficulty your staff encounters while trying to maintain it. Evaluate Microsoft's content creation and management tools to see how they can speed this process and make it more efficient.

❑   Examine your IT infrastructure. Find out whether your organization's platform has the capacity to handle electronic commerce applications that are likely to grow quickly. Look at Microsoft's Windows 2000 Server product line to find out how Microsoft can help you build a solid infrastructure foundation for future growth.

❑   Talk your customers and business partners to find out how they feel about your ability to process and electronic commerce business transactions. Visit the BizTalk Framework Web site to find out how this industry standard is evolving and how Microsoft can help your organization meet the challenge of the evolving e-world. Check out Microsoft's BizTalk server Web site.

❑   Make sure that your security plan addresses strategic implementation of key technologies, procedures, and techniques to reduce risks. Your plan should also include incident response measures to address known or suspected incidents in which vulnerabilities may have been exploited.

❑   Visit *www.microsoft.com.*

Chapter 11

Web Portals

Portals serve as friendly gateways to the Web and the Internet. Portals can help organizations communicate efficiently with employees, business partners, and customers. Organizations should develop portals that present information and services that are easily accessed and that supply useful, timely information.

A portal is a site on the Internet that provides a one-stop experience for visitors, allowing them to check e-mail, search the Web, get news and stock quotes and more, all in a personalized arrangement. Portals also provide a starting point for Web surfers to go other places. A portal may have links to travel sites, entertainment resources, and search engines. The best portal sites organize information so that Web visitors can find what they need quickly and easily. A portal is much more than a search tool, although a good search tool is always part of an effective portal. Some portals provide information on particular topics. For example, MSNBC, a joint venture between Microsoft and NBC, is a news portal, although it contains links to other topics as well. Some portals are based on Internet access, such as the Microsoft Network (MSN). Organizations may also create internal portals as part of their intranet to help employees find information on benefits, organizational events, and job postings. Portals may also serve as places for advertisers and sponsors to place ads or links to drive traffic.

MSN: THE MICROSOFT NETWORK

Microsoft's goal is to make MSN the most useful network of services on the Internet. The company wants to help consumers get things done more quickly. Microsoft is in the business of making people's lives easier through personal computing, and MSN provides access to products and services that enable consumers to accomplish more tasks more quickly. MSN is more than a portal; it's a true network of services. The major distinction between MSN and other portals is that MSN helps users get things done more easily and quickly than any other place online by focusing more on integration of services and less on aggregation or links to sites. Microsoft is integrating its best-of-breed services so that the whole of MSN is worth much more to the consumer than the sum of its parts. Microsoft measures the success of MSN in three main ways:

- **Member relationship** User registrations, repeat visits, degree of personalization: These are the measures of loyalty and customer satisfaction that Microsoft cares about most. These are also critical for targeted advertising, which is what advertisers care about most.

- **Traffic** Reach and frequency as measured by Media Metrix in U.S. households only.

- **Revenue** MSN is already seeing measurable results on this front, having signed some of the major ad deals on the Internet in 1999.

Microsoft continues to add products and services, including Internet access to continually increase its membership. By increasing membership, MSN's advertising worth grows, which helps Microsoft, its business partners, and its customers.

Alliances

MSN has more than 10,000 alliances and is adding more each day. These alliances help MSN continue to grow; currently, it facilitates $6 billion in electronic commerce annually. MSN has recently teamed up with AltaVista, licensing MSN to Compaq's new portal site and incorporating AltaVista's powerful search engine into MSN Search. MSN also has business alliances with John Hancock Mutual Life Insurance Co., Unilever PLC, and Barnes & Noble, Inc., all of which sponsor content and service segments across the MSN network. These and other businesses use a combination of banner ads, tailored promotions, and cross-network advertising packages to reach a broad range of demographic targets on MSN. MSN has also created alliances with companies for the network's best-of-breed services, including Merrill Lynch & Company, Inc.'s sponsorship of the

MSN MoneyCentral personal finance online service and Kelley Blue Book's presence on MSN CarPoint.

MSN Products

MSN is a comprehensive, integrated set of services that match the top needs of consumers and businesses. MSN expands opportunities for consumers to communicate, search, and shop on the Web. It also helps businesses get connected to the Internet and promote and manage their companies. Microsoft is integrating these services with software to provide users, whether they work on-line or offline, with opportunities for greater speed and productivity in their online activities.

MSN's Hotmail is a Web-based e-mail service. With a Hotmail e-mail account, users can send and receive e-mail from almost any computer connected to the Internet, including those at home, work, or at an airport kiosk. Their Hotmail-based messages are stored in a central location, so their Inbox is up to date. Hotmail also provides its users with a permanent e-mail address that likely will not change as long as they continue to use Hotmail.

MSN sponsors Web Communities—clubs built around a specific interest about which groups of people communicate and collaborate online. Users can join an existing community on one of thousands of topics, or set up one of their own. Each community offers a full set of communication tools, including a custom home page, chat room, photo albums, message boards, and mailing list capabilities. Users can make their community public or limit it to the people they invite.

MSNSearch helps users easily find exactly what they're looking for on the Web by combining IntelliSense technology with human intelligence to make smart assumptions about what most people want when searching. MSNSearch is designed to deliver the most relevant results to the most popular queries on the Web. Users need only type in one or two words and let MSNSearch do the work for them.

MSN MoneyCentral

The MSN MoneyCentral Web site provides information and guidance on virtually every aspect of personal money management, including saving, taxes, home buying, online banking, investing, and retirement planning. The site offers informative articles, practical tools, useful resources, and more. For instance, MSN MoneyCentral can help you

- Learn how to get started if you're new to investing, using Investor Workshop.

- Read today's financial news from MSNBC.

- Search for a real-time quote on a stock that interests you.

- Survey the performance of key indices, such as the Dow Jones industrial average.

- Research potential investments as the experts do with stock and fund research wizards.

- Dig into expert guidance about retirement and wills, real estate, smart buying, money and banking, taxes, family finance, and insurance.

- Check out Investing Highlights including Your Portfolio, Top Funds, Get Started, and more.

- Use Investment Finder to help you find stocks that may suit your needs.

- View a calendar of upcoming earnings announcements, stock splits, and other investment events.

- Tap into Quick Reference, which contains answers to more than 2,800 questions about personal finance.

- Set up online banking and bill paying.

MSN Money Central also offers tips on saving and spending, and on settng up family budgets. Visitors can work through college finance planning and use the income calculator to arrange the family's income in anticipation of that big expense. There's information on retirement planning and wills, including topics such as 401(k) plans, annuities, estate planning, investing, IRAs, and living trusts. The site offers guidance on how to find and buy the right insurance for family, cars, and homes. Real estate information includes interest rates, loan information, a home locator service, and a mortgage calculator.

MSN MoneyCentral bill paying service

MSN MoneyCentral provides online bill presentation and payment service, offering convenience and savings to businesses and consumers. E-bills are presented and paid over the Internet, eliminating the need for paper-based transactions. E-bills contain the same level of detail as paper, but they are rendered and delivered electronically; bill payment is accomplished through a simple Web-based interface that tracks and confirms payments.

E-billing is catching on slowly but surely. Both consumers and businesses are discovering the advantages of e-billing, including

- **Guaranteed on-time payment**   Online payments are guaranteed to arrive when the consumer specifies.

- **Flexible payment scheduling** Bills can be paid from several types of accounts and can be scheduled weeks in advance or at the last minute.

- **Privacy and protection** Financial information is kept confidential and consumers are protected against unauthorized charges over $50, a policy similar to those of most major credit cards.

- **Customer support** Consumers can contact customer support 24 hours a day, online or by phone.

Microsoft bCentral

Microsoft bCentral builds on the content and services Microsoft has offered small businesses to date, such as LinkExchange and the MSN Small Business Channel. The Microsoft bCentral portal delivers services and valuable tools in three key areas:

- Starting an online business and building a Web site
- Promoting and marketing an online business
- Managing business more efficiently

Microsoft bCentral provides Web services to expand your business. bCentral shows you how to get Internet access via MSN, build your own Web site, receive free e-mail service, and even to register your domain name. It also offers guidance on how to buy advertising and be listed on search engines to drive traffic. A free banner network lets small businesses start reaching potential customers quickly and easily. Additionally, this service provides help for obtaining loans and financing and for recruiting employees, among other things. Check out *www.bcentral.com*.

Other Services

As part of its ongoing effort to make the Web more productive for users, Microsoft is sharing a number of services and software with other online providers and software developers. These megaservices will cross the boundaries of proprietary Web sites to give users a more familiar and seamless Web experience. Two examples of current megaservice offerings are MSN Messenger Service and Microsoft Passport. With MSN Messenger Service, users can see when their family and friends are online and exchange instant messages with them. Messenger Service works with tools such as Hotmail, Outlook Express, and Microsoft Internet Explorer browser software. Microsoft Passport is an e-commerce service that makes using the Web and shopping online more secure for consumers.

Microsoft Passport reduces the number of steps necessary to access sites and make purchases on the Web by allowing consumers to create a single *wallet*, which includes a name and password for use with any Passport-enabled Web site. Using strong encryption and privacy policies, Passport helps ensure the security of consumers' personal data and online transactions.

Another MSN service is mobile service for cell phones, pagers, and other handheld devices. MSN Mobile lets users keep up-to-date even when they are not online. It does so by providing users with a suite of customizable information services that can be automatically delivered right to their digital pager, digital cellular phone, or handheld wireless device. With MSN Mobile, users can keep abreast of news, sports, weather, stock quotes, horoscopes, and lottery information; they can even be alerted to events such as birthdays and anniversaries. MSN Web Companion gives users who don't need a PC's power or flexibility a way to take advantage of Web-based services, browsing, and e-mail. Powered by MSN and the Windows CE operating system, Microsoft plans to make the MSN Web Companion available in desktop and laptop forms.

Microsoft will also continue to develop the WebTV Network service, enabling ever-greater capabilities for viewer interactivity and content personalization. These capabilities include interactive television that lets viewers participate in television programming and creating Personal TV, which gives viewers the freedom of choosing what to watch, and when. Also, the new version of MSN Internet Access will be fully integrated with MSN, making it an easy way for consumers to connect to the Web and have instant access to premier sites and services. In addition to around-the-clock, toll-free technical support, the service provides new users with the latest Internet technology, including the Outlook Express e-mail client, Microsoft Chat, and Internet Explorer 5 browser software for navigating the Web.

MSNBC

MSNBC is an information portal, supplying various types of news and information to consumers. The MSNBC Web site, *www.msnbc.com,* is a joint venture between Microsoft and NBC and a co-production of MSNBC on the Internet, and NBC and MSNBC on cable TV. MSNBC combines the worldwide resources of NBC News and the technological expertise of Microsoft Corporation to provide news and information tailored for online consumption. The site delivers the content from NBC, MSNBC, and CNBC along with original coverage. The content is provided free to visitors on the site. The various sections of MSNBC on the Internet are accessible from the menu bar on MSNBC's front page, allowing navigation from one section or story to another.

Content Sections

The News section of MSNBC on the Internet displays top stories from across the country and around the world in multimedia, complete with photos, graphics, video, and audio clips, and an automated slide show with news stories on topics chosen by visitors to the site.

The Business section features current business news, enterprise stories, and collaborations with *The Wall Street Journal*, CNBC, and MSN Investor, all displayed on one easy-to-use, dynamic front page. The quote look-up feature taps into MSNBC Tracker service and provides news relevant to the quote requested.

The official NBC Sports Web site delivers coverage of stories and major sports events, with exclusives from NBC Sports commentators and analysts, interactive special reports, and interaction with viewers.

The Technology section is designed to help keep users on the cutting edge by exploring the latest developments and profiling the individuals and companies that are making things happen. The section features reviews of hardware, software, and games complete with debates, bulletin boards, and e-mail feedback. ZDNet works with MSNBC Technology to provide content.

The Health section offers information to help visitors live healthier lives. Virtual Checkup provides quizzes to help people determine whether they might be at risk for various disorders. The Health Library provides users with a comprehensive medical library. "On the Cutting Edge," a regular column by Health Editor Charlene Laino, details recent medical breakthroughs.

MSNBC offers visitors the chance to explore interactively the virtual worlds of movies, music, health, travel, the arts, and food. The Living*Travel section keeps users up-to-date on the latest lifestyle news with opportunities for interactivity such as taking a tour through a virtual art museum, perusing chapters of popular books, reading gossip from former Esquire writer Jeannette Walls, or taking a quiz on Broadway trivia.

The Opinions section combines op-ed sites with a leading-edge "community desk" operation that provides easy access to MSNBC on the Internet's online bulletin boards and chats. A dozen regular columnists and periodic contributors provide commentary on the day's political, social, economic, and international events.

Offering coverage of local, national, and international events, MSNBC on the Internet provides all the news in one place. Links are provided to local news sources in cities across the nation, giving users access to a wide variety of coverage, from high school sports to the newest zoning regulations. Nearly 100 NBC affiliate stations provide this comprehensive local coverage, with additional cities being added continuously. Information on local and global current weather conditions is available for virtually any spot on the globe. As with all other sections, users can customize it by selecting their local weather report.

Personalization

MSNBC's Personal Toolkit allows visitors to personalize the news and enhance delivery using the latest "push" technology, which delivers prerequested information without the user requesting it over and over. Composed of Personal Front Page, Personal Delivery, Personal News Alert, and Personal Desktop Tickers, the news report can be designed by visitors to be most relevant to them. The MSNBC Front Page, using Zip Personalization, features breaking stories, top headlines, stock quotes, weather, sports scores, and local news. MSNBC's Cool Tools feature and Choose Your News offer customized news on a personalized front page. Today's Headlines delivers the top headlines of the day by e-mail at preferred delivery times.

Personal Desktop Ticker tracks sports scores, stock prices, and top headlines, all of which are updated automatically. Personal Front Page offers news and information most relevant to individual users. From top headlines, local weather reports, and stock quotes to favorite sports scores and local news, the Personal Front Page is delivered on one page. Personal Delivery sends a Personal Front Page via e-mail every day, delivering a customized edition of today's news. Personal News Alert instantly notifies users of breaking news via the alert icon, which flashes in the taskbar as news breaks, stocks fluctuate, or events occur related to user-defined topics. With a single mouse click, News Alert delivers the headline in a window with a hot link to the story.

ADVERTISING AND SPONSORSHIP

Microsoft assists organizations with advertising through its consulting services and through MSN. MSN Sales and Marketing offers online advertising, sponsorship, electronic commerce, and distribution opportunities within the MSN network. In addition to consumer reach, MSN properties deliver audiences to advertisers, helping them achieve their sales and marketing goals. MSN offers a variety of services that can be customized to help consumers do the things they want to do online. In combination, the MSN network of Internet Services and the LinkExchange Banner Network services reach nearly three-fourths of the total Web universe. MSN provides organizations with audiences that are tailored to the demographic needs of the product or service. The MSN audience spends an average of 13.1 hours per week online and is twice as likely as average Internet users to make online purchases.

Microsoft also provides opportunities for advertising in sponsorship associated with its products. For example, an organization may associate itself with Microsoft FrontPage as a FrontPage developer. Microsoft provides guidelines on how to use the FrontPage product name and provides marketing assistance by listing the organization on its Web site. Organizations can also receive assistance from Microsoft by having their professionals become Microsoft certified. The Microsoft Certified Professional (MCP) and Microsoft Certified Systems Engineer (MCSE) certifications provide organizations with specific credibility on the products in which they specialize. Microsoft also provides opportunities for organizations to become Certified Technical Education Centers (CTEC), which provide training on Microsoft products.

Microsoft provides consulting services that can help organizations build a better Web presence. Microsoft offers these services both through Microsoft's Professional Services division and through third-party service providers. Organizations that possess the Microsoft Certified Solution Provider (MCSP) logo are endorsed by Microsoft as technology solution providers. An MCSP can help you install a new network, upgrade a few machines, or change your company's technology framework entirely. For company-wide or individual training, Microsoft offers courses in a variety of formats. Instructor-led classes, online instruction, and self-paced training are available at thousands of locations worldwide. Organizations can find product and technology training at the right level, in the format that best fits the organization's schedule.

Microsoft works closely with leading companies to deliver products and services that interoperate with Microsoft's own products, broadening the appeal and application of Internet technologies and other Microsoft solutions. Organizations can partner with Microsoft and announce products and services that work with and enhance the use of Microsoft's products. These products include PCs, network hardware, gateways, firewalls, conferencing servers, compatible conferencing clients, directory services, and Internet and other custom software solutions. Organizations can contact Microsoft for more information on how to get started as a product or service partner.

SMALL BUSINESS SERVICES

Microsoft provides small businesses with the ability to get started in e-commerce quickly and easily. The Microsoft Advantage site is created specifically for small- and medium-sized businesses and provides resources designed to help small businesses make smart business decisions. Small businesses can find software solutions to build their IT infrastructure, locate a technology expert in their area, and shop for volume discounts on software. The site also provides expert advice and business tips, such as the value of a value-added provider, and it offers technology guides, tips for running a business online, expert book reviews, and discounts from Barnes & Noble. A value-added provider (VAP) or technology consulting firm can help you maintain your business technology infrastructure, support end users, and implement new solutions to meet the needs of your growing business.

Microsoft provides small businesses with tips such as how to capture e-mail addresses to bring visitors back and how use ListBot for free. ListBot provides a way for businesses to keep in touch with their Web site visitors by offering a Web-based e-mail list management system. ListBot helps small businesses by performing tasks that help build a small businesses Web presence. ListBot does the following:

- Collects visitor e-mail addresses automatically
- Sends e-mail to all visitors with just one click
- Provides demographics such as age and occupation on visitors to a site
- Manages you're a business's mailing lists
- Conveniently stores messages for re-use

Small businesses know that every customer counts and bringing customers back as often as possible is important. After visitors leave your site, they're gone unless you bring them back with e-mail. Small businesses can spread news about themselves using promotional e-mails or just keep in touch through a friendly e-mail newsletter. ListBot performs all these functions free by including small, unobtrusive ads from other small business like yours that are trying to grow.

Microsoft provides a variety of other services for small businesses as well. It offers Internet chat sessions that small businesses can use to ask questions of e-commerce experts. Microsoft also provides links to its technology partners that specialize in helping small businesses grow their online presence. Microsoft knows that small businesses play an integral part in its growth and is dedicated to helping small businesses get online as quickly and easily as possible.

ENTERPRISE INFORMATION PORTALS

Organizations can build their own enterprise information portals to serve employees, business partners, and even customers. Enterprise information portals provide site visitors with directions and links to information that's useful to them. Portals may contain links to business intelligence (for example, reports that would normally be printed), content and document management, enterprise resource planning systems, data warehouses, data-management applications, search and retrieval, and just about any other application that can be accessed via a Web browser. Portals can also provide data warehouse and decision support system access, as well as access to knowledge worker collaboration systems such as Microsoft Exchange 2000 Server.

For Employees

Internal portals are usually deployed over an organizational intranet, even if that intranet spans global borders. Some portals provide employees with structured data; others focus on unstructured information in documents and e-mail. Portal content may be aimed at general users, decision-makers, executives, partners, or teams. Some internal portals may be specific to a line of business or a vertical market, or customizable for each individual user. Content sources include everything from corporate operational systems and document stores to competitive intelligence. Corporate operations use include human resource (HR) departments that use internal portals for access to job postings, benefit information, and other HR-related material. Organizations are also using intranets for time-card entry, expense reporting, and travel arrangements.

Employees can also use enterprise information portals to access operational systems that would normally require multiple logons. The organization's intranet provides access to the portal (with a single sign-on), which, in turn, provides a link to the system that the employee needs to use. Portals can be used to access systems such as decision support and data warehousing applications, enterprise resource planning (ERP) software, organizational scheduling software, and a variety of others. By providing this single point of access, a portal makes an employee's job easier by reducing the effort required to access multiple systems. Portals also help organize information by providing employees with the ability to bring multiple systems' information together in the single, browser-based window. This type of organization enables employees to view data in an integrated fashion, which may lead to new insights.

Microsoft provides organizations with the ability to develop portals using the Windows 2000 platform and FrontPage 2000. Windows 2000 Server contains the functionality found in Internet Information Server (IIS), which allows organizations to quickly and easily deploy intranet-based portals. Windows 2000 Server technologies such as Web Distributed Authoring and Versioning (WebDAV) make it as easy to carry out standard file operations on a shared Web, which allows organizations to provide persistent URL reports and system access. Windows 2000 Server provides internet-aware application development tools with IIS, an efficiency that extends applications to the Web and eliminates awkward bridges between internal and external processes. They assist creating Web-based applications that integrate well into traditional business applications such as HR functions. FrontPage 2000 provides all employees with the ability to create and publish Web content to intranets. The Web-oriented interface of Office 2000 also allows organizations to access information from disparate sources using Microsoft's Digital Dashboard technology.

For Business Partners

Organizations can use extranet technology to create portals through which business partners can access internal data. These portals provide an organization's business partners with the ability to get the information they need at the business partners' convenience. By providing a business partners with a link to an organization's data, organizations increase their supply-chain efficiency. Business partners can get the information they need quickly and easily, without making phone calls and exchanging paper. Organizations are starting to use the XML standard as a data communications technique over the Web. This standard allows organizations and their business partners to exchange data in a standard format similar to well-established electronic data interchange (EDI) standards.

As mentioned in Chapter 9, Microsoft supports the BizTalk framework XML standard. Microsoft Windows 2000 Server and Advanced Server provide organizations with a solid, reliable operating platform that contains integrated Web technologies for linking supply chain partners. Microsoft BizTalk Server provides transmission and translation capabilities that allow organizations to exchange data with their business partners in the BizTalk XML standard format. BizTalk Server allows organizations to quickly and easily create business-to-business portals and extranets, trading communities, electronic catalog management, content syndication, and other supply chain capabilities. Organizations can also use other tools such as FrontPage 2000 and Commerce Server 2000 to create and publish content and transact business online.

For Customers

Organizations can build information portals for customers as well. Although most Web sites only sell things to customers, organizations have the opportunity to provide value-added services as well. Besides selling the organization's products to its customers, the organization can provide links to its business partners or advertising partners that make it easy for the customer to find complementary products for an organization's specific items. Customers appreciate being pointed in the right direction and having their Web searches made easier. Because there are so many sites with so many different products, customers will appreciate your organization's help in reducing the amount of effort required to find the products they want and need. Microsoft's FrontPage 2000 and Commerce Server 2000 products enable organizations to quickly and easily build customer-service applications. These products can help organizations serve their customers better by providing direction and even answers to customer questions. This kind of service helps improve the organization's relationship with its customers.

WRAP UP

- **The Microsoft Network (MSN) provides access to Microsoft products and services, as well as those of their business associates.** MSN provides consumers and businesses with access to Microsoft's alliance partners, specific MSN products and services, as well as MSN MoneyCentral and Microsoft bCentral.

- **MSNBC is a news portal that provides current news and information on a global and local basis.** This joint venture between Microsoft and NBC provides content that is both generalized and targeted for various audiences. Content sections include business, sports, entertainment, and local news and weather.

- **Microsoft provides small and large organizations with advertising opportunities through online services and product associations and sponsorship.** MSN provides organizations with standard banner advertising as well as targeted advertising for specific audiences. Microsoft also provides organizations with the opportunity to get involved with specific products and product lines and to become certified specialists on those products. Microsoft also provides professional services that can help organizations increase their Web presence through effective advertising.

- **Enterprise information portals are becoming an important part of an organization's Web strategy.** Employees, business partners, and customers can all benefit from an organization's information portals. Employees can bring together information from multiple systems into one integrated view. They can also access organization information such as job postings and benefits administration information. Business partners access an organization's data through extranet technologies, which allows them to communicate with the organization more easily. Customers benefit from an organization's portal when the organization assists the customer in finding the products and services they need more quickly and easily.

Taking Stock

1. Do you have an enterprise information portal strategy?

2. Can your employees, business partners, and customers easily find what they need on your Web site?

3. Do your employees need to access to multiple systems to get a single answer to a simple question?

4. Could your organization benefit from working with TransPoint?

5. Does your software platform support intranet, Internet, and extranet-based portals?

6. Do you have software tools that allow you to develop portals easily?

7. Could you benefit from effective advertising on MSN or other Microsoft Web sites?

8. Are you familiar with the advantages of Microsoft's products and services?

ACTION PLAN

❑ Develop an enterprise information portal strategy.

❑ Check the effectiveness of your online advertising and see whether it could be improved using MSN or another Microsoft service.

❑ Check out Microsoft's alliance program to see whether your organization could benefit from becoming a Microsoft partner.

❑ Assess the capabilities of your operating platform and determine whether it can support flexible, high-volume portals.

❑ Assess the capabilities of your software tool kit to see whether your employees can quickly and easily develop Web portal applications.

❑ Visit your own Web site to see whether you can easily find what you need.

❑ Survey your business partners and customers and find out that what they're saying about your Web site.

❑ Visit the Microsoft, MSN, and MSNBC Web sites.

Chapter 12

Partnering

It has become evident that no organization can go it alone in the race to succeed online. Microsoft and its business partners comprise a complete electronic commerce solution. Organizations must know how to pick partners and set the terms and conditions of cooperative efforts. Microsoft's partners are dedicated to helping customers build quick, flexible, and reliable e-commerce solutions.

Microsoft is dedicated to serving its customers through its product and service offerings and to fill gaps with its business partners. Microsoft makes every effort to find the best business partners in each industry and technology. Microsoft certifies its top business partners, which lets customers know that a specific business partner knows a specific Microsoft technology well enough to pass Microsoft's rigorous testing and certification process. Organizations must choose their business partners carefully, and Microsoft does—by considering the individual factors inherent in each type of business partner, industry, and technology. Microsoft works with only the best in each field and screens its partners carefully. Microsoft's customers can depend on the company to provide integrated solutions that leverage and support those of its business partners.

PARTNERING ISSUES

Forming effective partnerships is critical to the success of any organization working in the electronic commerce arena. No such thing as the status quo exists anymore. Technology markets are extremely unstable, driven by the fantastic pace of change in information technology (IT). This pace means that end-users are vulnerable to obsolescence faster than ever, so they want solutions fast! With much of the equipment purchased today being driven by project growth, few organizations purchase that extra piece of equipment to keep around as a utility machine. The government no longer grants equipment depreciation write-offs, as was the case prior to the so-called tax reform of 1986. Thus, today's IT decision-makers concentrate more on the business aspects of purchasing. Equipment acquisitions are better planned and justified, with emphasis on total cost and total support rather than just price. Microsoft's products and partnership are aimed at showing real business value through integrated technology solutions.

IT managers are moving toward being more sensitive to the needs and input of others in their organizations, including business users and sales force teams. Satisfying these needs takes more human or financial resources than one organization can supply. Meeting these needs requires the combined efforts of many partners working together to create a complete e-commerce solution. A highly effective partnering program reinforces brand loyalty and gives your customers justification to pay for complete solutions that are supplied to them, as opposed to those they have to create themselves. Technology is running ahead of users' ability to learn about it. Although the benefits of more technologically advanced machines outweigh the negatives, many end users fear it and some wish it would just go away. Effective partnerships solve problems for customers and provide solutions that are simple, integrated, and flexible. Microsoft is constantly looking for new partners to supply value-added services and help to create complete solutions for customers.

Choosing a Partner

Reasons to choose or not to choose a business partner abound. These reasons generally fall into five categories:

- **Trust** Organizations must trust that their business partners will honor the terms of partnership agreements, including maintaining confidentiality where necessary.

- **Culture** Business partners must also have cultures that fit together well enough to work together, although they certainly don't have to be perfectly aligned philosophically.

- **Reputation and image** Business partners must know the reputation of the organizations with whom they transact business. Sometimes, an organization's reputation on the grapevine is almost more important than what is printed in its annual report.

- **Technology** Business partners must have compatible technologies or at least use standard communication mechanisms to exchange data.

- **Financial stability** Business partners exchange goods and services based on credit. Both organizations must be able to financially support their end of the agreement.

Microsoft builds solid, long-lasting relationships with well-known companies that supply value-added products and services and works hard to provide leadership in these areas.

Trust

Perhaps the biggest issue in choosing business partners is trust. Before a partnership can start delivering benefits, a trusting relationship needs to be in place between the business partners. Partners trust one another to feed them accurate information on a timely basis. If each partner trusts the other to use the information correctly and appropriately to meet their customers' demands, then the partnership works. The partners must also trust that the information they share with each other is kept confidential from the marketplace and competitors. If any element of the relationship is missing or breaks down, the relationship can be adversely affected. Microsoft is careful to ensure that all its business partners are trustworthy and deliver what they promise to customers.

Culture

How business partners fit together culturally can be an issue. Organizational culture clashes create a tension between business partners. Culture clashes should be resolved early in the relationship. Interpersonal problems that are left to fester will cause increasing friction and discord between the two partners. The principals in any agreement between two organizations must work together to ensure that both business partners agree to the working conditions and terms of the partnership. Culture clashes occur concerning various factors. One organization may be more formal in its dress or communication methods while another may have a more laid-back approach to business. Another potential problem is the difference in how organizations approach technology deployments. If a partnership requires that two organizations decide on a specific technology to communicate or process the data, both organizations must have that technology deployed by the agreed-upon date. By agreeing on deliverables and work schedules, organizations can avoid having organizational culture or work styles affect the results of the combined effort. Microsoft makes sure that the organizations with which it partners have cultures that are dedicated to providing customers with high-quality products, services, and support.

One cultural issue that organizations often encounter when working together is work styles. Manager buy-in can reduce the amount of friction between the two organizations by setting an example for the rest of the workforce on the joint project. Often, joint efforts require organizations to change cultural work styles and meet in the middle. Management commitment can facilitate this change by bringing the two organizational workforces together. Key stakeholders in joint efforts can help set priorities for work deliverables and deadlines, a process that clarifies the team's project requirements. Key stakeholders and management should work together to make sure that all team members clearly understand the vision behind the project and the expected results. Continuous communication facilitates this process by keeping everyone on the team informed and their roles clarified. Microsoft provides continuous communications to business partners through e-mails, newsletters, contract updates, and product release notes to keep business partners appraised of Microsoft's direction and vision.

Reputation and Image

An organization's reputation is as important as its financial condition. Organizations must jealously guard their reputation and the image they present to both the public and their business partners. When organizations are considering taking on a business partner, they should carefully check the reputation of their prospective business partner. Does the prospective business partner have good customer relations? Does it meet the deadlines that it sets and announce its product releases or service offerings? Does the prospective business partner follow through on its commitment customers? All these questions and more should be asked before announcing a partnership publicly. If one of the business partners does not follow through on its commitments, it generally harms both partners in the relationship. Microsoft carefully screens all its business partners before announcing any new relationships, partnering only with those who are known for good customer relationships.

Technology

For business partners to deliver high-quality, integrated products and services, they must fit together technologically. Business partners must be able to share technology, communicate electronically, and provide solutions that allow customers to access the joint resources of the business partners seamlessly. This means that the partners must at least adopt the same standards, if not the same technology. Microsoft certifies only those business partners that it knows are compatible with Microsoft's technology. Microsoft's business partners must show that they can reliably support their products on Microsoft platforms. When an organization demonstrates that its products run on Microsoft's platforms, it receives a certification seal to display on its products and Web site. Microsoft monitors the vendor's customer service continuously to ensure customer satisfaction with Microsoft's products. Microsoft will continue to add strategic business partners only if they can meet the rigorous testing and certification requirements of the Microsoft seal of approval.

Financial Stability

All of Microsoft's business partners must show that they are financially stable and will be there to support their customers over the long haul. Making sure that business partners are not going to simply disappear after a product is sold is critical, and Microsoft carefully examines each business partner for stability, customer reputation, sales, and financial management. Regardless of the product or platform the business partner is supporting, it must show that it is financially stable or has solid financial backing if it is a start-up. Microsoft recognizes that many of the big innovations in electronic commerce come from Internet start-ups. Nonetheless, Microsoft is dedicated to ensuring high-quality customer support for installed products and screens even small start-ups carefully.

Restructuring an Organization to Fit a Partnership

There may be times when a part or even all of an organization must be restructured to fit a partnership. Most often, this effort is required to create a new division that works with the new business partner. All the normal tasks associated with forming a new part of an organization must be completed, including staffing, financing, securing office space, and sometimes even moving. For situations in which a vision must be created, organizational staff must be flexible enough to face potential changes in work style, hours, and even dress. For joint efforts in which a new entity is created from two or more different organizations (such as MSNBC, TransPoint, or CheckFree), staff from the forming organizations must be allocated to the new effort. Creating this new staff can sometimes be difficult if current staff from the foregoing organizations are allocated to the new effort. There may be both cultural and task-related changes. In such a situation, the forming organizations must be flexible in their requirements for the new effort.

Microsoft allocates both executive and line-level staff to its joint efforts. Microsoft ensures that its joint efforts provide value-added products and services to its customers. Microsoft monitors the joint ventures for quality and reliability. The Microsoft culture of innovation and high-quality support is infused into each of its new joint efforts. Microsoft partners only with those organizations that have a reputation for high customer satisfaction and high-quality products and services. Microsoft supplies the software and other technology infrastructure elements that make its joint efforts technologically advanced. Microsoft partners with hardware vendors that supply products compatible with its platforms and user products.

Writing the Contract

In many cases, the organization that writes the contract controls the joint effort. The organization that controls the contract can set terms favorable to itself. This allows the organization to control the quality of deliverables as well as the deadlines in the schedule. In an ideal situation, however, the organization with the greatest amount of expertise in the particular product or service area should own the contract because that organization is more likely to create a realistic picture of the joint development efforts. The organization that has the greatest expertise should also understand the resources, both financial and human, required to complete the project, thereby ensuring a more realistic project plan and ultimately a better-quality product as the end result. Microsoft product partnerships monitors closely to ensure the highest quality of value-added products from its business partners.

Microsoft makes sure that all business partnerships are aligned with Microsoft's vision of the customer's use of the product. To ensure both up-to-date customer support for all platforms and high-quality products and services, Microsoft sets the parameters under which partnerships are formed and monitors the quality standards of its business partner's value-added products and services. Microsoft ensures that business partners only enhance its products, not reduce or eliminate the products' usefulness to its customers. Microsoft contracts with all its business partners to ensure that add-on products are fully compatible with Microsoft's platforms. Microsoft requires that all its business partners provide quality support for all products compatible with Microsoft platforms. These Microsoft certification requirements ensure high-quality products and services for Microsoft customers.

Controlling the Joint Development

Microsoft keeps careful track of joint development efforts for several reasons, but the most important is Microsoft customer satisfaction. By monitoring joint development efforts, Microsoft is able to hold projects to its quality standards and ensure that services and support from Microsoft and its business partners meet Microsoft's customer-service goals. Microsoft partners only with top organizations in their fields, such as NBC for MSNBC and CheckFree, FirstData, and Citibank for CheckFree/TransPoint. Microsoft has the resources to fund joint development efforts that it thinks will contribute to the utilization of its products and services. By controlling the joint effort, Microsoft is able to ensure that the resources are used effectively and efficiently. Microsoft has the products, services, and resources to meet the demands of joint e-commerce efforts that must stay current and evolve over time with the rapidly changing e-landscape.

Knowledge Management

Microsoft makes sure that its business partners are well trained on its strategies, products, and services. Microsoft has created a knowledge-transfer program specifically for its business partners. The program focuses on training recommendations for those specific areas needed by the business partners. A variety of training methods are used, based on the unique corporate culture and specific technology training needs. These methods can include any or all of the following: self-study guides, instructor-led training, online training, mentorship programs, project-based workshops, custom labs, and private classes. The goal, of course, is to use this highly integrated plan to move the business partner toward higher productivity and customer service.

Microsoft provides all its business partners with access to complete documentation libraries and provides guidance on standards, tools, and techniques for third-party software development. Microsoft's certified business partners go through rigorous training on their way to becoming active in Microsoft's business partner program. Microsoft's program offers complete, thorough communication and understanding between the Microsoft, its business partners, and its customers. This means that Microsoft's customers get excellent training, products and services, which helps customers bridge the gap between tactics and execution, enabling staff to create systems that serve the organization's needs and provide it with a competitive advantage.

Security

Security is just as important with business partners as it is with any other e-commerce arrangement. Verifying an organization's integrity and solidity is necessary before forming a partnership with it. The fact that an organization has a D&B entry doesn't guarantee that it's legitimate. One major failing of business partnerships is the lack of due diligence completed before organizations are accepted as customers, suppliers, or other type of business partners, especially for big orders. Microsoft is extremely thorough in its examination and certification of business partners. It performs a complete risk analysis to determine specific vulnerabilities, but also makes the security and risk management policies and technology flexible to cover new needs as they arise.

Microsoft also makes sure that all business partners in its electronic commerce chain are tightly monitored and controlled. Having someone exceed his or her authority and hack the communication channel is nearly impossible, and

Microsoft protects both itself and its customers from bad faith between business partners. Microsoft's campus security is also quite thorough. Microsoft avoids hiring people who aren't trained and may cause a compromise (for example, someone just lets Joe Smith walk past the guard). Although many commercial organizations have poor security measures in place, Microsoft is careful about protecting its assets. Further, many organizations still think locally and don't understand that risk can come from anywhere in the world via the Internet. Microsoft protects itself with its own products that control access and ward off hacks.

INDEPENDENT SOFTWARE VENDORS

Independent software vendors (ISVs) are the backbone of Microsoft's partnerships. ISVs create software that utilizes Microsoft's platforms, such as Windows 2000 Server, and extends products such as Microsoft Office. ISVs include:

- ERP vendors such as SAP, Oracle, PeopleSoft, and Baan
- Database software manufacturers including Oracle and Sybase
- Web software companies such as iFront and Mercado
- Home and office productivity software companies such as Intuit and Norton

All these organizations provide Microsoft customers with options that offer complete, integrated solutions for creating and extending a digital nervous system. As mentioned, Microsoft screens strategic partners carefully and works with the best providers in each technological and functional area. Microsoft customers should be aware of the issues that are part of selecting and integrating ISV products with Microsoft's platforms and products.

Independent software vendors face several issues when developing software for Microsoft platforms. Among those issues are compatibility and interfaces on current products and upgrades, connectivity, and system performance. Microsoft makes products compatibility easy as long as independent software vendors follow the specifications published for the Microsoft application programming interfaces (APIs). These specifications tell independent software vendors how to pass data between their applications, and between their applications and the Microsoft platform. If the independent software vendors follow the API specifications, upgrades are fairly easy. Simplified upgrades ensure that Microsoft's customers and those of the ISVs can continue to take advantage of new features offered by upgrades.

Connectivity issues are similarly resolved through the use of APIs, as well as the use of Microsoft's BizTalk Server for business-to-business e-commerce. BizTalk Server provides ISVs with the ability to move data between organizations using the XML translation facility. BizTalk Server is with 100 percent compatible with the BizTalk framework that is being backed by large independent software vendors and organizational IT departments. Microsoft's open Windows 2000 Server standards and APIs assist ISVs in connecting their products to other products and platforms across a variety of hardware configurations Microsoft also provides its customers with services to help them connect products from various independent software vendors. These services are provided through Microsoft partnerships and Microsoft's Professional Services Division.

System performance is often an issue, particularly with respect to large software packages such as ERP systems. Microsoft partners provide tuning tools to help customers optimize performance of their software. Microsoft also provides console management and monitoring tools in Windows 2000 Server. These tools enable organizations to monitor the performance and uptime of their applications, as well as generate reports that analyze performance over time. Microsoft partners, including ERP vendors, database software companies, and third-party performance-management tools, work with Microsoft to ensure that their tools are Windows compatible and provide the information that organizations need to make good decisions to optimize the performance of their applications.

WEB DEVELOPERS

Web developers are truly at the heart of today's technology. As Web technology continues to permeate organizational infrastructures, Web developers will become the core development teams for most organizations. Microsoft works with the top Web development companies to provide its customers with the best possible solutions. Organizations need to screen potential Web developers carefully. Someone can easily hang out a shingle and say that he or she can develop Web pages. Developing Web sites that serve an organization's business needs and provide real value to an organization's employees, business partners, and customers requires more than just knowing how to program in a Web-based language. A good Web development company knows how to create a Web design that enables quick and easy navigation, provides content that is useful to visitors, and is flexible enough to change as required over time. Microsoft's customers can rest assured that Web developers recommended by Microsoft provide high-quality services at a reasonable cost.

Web design firm staffs generally have a mix of skills, ranging from highly analytical, technical people to very creative, artistic people. An organization should choose its Web design firm based on the design firms capabilities, skill sets, and style. It's important to review a prospective vendor's Web sites to see how the vendor designs and creates a site. Is the prospective vendor's style compatible with your organization's culture? Is navigation easy and are the colors aesthetically pleasing? The design firm's style must match the expectations of the organization and, perhaps more important, the expectations of the organization's customers and/or site visitors. By examining a portfolio of the design firm's previous work, an organization can get a good idea of whether the design firm can meet the organization's requirements.

Examining a portfolio of the design firm's work also provides organizations with a look into the experience of that design firm. The design firm should have sufficient experience to understand the organization's needs, design a creative but cost-effective solution, and manage the implementation of that solution. The design firm must also have a blend of marketing and technology skills, which may be difficult to find given the current IT staffing shortage. The design firm should have a strong team of individuals who can work together well to create an integrated solution that is both artistically pleasing and technically solid. Design firms must understand the Microsoft Windows platform and the capabilities of its Web products. Their technical staff should be fluent in the Microsoft products that are required to create e-commerce solutions.

As mentioned in Chapter 4, e-commerce solutions are not cheap. A design firm's rates should be within market limits and within the organization's ability to pay. Organizations should never pay more than they expect to get in return on their Web site, although again, as mentioned in Chapter 4, this can be very difficult to calculate. The competitive bidding process can often provide organizations with some leverage to use in negotiations. Microsoft's Professional Services Division can help you create a request for proposal (RFP) that assures you the best-quality design firms at a reasonable price. Organization should do their homework and set return on investment (ROI) goals and a budget to prevent cost overruns and unmet expectations.

ENTERPRISE SERVICES

Enterprise service firms provide complete, integrated solutions to mid- and large-sized organizations. These firms may provide hardware, software, and services that include project management, software development, and training. Some enterprise service firms are part of the Microsoft Service Advantage team. Microsoft Service Advantage, introduced in early 1996, includes a full line of services from Microsoft and key industry partners and is aimed at meeting the information technology needs of large organizations. Whether enterprise service firms are specifically members of the Microsoft Service Advantage team or not, all such firms are carefully screened by Microsoft to provide customers with high quality, value-added products and services.

To choose the right consultant, you need to know the types of consultants available, the services they offer, and what you want to accomplish. Many enterprise service firms work in two or more broad areas; others specialize or subspecialize. Also, your local market and the extent of your own knowledge influence the type of consultant services you will need. Consultants are usually more effective when they are working with organizations that have some awareness of the market and at least a basic understanding of the projects and technology they're implementing.

An enterprise service provider is typically a large consulting company that operates worldwide. The two most important characteristics to consider when choosing an enterprise service provider are the ability to deliver and the cost. A consulting company's ability to deliver on its commitments is based on the skill level and skill currency of its consultants. Large consulting firms typically have a good base of skills in most of the hot technology areas. The problem is that some of these firms put their less experienced consultants on projects to learn the technology at the expense of the client. It is important for organizations to screen consultants carefully to make sure that their skill sets are appropriate in scope and level. Microsoft works with enterprise service providers that provide certified consultants for Microsoft products. Microsoft's customers can ask to verify the consultant's certifications for the products that the particular customer uses.

The other major factor to consider when choosing an enterprise service provider is cost. Large consulting firms typically charge premium rates for their consultants. This can often put those services out of the reach of small and midsized organizations. One alternative is Microsoft Consulting Services (MCS), which uses consultants with experience and expertise in Microsoft technology, methodologies, and tools and is chartered to help organizations capitalize on the benefits Microsoft's products. MCS consultants focus on solving problems for organizations transferring knowledge and skills to corporations, government organizations, and third-party Microsoft Solution Providers worldwide. MCS, in conjunction with third-party solution providers, offers organizations a number of services customized to their unique information technology environment. Such services include planning, design, development, integration, and implementation.

COMMERCE AND APPLICATION HOSTING

Application hosting by application service providers (ASPs) has become a hot information technology trend recently. Organizations are finding that it is less expensive for them to rent applications hosted by a service provider than it is to try to implement the application on the organization's platform. Also contributing to this trend is the shortage of information technology professionals to do the implementation work. Organizations that simply need or can use a vanilla version of software such as large ERP systems may find using a hosted application more efficient. Application service providers are building value-added services to extend access and data center facilities that provide a canned quick-start solution for organizations that need to implement new systems fast. "Software as a service" is providing a new model for outsourcing commerce applications, both for business-to-business and business-to-consumer outfits.

Before making the decision on application hosting for any particular application, organizations need to consider some factors, including:

- Uptime

- Connectivity

- Customization requirements

- Cost comparison between outsourcing and keeping the work in-house

Considering uptime and connectivity is part of creating a good service level agreement (SLA). The organization must come to an agreement with the application service provider as to what percentage of uptime is sufficient and what penalties and rewards will be handed out for exceeding or missing those goals.

Customization requirements are a major issue for organizations to consider. If your organization cannot easily use the vanilla version of the application, the customization requirements may drive the cost of outsourcing the application higher than doing it in-house. Organizations must also identify their motivation for considering outsourcing e-business applications, such as staffing shortages and upgrade frequency. If these applications are considered mission critical and contribute to the competitive advantage of the organization, the organization may be giving up an advantage by using a noncustomized version of the software. If your competitors are using the same version of the software, then you may be giving up the competitive advantage.

Microsoft has a complete set of services and products for both application service providers (ASPs) and customers wishing to utilize application service providers. Microsoft is committed to making Windows 2000 the best ASP platform for commercial hosting. Microsoft is dedicated to building strong relationships with ASPs and providing them with the platform and products needed to help customers accomplish their goals. Microsoft has also built a series of partnerships, equity investments, and pilots, which lead to ASPs offering additional application hosting services, including:

- Managed Microsoft Exchange messaging

- Office 2000 collaboration

- Corporate purchasing

- Media streaming

- Line of business application services

Microsoft considers ASPs to be customers and will continue to expand its product and service offerings to enable ASPs to service their customers. Because no single solution exists that spans the myriad of applications, from small business or department level to enterprise-wide customer needs and e-business models, Microsoft is pursuing a generalized platform approach for hosting in anticipation that software will be offered within a service. This platform will offer a new generation of programmable Web services in which software, regardless of where it is hosted, can work with other applications and services.

WRAP UP

- **Developing strong business partnerships requires an organization to navigate through a number of obstacles.** Microsoft chooses its partners based on culture compatibility, technical savvy, and the stability of the partner. Microsoft monitors and maintains control of the quality of its business partnerships by certifying vendors. Microsoft manages its business partnerships over time by maintaining control of the contract and establishing a strong presence in any joint efforts. Microsoft also makes sure that all its business partners have access to the information they need to help Microsoft's customers deploy successful solutions based on Microsoft products.

- **Independent software vendors provide Microsoft customers with the value-added products and services they need to leverage Microsoft's platform.** Independent software vendors include makers of ERP, database, utility, and home/office productivity software. Independent software makers must resolve issues of compatibility, connectivity, system performance, and ease of upgrades to provide their customers with high quality software and services. Microsoft assists its independent software vendor partners with standard, published APIs and a complete library of software interfaces and documentation.

- **Selecting Web developers is as much a matter of style as technology.** Microsoft recommends only the best Web design firms to its customers, but customers must still evaluate each Web design for cultural fit and technological experience and prowess. Web design firms should have a blend of marketing, design, and technological skills. Organizations should review a Web design firm's portfolio of sites to determine whether it has the particular skill and style that best fits the organization.

- **Enterprise service firms provide large Microsoft customers with a wide variety business and technical services.** Organizations must carefully evaluate each consultant from each enterprise service firm to ensure that they receive the skill set that is most cost effective and best fits the organization's needs. The Microsoft Service Advantage team is made up of the best enterprise service firms that are certified in Microsoft products.

- **Application hosting is the next big thing in technology.** However, organizations must carefully evaluate whether outsourcing a particular application or commerce function is cost effective for them. Microsoft provides a complete set of products and services for application service providers and their customers to leverage the Microsoft platform.

Taking Stock

1. Are your independent software vendors Microsoft certified?

2. Does your IT department have a formal process for selecting and evaluating software and software vendors?

3. Have you seen Microsoft's product and service evaluation kits?

4. Have you looked at your Web site through the eyes of a customer recently?

5. Does your Web design firm meet your expectations?

6. Does your Web site use Microsoft products for both business-to-business and business-to-consumer electronic commerce?

7. Do your software and service vendors make sure that you have all the information you need to support your software products?

8. Do your enterprise service firms supply high-quality, cost-effective consultants?

9. Would it be cost effective for your organization to outsource some or all of its application portfolio?

10. Have you visited Microsoft's Web site at *www.microsoft.com?*

ACTION PLAN

❑ Formalize the process by which you select business partners.

❑ Check to see whether your software vendors are certified Microsoft business partners.

❑ Browse Microsoft's business partner list to see how prospective partners can help you to leverage your technology investments.

❑ Make up a formal list of characteristics that you desire in a software vendor and evaluate Microsoft and its business partners against that list.

❑ Look at the evaluation kit for each Microsoft product and solution set.

❑ Before selecting a Web design firm, check some of its other work to see whether it meets your expectations and organizational style.

❑ Check your security system to see whether it needs patching or replacing.

❑ Ask for—no, demand—résumés and certification materials from your enterprise service firms.

❑ Do a cost/benefit study on the possibility of outsourcing some or all of your application portfolio.

❑ Visit Microsoft's Web site at *www.microsoft.com.*

Part III

Appendixes

Appendix A

References

Aaker, David. *Building Strong Brands*. New York: Free Press, 1995.

Adams, Charles (ed.). *The Beginner's Illustrated Internet Dictionary: From A to Zine*. Sarasota, FL: Bookworld Services, 1997

Blum, Daniel. *Understanding Active Directory Services*. Redmond, WA: Microsoft Press, 1999

Boni, William C., and Kovacich, Gerald L. *I-Way Robbery : Crime on the Internet*. New York: Butterworth-Heinemann, 1999.

Boni, William C., and Kovacich, Gerald L. *High Technology Crime Investigator's Handbook: Working in the Global Environment*. New York: Butterworth-Heinemann, 1999.

Boni, William C., and Kovacich, Gerald L. *The Information Systems Security Officer's Guide*. New York: Butterworth-Heinemann, 1998.

Bucki, Lisa. *Computer & Internet Dictionary*. New York: DDC Publishing, 1998.

Carptenter, Frederica. 1999. "Customer Management: A Key Part of the Digital Nervous System," *Microsoft CRM Highlights*. Redmond, WA: Microsoft Corporation, 1999.

CommerceNet. *Barriers & Inhibitors to the Widespread Adoption of Internet Commerce 1997*. CommerceNet Research Report #97-05, April 1997.

CommerceNet. *Overview of the 1998 Barriers and Inhibitors Research project*. CommerceNet Research Bulletin #98-08.

Eckhouse, John, and Vance, Ashlee. "Presenting Your Bills on the Web." *InformationWeek, August 9, 1999*.

"E-Business Exponential Growth." *CIO Magazine*, February 15, 1999.

Ernst & Young. "2000: Third Annual Ernst & Young Internet Shopping Study." New York: Ernst & Young, Fall 1999.

Freedman, Alan. Computer Desktop *Dictionary*. New York: Amacom, 1999.

Freedman, Alan. *The Internet Glossary and Quick Reference Guide*. New York: Amacom, 1998.

Gates, William H, III. *Business @ The Speed of Thought*. New York: Warner Books, 1999.

Hammer, Michael, and Champy, James. *Reengineering the Corporation: A Manifesto for Business Revolution*. New York: HarperBusiness, 1994.

Hinkkanen, Aimo; Kalakota, Ravi; Saengcharoenrat, Porama; Stallaert, Jan; Whinston, Andrew B. *Distributed Decision Support Systems for Real-Time Supply Chain Management Using Agent Technologies*. Auston: University of Texas Press, 1998.

Ind, Nicholas. *The Corporate Brand*. New York: New York University Press, 1997.

Kalakota, R., and Whinston, A.B. *Electronic Commerce: A Manager's Guide*. Boston: Addison-Wesley Publishing, 1997.

Kappferer, Jean-Noel. *Strategic Brand Management: New Approaches to Creating and Evaluating Brand Equity*. New York: Free Press, 1994.

Keller, Kevin Lane. *Strategic Brand Management: Building, Measuring, and Managing Brand Equity*. Englewood Cliffs, NJ: Prentice Hall, 1997.

Kwano, Hirobumi. "Dismantling the Barriers to Global Electronic Commerce." Keynote Speech at the OECD Conference, November 1997.McConnell, Steve. *Software Project Survival Guide*. (*www.construx.com/survivalguide*), 1997.

MacRae, Chris. *World Class Brands*. Boston: Addison-Wesley Publishing, 1991.

McWilliams, Gary, and Stepanek, Marcia. "Taming The Info Monster." *Business Week Online*, June 11, 1998.

Meta Group. Meta Group Web site (*www.meta.com*), 1999.

Microsoft Corporation. Value Chain Initiative FAQ. Redmond, WA: Microsoft Corporation, 1999.

Microsoft Corporation. "Microsoft Strategy for Internet Corporate Purchasing." White Paper, Redmond, WA: Microsoft Corporation, 1999.

Microsoft Corporation and KPMG Peat Marwick LLP. *Microsoft Business Benefits Study*. Red- mond, WA: Microsoft Corporation, 1999.

Mougayar, Walid. *Opening Digital Markets*. New York: McGraw-Hill, 1997.

Nilson, Torsten H. *Competitive Branding: Winning in the Market Place With Value-Added Brands*. New York: John Wiley & Sons, 1999.

Organization for Economic Cooperation and Development (OECD). "Dismantling the Barriers to Global Electronic Commerce." OECD Discussion paper, November 1997.

Porter, Michael E. *Competitive Strategy: Techniques for Analyzing Industries and Competitors*. New York: Free Press, 1998.

Roberts-Witt, Sarah L. "Making Sense of Portal Pandemonium." *Knowledge Management Magazine*, July 1999.

Summit Strategies Web site (*www.summitstrat.com*), 1999.

Temkin, Bruce. Interview with Research Director of Business E-Commerce at Forrester Group, September 22, 1999.

Trepper, Charles. "Requirements Gathering for Web-Based Development. Application Development." *Application Development Trends Magazine*, March 1998.

Trepper, Charles. "Structured Interviewing: Getting It Right The First Time." *Application Development Trends Magazine*, June 1998.

Trepper, Charles. "Training for Retention." *Application Development Trends Magazine*, August 1998.

Trepper, Charles. "Internet content management: Untangling the 'Net." *Application Development Trends Magazine*, December 1998.

Trepper, Charles. "Training for ERP." *Application Development Trends Magazine*, April 1999.

Trepper, Charles. "CRM gets personalized." *Application Development Trends Magazine*, September 1999.

Trepper, Charles. "The road to enlightenment." *Application Development Trends Magazine*, November 1999.

Upshaw, Lynn B. *Building Brand Identity: A Strategy for Success in a Hostile Marketplace*. New York: John Wiley & Sons, 1995.

U.S. Government, Commerce Department, "The Emerging Digital Economy," 1998.

U.S. Government, Office of Management and Budget (OMB) *Cost-Benefit Analysis Handbook*. (U.S. Information Infrastructure Project) .

Wilder, Clinton. "E-Transformation." *InformationWeek*, September 13, 1999.

Wells, William; Burnett, John; Moriarty, Sandra. *Advertising Principles and Practice*. Englewood Cliffs, NJ: Prentice Hall, 1995.

Winkler, Agnieszka. *Warp-Speed Branding : The Impact of Technology on Marketing*. New York: John Wiley & Sons, 1999.

World Trade Organization. "Electronic Commerce and the Role of the WTO." *WTO Secretariat*, March 1998.

Appendix B

Web Site References

This appendix presents the Web site addresses (URLs) of key organizations discussed or mentioned in this book. These addresses are current as of this writing, but the Web is a dynamic entity and addresses are subject to change without notice and without redirection. If a company is discussed in more than one chapter, its URL is listed here only under the chapter in which it first appears.

Chapter 1

American National Standards Institute (ANSI)   *www.ansi.org*

barnesandnoble.com llc   *www.barnesandnoble.com*

CheckFree Corporation   *www.checkfree.com*

CIO Communications, Inc.   *www.cio.com*

Ernst & Young   *www.ey.com*

First Data Merchant Services Corporation   *www.firstdata.com*

Jupiter Communications, Inc.   *www.jup.com*

META Group, Inc.   *www.metagroup.com*

Microsoft Corporation   *www.microsoft.com*

Toysrrus.com   *www.toysrus.com*

TransPoint   *www.transpoint.com*

United Nations   *www.un.org*

United States Department of Defense   *www.defenselink.mil*

World Trade Organization (WTO)   *www.wto.org*

Chapter 2

Ask Jeeves, Inc.   *www.askjeeves.com*

SportsLine.com, Inc.   *www.sportsline.com*

Cinergy Corp.   *www.cinergy.com*

Ticketmaster Online – CitySearch, Inc.   *www.citysearch.com*

Clarus Corporation   *www.claruscorp.com*

Dell Computer Corporation   *www.dell.com*

Exabyte Corporation   *www.exabyte.com*

EXE Technologies, Inc.   *www.exe.com*

General Mills, Inc.   *www.generalmills.com*

Giga Information Group, Inc.   *www.gigaweb.com*

H&R Johnson Tiles, Ltd.   *www.johnson-tiles.com*

InformationWeek Magazine (CMP Media Inc.)   *www.informationweek.com*

MasterCard International Incorporated   *www.mastercard.com*

Mayne Nickless Limited   *www.maynick.com.au*

Merisel   *www.merisel.com*

Northwest Airlines   *www.nwa.com*

Office Depot, Inc.   *www.officedepot.com*

SAP AG   *www.sap.com*

Sintaks   *www.sintaks.com*

Sony Corporation of America   *www.sony.com*

Telxon Corporation   *www.telxon.com*

Unilever PLC   *www.unilever.com*

United States Department of Commerce   *www.doc.gov*

United States Federal Trade Commission   *www.ftc.gov*

United States Justice Department   *www.usdoj.gov*

Webridge, Inc.   *www.webridge.com*

Chapter 3

American Express Company   *www.americanexpress.com*

CommerceNet   *www.commerce.net*

Georgia Institute of Technology   *www.gatech.edu*

Georgia Tech Lorraine   *gtlntback.georgiatech-metz.fr*

Jill Spiegel   *www.spiegelspeak.com*

National Institute of Standards and Technology   *www.nist.gov*

Organisation for Economic Co-operation and Development   *www.oecd.org*

The Pillsbury Company   *www.pillsbury.com*

PricewaterhouseCoopers   *www.pwcglobal.com*

United Nations International Computing Centre   *www.unicc.org*

Visa International   *www.visa.com*

Chapter 4

Construx Software Builders, Inc.   www.construx.com

The Forrester Group Inc.   www.forrestergroup.com

HomeSource.com   *www.homesource.com*

International Data Corporation   *www.idc.com*

Chapter 5

Apple Computer, Inc.   *www.apple.com*

International Business Machines Corporation   *www.ibm.com*

Network Solutions, Inc.   *www.networksolutions.com*

Oracle Corporation   *www.oracle.com*

RealNetworks, Inc.   *www.real.com*

Sun Microsystems, Inc.   *www.sun.com*

Chapter 6

AltaVista Company   *www.altavista.com*

Amazon.com, Inc.   *www.amazon.com*

bivings woodell, inc.   *www.bivwood.com*

The Chase Manhattan Corporation   *www.chase.com*

Chemdex Corporation   *www.chemdex.com*

ConAgra, Inc.   *www.conagra.com*

Delta Air Lines   *www.deltaairlines.com*

Excite, Inc.   *www.excite.com*

Hewlett-Packard Company   *www.hp.com*

HotBot   *www.hotbot.com*

InfoSeek (Go, Inc.)   *www.infoseek.go.com*

Kraft Foods, Inc.   *www.kraft.com*

Lycos, Inc.   *www.lycos.com*

Monsanto Company   *www.monsanto.com*

The Procter and Gamble Company   *www.pg.com*

Purdue University *www.purdue.edu*

Sprint Spectrum, L.P. *www.sprintpcs.com*

Time Inc. *www.pathfinder.com/time/*

TradeMatrix *www.tradematrix.com*

Wal-Mart.com, Inc. *www.walmart.com*

Yahoo! Inc. *www.yahoo.com*

Chapter 7

Direct Marketing Association, Inc. *www.the-dma.org*

IMT Strategies, Inc. *www.imtstrategies.com*

Tandy Corporation *www.tandy.com*

U.S. Bancorp *www.usbank.com*

Chapter 8

America Online, Inc. *www.aol.com*

Cambridge Information Network (CIN) *www.cin.ctp.com*

Cambridge Technology Partners *www.ctp.com*

eBay Inc. *www.ebay.com*

Intel Corporation *www.intel.com*

ivillage, Inc. *www.ivillage.com*

priceline.com Incorporated *www.priceline.com*

RealNetworks, Inc. *www.realnetworks.com*

University of Minnesota *www.umn.edu*

Chapter 9

BizTalk *www.biztalk.org*

The Boeing Company *www.boeing.com*

BP Amoco p.l.c. *www.bpamoco.com*

CommerceOne Inc. *www.commerceone.com*

Microsoft bCentral *www.bcentral.com*

The Microsoft Network (MSN) *www.msn.com*

Chapter 10

Massachusetts Institute of Technology *www.mit.edu*

Netscape Communications Corporation *www.netscape.com*

Open Applications Group *www.openapplications.org*

Rational Software Corporation *www.rational.com*

Sybase, Inc. *www.sybase.com*

Chapter 11

Citibank *www.citibank.com*

CNBC *www.cnbc.com*

Compaq Computer Corporation *www.compaq.com*

MSN Hotmail *www.hotmail.com*

John Hancock Financial Services, Inc. *www.johnhancock.com*

Kelley Blue Book *www.kelleybluebook.com*

Merrill Lynch & Co., Inc. *www.merrilllynch.com*

National Broadcasting Company *www.nbc.com*

WSJ.com (The Wall Street Journal interactive edition) *www.wsj.com*

ZD Inc. *www.zdnet.com*

Chapter 12

Baan Company N.V. *www.baan.com*

iFront *www.ifront.com*

Intuit Inc. *www.intuit.com*

Mercado Software, Inc. *www.mercadosw.com*

Symantec Corporation *www.symantec.com*

PeopleSoft, Inc. *www.peoplesoft.com*

Appendix C

Microsoft E-Commerce Product and Services Briefs

This appendix presents an alphabetized listing and high-level summary of the Microsoft products and services mentioned in this book. The products and services listed are constantly upgraded, and some of them are still in initial development at the time of this writing, so be sure to check the Microsoft Web site at www.microsoft.com frequently for details and updates on these and all Microsoft products and services.

Active Directory

Active Directory directory services is the part of the Windows 2000 Server operating system that manages and controls directories. For more information, see the section toward the end of this appendix on Windows 2000 Server.

Application Center 2000

Microsoft Application Center 2000 is the deployment and management environment for high-availability Web applications built on Windows 2000. It enables administrators to achieve on-demand scalability and mission reliability for their Web applications by running them on multiple servers, and it reduces operational complexity and cost by allowing centralized administration of a Single Application Image. Application Center makes managing groups of servers as simple as managing a single machine. Key features include a replication engine, centralized performance and event monitoring, self-tuning, self-healing application health tools, load testing, capacity planning, dynamic load balancing, and tight integration with Windows 2000 Network Load Balancing (NLB).

BackOffice Server 2000

BackOffice Server 2000 is used for the integrated development, deployment, and management of BackOffice applications in departments, branch offices, and mid-sized businesses. BackOffice Server 2000 provides a set of tools that allow organizations to leverage the Windows 2000 Server platform. These tools include

- **Exchange Server** for complete messaging and enterprise collaboration
- **Proxy Server** for extensible firewall and network security
- **Commerce Server 2000** for Web publishing, management, and search, and comprehensive Internet transactions services
- **SNA Server** for the integration of existing and new systems and data
- **SQL Server** for database and data-warehousing solutions
- **Systems Management Server** for centralized change- and configuration-management
- **Small Business Server,** which rounds out the complete network solution for small business

This set of tools provides all the needed functionality for processing business transactions. Combined with the Web, application, and file and print services of Windows 2000 Server, this toolkit creates a complete server platform, able to grow and adapt as your organization does.

BizTalk Server 2000

BizTalk Server provides the tools and infrastructure that enable business process integration. Companies currently conducting traditional business-to-business e-commerce like EDI will find that BizTalk Server has all the required product components, such as trading partner management, document mapping and translation, reliable document routing and delivery, data extraction and storage for analysis and business process automation, to carry their legacy processes forward. BizTalk Server also extends the feature set of traditional e-commerce and EDI products to include extensive support for XML and Internet transport technologies, such as SMTP, HTTP, FTP, encryption, and certificate exchange.

BizTalk Server makes business process integration easier and provides a clean migration for companies to integrate XML into their business processes. In addition to solving platform issues, BizTalk Server also offers organizations the following:

- Document interchange services via XML translators
- Support for existing industry data formats

- Support for existing industry data communication protocols

- Security by means of digital signature and encryption

Security is often mentioned as a critical component, and BizTalk Server uses Microsoft Windows 2000 security features, including full support for public-key infrastructure and Windows 2000 Microsoft Transaction Services (MTS). Public-key certificate management includes requesting certificates, processing certificates in a certificate-request response, and exchanging certificates with trading partners. These certificates are available for both digital signature and encryption.

The core component of BizTalk Server is the document/data exchange mechanism. For Hypertext Transfer Protocol (HTTP), the SendHTTP component provides transport of documents over an HTTP connection. The ReceiveHTTP service uses Active Server Pages (ASP) to receive a document and submit it to BizTalk Server. For HTTP/S, the SendHTTP/S component provides transport of documents over an HTTP connection that uses a Secure Sockets Layer (SSL). The ReceiveHTTP/S service uses an ASP page to receive a document, which is secured with an SSL certificate, and submit it to BizTalk Server.

For Simple Mail Transfer Protocol (SMTP), the SendSMTP component creates an SMTP-based e-mail message, which contains the document in the body of the message or as an attachment. The e-mail message is then sent to the target e-mail address that is configured as a property of the SendSMTP component. The ReceiveSMTP service uses an e-mail message to receive a document and then calls BizTalk Server to submit the document.

BizTalk Server supports the Windows 2000 Microsoft Message Queue Services (MSMQ) 2.0. The SendMSMQ transport provides transport of documents over MSMQ 2.0. The transport reads a configurable key on the transport dictionary and transports that data as an MSMQ message. The destination queue, which can also be thought of as the recipient address, can be configured on the component property page. The ReceiveMSMQ service checks the queue on a periodic basis and when a message arrives, it passes the message by calling BizTalk Server. Upon completion of that task, it dequeues the documents (MSMQ messages).

BizTalk Server also supports the File Transfer Protocol (FTP). The SendFTP component sends the document in the configurable key on the transport dictionary to a destination FTP server, which saves the document as a file. The component does this through an FTP PUT command, putting the file on the trading partner's server. Alternatively, the SendFTP component can pick up a file from the file system and do an FTP PUT of that file. The ReceiveFTP service does an FTP GET of a file from the trading partner's FTP server and then calls BizTalk Server. This component periodically checks for the file on the trading partner's FTP server. When it finds a file or files, the ReceiveFTP service creates a transport dictionary, places the contents of the file in the Received- Data key, and calls BizTalk Server.

Commerce Server 2000

Commerce Server 2000 is an improved edition of Site Server 3.0 Commerce Edition. Commerce Server 2000 integrates with Windows 2000 Server and Biz-Talk Server, as well as other Microsoft DNA platform products. The features of Commerce Server 2000s features include

- **Commerce Interchange Pipeline (CIP)** The Commerce Interchange Pipeline is a new system, enhancing the existing Order Processing Pipeline, for enabling application-to-application interchange of structured business data using the Internet or existing EDI systems. This particular piece will work with BizTalk Server for business-to-business electronic commerce.

- **Ad Server** A server for hosting online advertisements that includes support for targeted delivery, ad schedule management, and exposure limits.

- **Improved Integration with Windows 2000 Server** Integration with IIS and Microsoft Transaction Server (MTS) provides resource utilization services as well as two-phase-commit type transaction properties over a distributed set of operations in the Order Processing and Commerce Interchange Pipelines.

Commerce Server 2000 provides better usage reports that can be created from integrated commerce, personalization, search, and content data. In addition, content analysis tools can import usage data to allow sites to analyze usage data interactively and visually. Administrators will find Commerce Server 2000 to be easier to install, monitor, and administer with a new set of tools for electronic commerce management. Some Internet Information Server (IIS) features are also bundled in Commerce Server 2000.

Exchange 2000 Server

Exchange 2000 Server has many new features that provide highly scalable, reliable messaging and collaboration capabilities. Primary features include the following:

- **Active Directory integration** Exchange 2000 takes advantage of the full power of Windows 2000 Active Directory, enabling system administrators to create a single, unified enterprise directory for administration of all users, groups, permissions, configuration data, network login, and file and Web shares. Providing a single point of administration for e-mail and network resources should lower the total cost of ownership of a typical messaging and collaboration infrastructure.

- **Multiple message databases** Exchange 2000 takes this architecture to the next step, enabling administrators to split a single logical database across multiple physical databases.

- **Active/Active clustering** To increase Exchange Server's levels of reliability, Exchange 2000 and Windows 2000 Server enhance clustering to include Active/Active (multi-master) clustering. Windows 2000 Advanced Server will support two-way clustering, whereas Windows 2000 Datacenter Server will support four-way clustering.

- **Distributed configuration** A distributed configuration architecture enables services to be partitioned across multiple servers to provide scalability to hosted services that can potentially serve millions of users.

- **Fault tolerant SMTP-based message routing** Exchange 2000 Server provides routing of e-mail messages between servers using advanced algorithms and SMTP as a peer to X.400-based routing for reliability despite multiple network or machine failures.

- **Native Internet mail content** Exchange 2000 Server significantly increases the performance of Internet e-mail by enabling e-mail clients to store and retrieve MIME content directly from Exchange 2000 with on-demand format conversion, maintaining compatibility with existing MAPI messaging clients.

- **Single-seat administration with Microsoft Management Console** Administration of Exchange becomes easier through integration with the familiar, single-seat management interface of MMC in Windows 2000. Using a single console for managing all Microsoft servers, including Windows 2000 itself, means that administrators train once and reuse their expertise across management tasks.

- **Use of Windows 2000 Security** Exchange 2000 Server is the only messaging and collaboration system that uses the full power of Windows 2000 to ensure messaging and collaboration security, including native use of Windows 2000 security descriptors (ACLs) for setting permissions on all Exchange resources. System administrators can create and manage all user groups and permissions once for all network and messaging and collaboration scenarios.

- **Enhanced integration with Office 2000** Office 2000 users can store and retrieve Office documents directly to and from the Web Store using the standard Save As and Open dialog boxes on the File menu.

- **Built-in content indexing and search** The Web Store's built-in content indexing enables high-speed and accurate full-text searches across a diverse set of information types, such as e-mail messages, e-mail attachments, Web content, and documents including Microsoft Office files.

- **URL addressing** All data stored in the Web Store can be accessed through a Web browser.

- **IIS and ASP integration** The Web Store is tightly integrated with IIS and ASP technology, enabling developers to utilize known tools to build Web-enabled applications that include Web-based forms, business logic and workflow services.

- **Support for Web DAV** The Web Store supports the Web DAV interface. Web DAV enables client and server software to exchange documents across the Internet and provides a common model for storing properties on Web Store items.

- **Support for XML** Exchange 2000 Server uses Extensible Markup Language (XML) for the native representation of many types of data in many protocol situations (for example, HTTP support). In addition, Exchange 2000 uses the support for XML in Microsoft Internet Explorer Explorer 5 browser software.

- **OLE DB and ADO Integration** Exchange 2000 Server includes full support for OLE DB 2.5.

- **Data conferencing and application sharing** Exchange 2000 Server includes data conferencing services based on the T.120 standard, providing an enterprise-ready client/server solution for real-time conferencing and document authoring with client software such as the Microsoft NetMeeting conferencing software.

- **Multicast video teleconferencing** Exchange 2000 Server offers integrated scheduling and management services for multicast (multiple person) video teleconferencing.

- **Instant messaging** Users of Exchange 2000 Server can send ad hoc, urgent communications that appear on another user's screen.

25

Host Integration Server 2000

Microsoft Host Integration Server 2000 solves the problem of integrating the Windows platform with other non-Windows enterprise systems running on platforms such as IBM mainframes, AS400, and UNIX. It provides network, data, and application integration with a variety of legacy hosts. Host Integration Server 2000 provides the following:

- Real-time, bidirectional data and control flow between Windows 2000 Server platforms and host systems

- Seamless network protocol integration with multiple platforms

- Performance management, monitoring, and reporting of traffic between platforms

- A flexible distributed architecture

- Remote back-end database services and administration

- Seamless messaging capabilities

These features are designed to make the creation of a digital nervous system within an organization easier and to facilitate the seamless flow of information between people and technology. Host Integration Server 2000 makes accessing data from any PC or terminal transparent and enhances the ability of organizational staff to share and use information.

Management Console

Microsoft Management Console (MMC) works with other system and network management tools to provide organizations with the ability to manage resources from a single control point. MMC is a Windows-based multiple document interface (MDI) application that heavily leverages Internet technologies. Both Microsoft and ISVs extend the console by writing MMC Snap-Ins, which are responsible for actually performing management tasks.

The following features make MMC an easy way to create a simplified management console with a consistent look and feel.

- Capable of total customization

- Can manage multiple network products

- Offers easy extension of MMC with snap-in code chunks

- Hosts almost any network or system management tool

Office 2000

Office 2000 offers many new features and applications. Office 2000 provides a wide variety of levels and programs, tailored for home use, small business, and large enterprises. The following table shows which products are included with each version of Office 2000.

TABLE C-1. PRODUCTS INCLUDED WITH VERSIONS OF MICROSOFT OFFICE 2000

Standard	Small Business	Professional	Premium
Word	Word	Word	Word
Excel	Excel	Excel	Excel
Outlook	Outlook	Outlook	Outlook
PowerPoint	Publisher	Publisher	Publisher
	Small Business Tools	Small Business Tools	Small Business Tools
		Access	Access
		PowerPoint	PowerPoint
			FrontPage
			PhotoDraw

Office 2000 Premium provides integrated graphics, publishing, and communications tools to make it easy to create and share documents, presentations, printed materials, and Web pages. Office 2000 Premium offers everything you need to create and manage intranet sites and streamlines the process of working with people and information. For example, you can easily publish and collaborate on documents or build a home page with custom graphics created in PhotoDraw 2000.

Office 2000 Professional offers a set of tools that streamlines the process of processing and sharing information, making it easier to create, publish, and analyze important data regardless of where it is located. In addition to all the applications in Office 2000 Standard and Office 2000 Small Business, Office 2000 Professional includes Access 2000. Access 2000 is the desktop database tool that provides interactive analysis capabilities. Office 2000 Professional does not include FrontPage 2000 or PhotoDraw 2000.

Office 2000 Small Business provides a core set of tools to help manage and run a small business. It includes word processing, desktop publishing, and spreadsheet capabilities, as well as an e-mail and desktop information management tool. In addition, Office 2000 Small Business includes a set of analysis tools specifically designed to help small businesses make better decisions. These tools include the Small Business Customer Manager, Business Planner, Direct Mail Manager, and Small Business Financial Manager. (The Small Business Tools are in every Office 2000 suite except for Standard.)

Office 2000 Standard is designed for users who require only the core desktop productivity tools. It provides tools for creating, publishing, and analyzing information regardless of where it is located. It includes word processing and spreadsheet capabilities, as well as an e-mail and desktop information management tool. Office 2000 Standard is for users who do not need to manage and track business information or create Web sites. It is also the only suite that does not include the Office 2000 Small Business Tools.

Outlook 2000

Microsoft Outlook 2000 is a next generation personal productivity center. Besides scheduling and e-mail, Microsoft Outlook 2000 integrates with Microsoft's Digital Dashboard technology. Standard Office 2000 personal productivity features include personalized menus, personalized toolbars, and quick-customize toolbars. Outlook 2000 included the following features:

- **Read Receipts and Tracking** Users can control whether read receipts are returned, see all receipts received for a message, and print the receipts log.

- **Run Rules Now** Users can manually apply a rule to any folder at any time.

- **Rules Wizard** The built-in Rules Wizard offers significant enhancements to the add-on that was available previously for Outlook 97.

- **Automatically spell check in multiple languages** Microsoft Word can serve as an e-mail editor, offering language AutoDetect spell checker and proofing support.

- **Per-message Office e-mail from Outlook** Users can compose a particular message easily using any Office application and send the message as HTML so that the application isn't required to read the message.

- **Switch formats on the fly** Users can switch between HTML, RTF, or plain-text editing in Outlook at any time.

- **Independent editor and send format choice** The built-in Outlook editor or Microsoft Word helps edit messages. Users can choose to send mail independently in RTF, HTML, or plain-text format.

- **Preview pane** Users can quickly view messages without opening them. This feature includes support for attachments, hyperlinks in HTML, and signed and encrypted mail.

- **iCalendar (Internet group scheduling)** Group scheduling is possible over the Internet. Users can publish and download free/busy information for scheduling meetings, as well as send and receive meeting requests and responses over the Internet.

- **Message disposition notifications (Read Receipts)** Outlook generates and tracks Internet-standard read receipts.

- **LDAP** High-performance Internet directory access includes search and check names. Full multiple account support is also featured.

- **Microsoft Internet Explorer integration** Outlook features integrated setup of Internet Explorer.

- **Outlook Startup Wizard** This wizard automatically detects appro-appropriate installation options and imports existing accounts, profile information, folders, and personal address books from earlier Outlook versions, Outlook Express, Netscape Messenger or Eudora.

- **Send link to public folder** Users can easily send a link to an Exchange Server public folder.

- **Find Exchange Server Public Folder** Outlook can now search on Microsoft Exchange Server Public Folder properties.

- **QuickFind contact** Users can easily find and open a contact from anywhere in Outlook.

- **Improved InfoBars** InfoBars displayed in messages are more colorful and noticeable.

- **Internet group scheduling** Users can share calendar free/busy information and send and receive meeting requests and responses over the Internet between iCalendar-compliant applications.

- **Save as Web Page** Publishing a personal or team calendar as HTML is easy.

- **ScreenTips in Calendar views** Hovering the mouse displays pop-up ScreenTips containing complete subjects and details of appointments.

- **Calendar background color** Contrasting color between free/busy times is provided in daily and weekly views.

- **Enhanced Calendar printing options** Users can print word-wrapped details of appointments in daily, weekly, and monthly printouts, with the option to omit private appointments. Prints exactly one month per page.

- **Meeting planner enhancements** Enhanced features for working with distribution lists offer smarter auto-pick of next free time and more.

- **Adding and removing attendees** Users can easily change the list of attendees for an already scheduled meeting.

- **Direct booking of resources** Resources such as conference rooms can be reserved without dedicated resource computers running.

- **Easily open other users' calendars** The most recently used list of other users' calendars is immediately accessible.

- **Hide private appointments** Users can control whether a delegate, such as an administrative assistant, has access to details of private appointments.

- **Microsoft NetMeeting integration** Users can easily schedule real-time meetings and automatically start the NetMeeting conferencing software with an Office document to share during the NetMeeting-based conference.

- **Microsoft NetShow integration** Users can easily schedule times to watch broadcasts via NetShow services and automatically start NetShow at the designated time.

- **Personal distribution lists** Users can create distribution lists consisting of contacts from one or more Contacts folders and the Microsoft Exchange Server Global Address List.

- **Contact activity tracking** Users can keep track of all e-mail, tasks, appointments, and documents related (linked) to each contact.

- **Enhanced mail merge** Users can filter the Contacts lists in Outlook as desired and then pass the contacts to the Microsoft Word Mail Merge and merge on any Outlook fields.

- **AutoMerge contact information** Before adding a new contact, Outlook intelligently warns whether the contact might be a duplicate and gives the option to automatically merge the new information.

- **Outlook Bar shortcuts** Users can easily create a shortcut in the Outlook Bar to any file, folder, or Web page.

- **View the Web** Clicking an Outlook Bar shortcut to a Web page displays the Web page in the right-hand Outlook pane. Basic Web navigation is supported and the currently displayed page can be opened in the user's default Web browser.

- **Folder home pages** Users can associate one or more Web pages with any personal or Exchange Server folder.

- **Improved offline folder synchronization user interface** New user interface makes it easy to specify which Microsoft Exchange Server folders should be available offline.

- **Quick synchronization groups** Specify collections of Microsoft Exchange Server folders to be synchronized based on speed of connection or time available.

- **Synchronized message size limit** User can easily specify that large messages shouldn't be synchronized over a slow link.

- **Improved offline Address Book synchronization** The offline Exchange Server Address Book is synchronized using the same command and features Offline Folders.

- **Change connection type** The manual switch between LAN and dial-up connection has been simplified.

These features, along with Digital Dashboard integration, provide organizations with a platform for improving productivity and organizational effectiveness through better collaboration and activity management.

SQL Server

SQL Server 2000 Enterprise Edition offers scalability and availability up to the highest levels of the enterprise by taking full advantage of up to 64 GB of RAM, up to 32 processors, and four-node failover clustering supported out of the box with Windows 2000 Data Center. SQL Server 2000 takes advantage of the Windows 2000 Server architecture and performance features to deliver excellent database server performance and reliability. New features in SQL Server include the following:

- Integration with Active Directory services, providing quick, easy access to any physical database through a logical connection mechanism

- Automatic detection of new servers and users

- Improved security features

- Improved OLAP services

- Use of Microsoft's data warehousing framework standards for high-speed performance on DSS applications

- Ability to scale to large applications quickly and grow with an organization over time

- Easy Web integration

These features, combined with Windows 2000 Server, provide organizations with a scalable, reliable database platform that speeds development time, reduces project costs, and integrates well with other applications such as ERP software, Web applications, and others.

Visual Studio

Microsoft Visual Studio, with its Windows 2000 Readiness Kit, provides organizations with the ability to quickly design, develop, and deploy visual applications for both internal and Web-based systems. Standard features include

- **Visual Basic 6.0 Development System** For rapid development of Windows-based client/server applications, as well as Web applications and middle-tier business components.

- **Visual Source Safe 6.0** Complete team-based source code control system for components, applications, and Web sites.

- **Visual C++ 6.0 Development System** For building the highest performance applications and components.

- **Visual J++ 6.0 Development System** Microsoft's development tool for building applets, Windows-based applications, and components using the Java language.

- **Visual InterDev 6.0 Development System** An integrated, team-based development tool for building data-driven Web applications based on HTML, Script, and components written in any language.

- **Visual FoxPro 6.0 Database Development System** For building workgroup database applications and developing components using the XBASE language.

- **Windows NT 4.0 Option Pack** Application, communication, and Web services; includes Microsoft Transaction Server 2.0 and Microsoft Internet Information Server 4.0.

- **MSDN Library** Includes the MSDN Library (single edition) with development information and reference for Visual Studio. Plus, a one-year MSDN Library subscription.

- **Professional Visual Database Tools** View database objects (including tables, views, and data) and rapidly create queries within the development environment.

- **Windows 2000 Developer's Readiness Kit** With the Windows 2000 Developer's Readiness Kit, you'll learn how to take advantage of new Windows 2000 features through in-depth, step-by-step training and technical resources.

- **Microsoft Data Engine (MSDE) for Visual Studio** Build desktop and shared solutions that are fully compatible with SQL Server 7.0 and can migrate directly to SQL Server without changing a single line of code.

- **Visual Studio Installer** Build self-repairing, low-cost deployment applications with the new Visual Studio Installer.

- **Complete debugging support** Shorten development time with end-to-end debugging. Debug across languages smoothly with point-and-click breakpoints, drag-and-drop watch windows, and multiple call stacks.

- **RAD Web development** Get a jump on your Web development with prebuilt components, wizards, HTML, script, and data—in one integrated environment.

- **Microsoft Repository 2.0** Open repository for storing project elements created by Microsoft tools and by third-party tools. Repository is integrated with all tools in the suite through the Visual Component Manager.

- **Cross-platform deployment** Use HTML, script, and Dynamic HTML to reach any desktop platform, including 16-bit and 32-bit Windows clients, Macintosh, and UNIX.

- **Visual SourceSafe 6.0** Complete team-based source code control system for components, applications, and Web sites.

- **Enterprise Visual Database Tools** Visually create schema diagrams for Microsoft SQL Server 6.5+ and Oracle 7.3.3+ databases. View tables, modify data, and create SQL queries for high-speed access to any ODBC- or OLE DB–compliant database.

- **Visual Modeler** Visually model components in detail, as well as component relationships, methods, properties, and events; then, communicate this information to team members and generate code.

- **Visual Studio Analyzer** Profile distributed applications and isolate and fix performance bottlenecks.

- **Visual Component Manager** Find, track, catalog, and reuse application components stored in the Microsoft Repository.

- **Scalability** Upgrade your system to handle multiple concurrent users, manage secure transactions across disparate data sources, and develop and test database applications using Microsoft SQL Server 7.0 Developer Edition.

- **Interoperability** Use HTML, Script, and Dynamic HTML to reach Win16, Win32, UNIX, and Macintosh desktops. Access mainframe transactions using SNA Server and remote Oracle, DB/2, VSAM, and AS400 data sources using OLE DB.

- **Team-based development** Easily find, track, catalog, and reuse application components with the Visual Component Manager. Use Microsoft Visual SourceSafe version control system to collaborate, share, and secure source code.

- **Lifecycle support** Graphically define application architecture and communicate designs using Microsoft Visual Modeler diagrams; visualize distributed applications and optimize performance using animated event diagrams in Visual Studio Analyzer; and reduce costs with new automatic system build, installation script generation, and deployment tools.

These features form a complete toolkit for building scalable applications quickly and efficiently. Organizations can choose the best tool for each platform, application, or technology. Organizations can create a tightly integrated, scalable, reliable platform for their next generation of systems.

Windows 2000 Server

Windows 2000 Server is the next-generation operating system from Microsoft. Windows 2000 Server builds on and extends Windows NT technology and has the scalability and reliability to run devices from laptops to datacenters. There are various versions of Windows 2000 Server, including Windows 2000 Server, Windows 2000 Advanced Server, and Windows 2000 DataCenter Server. Windows

2000 Professional provides the client support and connectivity needed to work with Windows 2000 Server. The following new features are part of Windows 2000:

- **Integrated Web services** These enable users to easily host and manage Web sites to share information, create Web-based business applications, and extend file, print, media and communication services to the Web.

- **Active Server Pages (ASP) Programming Environment** Active Server Pages is consistently rated the easiest, highest-performance Web server-scripting environment available.

- **XML Parser** Create applications that enable the Web server to exchange XML-formatted data with both Microsoft Internet Explorer and any server capable of parsing XML.

- **Windows DNA 2000** With the Windows Distributed interNet Applications Architecture (Windows DNA 2000)—the application development model for the Windows platform—you can build secure, reliable, highly scalable solutions that ease the integration of heterogeneous systems and applications.

- **Component Object Model +** COM+ builds on COM's inte- grated services and features, making it easier for developers to create and use software components in any language, using any tool. COM+ includes Transaction Services and Message Queuing Services for reliable distributed applications.

- **Multimedia platform** With integrated Windows MediaTM Services, configure and manage high-quality digital media content across the Internet and intranets—delivering live and on-demand content to the maximum number of users.

- **Directory-enabled applications** Developers can use a number of standard interfaces to write applications that utilize information stored in the Active Directory service about users, other applications, and devices. This enables rich, dynamic applications that are simpler to develop and easier to manage. All Active Directory functions are available through LDAP, ADSI, and MAPI for extending and integrating with other applications, directories, and devices.

- **Web Folders** Web Folders brings the richness of Windows to the Web by using Web Document Authoring and Versioning (WebDAV) to enable drag-and-drop Web publishing.

- **Internet printing** Send print jobs across the Internet to a URL.

- **8-way symmetric multiprocessor support (in Advanced Server)** Scale up by utilizing the latest 8-way SMP servers for more processing power. Windows 2000 Server delivers support for up to 4-way SMP servers.

- **8 GB memory support (in Advanced Server)** Take advantage of larger amounts of memory to improve performance and handle the most demanding applications, with support for up to 8 gigabytes (GB) of RAM with Intel's Physical Address Extension (PAE). Windows 2000 Server delivers support for up to 4 GB of RAM.

- **Network Load Balancing (in Advanced Server)** Scale out quickly and easily by distributing incoming IP traffic across a farm of load-balanced servers. Incrementally expand capacity by adding additional servers to the farm using Network Load Balancing (NLB).

- **Terminal Services** Run Windows-based applications on the server, and access from a remote PC, Windows-based terminal or non-Windows dows device over LANs, WANs, or low-bandwidth connections, through terminal emulation software. In Windows 2000, Terminal Services are up to 20 percent more scalable and have dramatically improved performance for both high- and low-bandwidth connections.

- **Enhanced ASP performance** More scalable Active Server Page (ASP) processing, improved ASP flow control; and ASP Fast Path for scriptless ASP files enable faster Web page processing.

- **Multisite hosting** Internet Information Services (IIS) 5.0 allows you to host more Web sites per server with high performance.

- **IIS CPU throttling** Limit the amount of CPU time a Web application or site can use to ensure that processor time—and therefore better performance—is available to other Web sites or to non-Web applications.

- **High throughput and bandwidth utilization** With support for up to 1 GB networks, Windows 2000 Server delivers high-performance processing on high-performance networks. Increased throughput increases performance without having to increase network bandwidth.

- **Support for the latest security standards** Build secure intranet, extranet, and Internet sites using the latest standards, including: 56-

bit and 128-bit SSL/TLS, IPSec, Server Gated Cryptography; Digest Authentication, Kerberos v5 authentication, and Fortezza.

- **Active Directory integration** Active Directory integration with the underlying security infrastructure provides a focal point of security management of users, computers, and devices, making Windows 2000 easier to manage.

- **Kerberos authentication** Full support for Kerberos version 5 protocol provides fast, single sign-on to Windows resources as well as other environments that support this protocol.

- **Public Key Infrastructure (PKI)** The Certificate Server is a critical part of a public key infrastructure that allows customers to issue their own x.509 certificates to their users for PKI functionality such as certificate-based authentication, IPSec, and secure e-mail. Integration with Active Directory simplifies user enrollment.

- **Smart card support** Supports logon via Smart cards "out-of-the-box" for strong authentication to sensitive resources.

- **Encrypting file system** Increase security of data on the hard disk by encrypting it. This data remains encrypted even when backed up or archived.

- **Secure network communications** End-to-end encrypted communications across your company network using the IPSec standard. Great for protecting sensitive internal communications from intentional or accidental viewing. Active Directory provides central policy control for its use to make it deployable.

- **Routing and Remote Access Service** Connects remote workers, telecommuters, and branch offices to the corporate network through dial-up, leased line, and Internet links.

- **Virtual private networking (VPN)** A full-featured gateway that encrypts communications to securely connect remote users and satellite offices over the Internet. Now with an updated PPTP support and advanced security with Layer 2 Tunneling Protocol encrypted by IPSec.

- **Kernel-mode write protection** Helps prevent errant code from interfering with system operations.

- **Windows file protection** Prevents new software installations from replacing essential system files.

- **Driver certification** Identifies device drivers that have passed the Windows Hardware Quality Labs test and warns users if they are about to install an uncertified driver.

- **IIS application protection** Application protection keeps Web applications running separately from the Web server itself, preventing an application from crashing the Web server.

- **Cluster service (in Advanced Server)** 2-node cluster service supports fail-over, caused by hardware or software failure, of critical applications, including databases, knowledge management, ERP, and file and print services.

- **Network Load Balancing (in Advanced Server)** On Web or Terminal Services server farms, redistribute workload among remaining servers in the event of a server hardware or software failure in less than 10 seconds.

- **Job Object API** The Job Object API, with its ability to set up processor affinity, establish time limits, control process priorities, and limit memory utilization for a group of related processes, allows an application to manage and control dependent system resources. This additional level of control means that the Job Object API can prevent an application from negatively impacting overall system scalability.

- **Application certification and DLL protection** Applications certified to run on Windows 2000 Server are tested by Microsoft to ensure high quality and reliability. DLL protection protects DLLs installed by applications from conflicts that can cause application failure.

- **Multimaster replication** Active Directory uses multimaster replication to ensure high scalability and availability in distributed network configurations. *Multimaster* means that each directory replica in the network is a peer of all other replicas; changes can be made to any replica and will be reflected across all of them.

- **Distributed File System (DFS)** Build a single, hierarchical view of multiple file servers and file server shares on a network. DFS makes files easier for users to locate and increases availability by maintaining multiple file copies across distributed servers.

- **Disk quotas** The ability to set quotas on disk space usage per user and per volume to provide increased availability of disk space and help capacity planning efforts.

- **Hierarchical storage management** Automatically migrate data that hasn't been recently accessed to less expensive storage media, maximizing disk space for the most heavily accessed data on the disk.

- **Dynamic system configuration—Rolling Upgrade Support (in Advanced Server)** Using cluster service and NLB, you can avoid downtime caused by planned maintenance or upgrades with rolling upgrades. Migrate your applications or IP workload to one node, upgrading the first node and then migrating them back. You can roll out hardware, software, and even operating system upgrades without taking the application offline. Both Windows clustering technologies are backward-compatible with their Windows NT Server 4.0 predecessors.

- **Dynamic volume management** Add new volumes, extend existing volumes, break or add a mirror, or repair a RAID 5 array while the server is online without impacting the end-user.

- **Disk defragmentation** Over time, fragmentation can have a severe impact on the performance of a busy file or Web server. These tools increase disk availability and performance.

- **Safe mode boot** Booting in Safe mode allows users to troubleshoot the system during start-up by changing the default settings or removing a newly installed driver that is causing a problem.

- **Backup and recovery** Backup and recovery features make it easier to back up data and then recover data in the event of a hard disk failure. Windows 2000 allows backup to a single file on a hard disk and tape media.

- **Automatic restart** Configure services across the operating system, including IIS, to restart automatically if they fail.

- **Kill process tree** Stop all processes related to an errant process or application without rebooting the system.

- **Cluster service setup (in Advanced Server)** Quickly configure clusters with the improved and streamlined cluster service setup wizard. Perform remote installations using SysPrep support for cluster service.

- **Integrated Network Load Balancing configuration–(In Advanced Server)** NLB is now an integrated part of the Windows 2000 Advanced Server networking stack, allowing rapid configuration without the need for separate installation or system reboots.

- **Configuration wizard** Automatically set up file, print, Web, communications, networking, Active Directory, and DNS services with the Configure Your Server Wizard.

- **System Preparation Tool** Save deployment time by using SysPrep to create an image of a computer's hard drive, including the operating system and applications, that you can then duplicate onto other computers.

- **Windows Installer** Windows Installer monitors application installations and cleanly performs uninstall/removal tasks.

- **Plug and Play** Automatically detect and recognize newly installed components, simplifying network system configuration and reducing service down time.

- **Service pack slipstreaming** Simplify operating system updates by marinating one master image of the operating system on the network.

- **Dynamic DNS** The Active Directory integrated, Internet standards-based Domain Name System (DNS) service simplifies object naming and location through Internet protocols, and improves scalability, performance and interoperability. Systems that receive addresses from a Dynamic Host Configuration Protocol (DHCP) server are automatically registered in DNS. Replication options with legacy DNS systems and through Active Directory can simplify and strengthen name replication infrastructure.

- **Microsoft Connection Manager Administration Kit and Connection Point Services** These wizard-driven tools let admin-administrators centrally configure and deploy customized remote access dialers that can integrate automatic-update phonebooks, custom connect actions (such as firewall authentication and client virus inspection), driver updates, and more.

- **Internet connection sharing** Enables multiple users within small business or workgroups to share a single external Internet connection, making connection to the Internet easier.

- **Search for and connect to printers from a desktop** Publish printers in the Active Directory service, enabling users to locate and connect to printers based on criteria such as location, ability to print color, or speed.

- **Cluster Administrator (in Advanced Server)** Run Cluster Administrator from any Windows NT or Windows 2000 system to remotely control multiple clusters from a single location.

■ **Integrated Directory Services** Windows 2000 introduces Active Directory, a scalable, standard-compliant directory service that makes Windows 2000 easier to manage, more secure, and more interoperable with existing investments. Active Directory centrally manages Windows-based clients and servers through a single, consistent management interface, reducing redundancy and maintenance costs.

■ **Windows Management Instrumentation** A uniform model through which management data from any source can be managed in a standard way. Windows Management Instrumentation (WMI) provides this for software, such as applications, whereas WMI extensions for the Windows Driver Model (WDM) provide this for hardware or hardware device drivers. WMI in Windows 2000 enables management of even more functions.

■ **Delegated Administration** Active Directory enables administrators to delegate a selected set of administrative privileges to appropriate individuals within the organization to distribute the management and improve accuracy of administration and ease of administering multiple domains globally.

■ **Microsoft Management Console** is incorporated into Windows 2000 Server

■ **Remote management with Terminal Services** Safely enable Terminal Services for remote administration purposes. Up to two concurrent sessions are supported, with no impact on performance or application compatibility.

■ **Windows Script Host (WSH)** Administer the server and automate tasks via the command line rather than graphical user interface tools with scripts.

■ **Group Policy** Group Policy allows central management of collections of users, computers, applications, and network resources instead of managing entities on a one-by-one basis. Integration with Active Directory delivers more control.

■ **Centralized Desktop Management** Manage users' desktop resources by applying policies based on the business needs and location of users. IntelliMirror management technologies install and maintain software, apply correct computer and user settings, and ensure that users' data is always available.

- **Security Configuration Toolset (SCTS)** Reduce costs associated with security configuration and analysis of Windows-based networks. In Windows 2000, use Group Policy to set and periodically update security configurations of computers.

- **PKI Group Policy Management** Centrally manage domain-wide-PKI policies. Specify which Certificate Authorities a client will trust, distribute new root certificates, adjust IPSec policy or determine whether a user will be required to use smart cards to log on to a particular system.

- **Windows NT 4.0 domain migration tools** Simplify the upgrade process to a Windows 2000 domain.

- **Directory interoperability** Meta directory technologies enable companies to use Active Directory to manage identity information stored in heterogeneous directory services.

- **Directory synchronization tools** Maintain and synchronize data between Active Directory and Microsoft Exchange and Novell NDS directories.

- **High interoperability with client computers** Supports Windows NT Workstation, Windows 9*x*, Windows 3.*x*, Macintosh, and UNIX operating systems. TCP/IP Appleshare support improves resource sharing for the Macintosh operating system.

- **Applications and directory interoperability** Windows 2000-compatible applications will install and upgrade onto the Windows 2000 operating system. Active Directory can interoperate or synchronize date with other directory services using Lightweight Directory Access Protocol (LDAP), Meta directory technologies, Microsoft Directory Service Synchronization, or Active Directory Connector.

- **Server and mainframe interoperability** Message queuing enables the exchange of information between applications running on mainframe platforms. Kerberos authentication protocol support enables interoperability with other systems using industry standard authentication protocol. Services for NetWare is an add-on product that increases interoperability with NetWare servers and clients with Windows-based servers and clients. Services for UNIX is an add-on product to integrate Windows NT 4.0 and Windows 2000 into a UNIX environment.

- **Latest server hardware (in Advanced Server)** Support for the latest advanced 8-way SMP servers running Intel's Profusion chipset and architecture and up to 8 GB of memory support with Intel's Physical Address Extension (PAE).

- **Networking** Windows 2000 Server works with networking devices that support the latest networking technologies, including Plug and Play, DSL, VPN, routing, NAT, DHCP, Quality of Services switches and routers, Directory-Enabled Networking devices, IPSec, SSL, and Asynchronous Transfer Mode.

- **Peripherals** Windows 2000 Server works with the newest peripherals such as storage management hardware, USB printers, network adapters, keyboards, and mice. It delivers advanced printer driver support as well as support for 1394, PCMCIA, infrared, and digital devices.

Windows NetMeeting

NetMeeting provides a conferencing solution for the Internet and corporate intranet. NetMeeting lets you communicate with both audio and video, collaborate on virtually any Windows-based application, exchange graphics on an electronic whiteboard, transfer files, use the text-based chat program, and much more. Standard features include:

- **Standards-based multipoint data conferencing** Users can collaborate and share information with two or more conference participants in real time. Users can share applications on their computer and work together by allowing other conference participants to see the same information on their screens.

- **Standards-based video conferencing** With a video-capture card and camera, users of NetMeeting can send and receive video images for face-to-face communication during a conference. The switchable audio and video feature allows users to switch among participants they communicate with.

- **Standards-based Internet telephony** Using a sound card, microphone, and speakers, participants using NetMeeting can talk to friends, family, and business associates over the Internet and corporate intranets.

- **Ability to change the size of the video window** You can dynamically change the size of the video window to reduce or enlarge the image being sent to another person. Also, you can choose whether to transmit video immediately when a call starts.

- **Compatibility with existing video capture hardware** NetMeeting supports video capture cards and cameras that are compatible with video for Windows drivers. This includes most commonly available video hardware.

- **High-quality video** NetMeeting produces high-quality, real-time video images using a standard 28.8 Kbps modem Internet connection, IP over ISDN connection, or local area network (LAN) connection.

- **Receive images without video hardware** Even if you do not have a video capture card or camera for sending video, you can still receive video images sent by other users.

- **Dockable video windows** To simplify video capabilities during a NetMeeting call, the Current Call window integrates the My Video and Remote Video windows. You can view the docked video windows from the Current Call window or you can undock them and drag them to another location.

- **Switchable audio and video** Have you participated in a meeting with many people and wanted to switch who you were seeing and talking to? Now you can. Simply right-click the person's name listed in the Current Call window and click Send Audio and Video.

- **Copy video images to the Clipboard** Copying video images into another application is simple. You can right-click either the local or remote video window, place a copy of the video image on the Clipboard, and then paste the video image into another application, such as a whiteboard.

- **Ability to adjust video quality** To remotely adjust video, click the Tools menu, click Options, click the Video tab, and then use the Video Quality slidebar. Based on what you see, you can adjust for higher quality or higher performance, depending on your preference.

- **Interoperability with other H.323 products** NetMeeting 2.0 supports the H.323 standard for audio and video conferencing, which includes the H.263 video codec. H.323 allows NetMeeting to interoperate with other compatible video phone clients, such as the Intel Internet Video Phone.

- **Support for Intel MMX technology** If you have an Intel MMX-enabled computer, specialized NetMeeting codecs for MMX provide enhanced performance for video compression and decompression. You will benefit from lower CPU utilization and improved video quality during a call.

NetMeeting's complete Internet conferencing capabilities allow users to share data via audio/video to conference in real time! NetMeeting supports all industry standards and compatible conferencing products.

Glossary

Access *See* Microsoft Access.

Active Directory services Microsoft's advanced, hierarchical directory service that comes with Windows 2000. Active Directory technology enables general-purpose directory functionality at the network operating-system level.

Active Server Pages Web technology developed by Microsoft that enables Web pages to contain scripting-language commands written in such languages as VBScript or JavaScript. When an Active Server Page is requested by a browser, the commands are executed on the server side before the page is delivered to the client-side browser.

ActiveX Prepackaged software components based on the Microsoft Component Object Model (COM) architecture. ActiveX enables a program to add functionality by calling ready-made components that work as normal parts of the program.

Advanced Ship Notice (ASN) An EDI transaction that tells an organization receiv-ing goods the schedule, destination, and other information concerning a shipment. *See also* Notice of Shipment (NOS).

American National Standards Institute (ANSI) An organization that administers and coordinates the United States private sector voluntary standardization system for 80 years. Founded in 1918 by five engineering societies and three government agencies, the Institute remains a private, nonprofit membership organization supported by a diverse constituency of private and public sector organizations.

Applets Small programs to do something on a Web site, usually written in Java.

Application Center 2000 *See* Microsoft Application Center 2000.

Application Program Interface (API) A language and message format used by an application program to communicate with the operating system or other programs.

Application server A computer in a network that processes business transactions. This server contains the business rules by which data is processed.

Application Server Provider An organization that hosts software applications on its own servers within its own facilities

Authentication The process of verifying security access via passwords, voice, or digital certificates.

Automated waste The money spent on computer systems that support bad business processes.

B2B Business-to-business.

B2C Business-to-consumer.

Backdoor A hidden security gap often exploited by someone intent on harming an organization's computer systems.

BackOffice *See* Microsoft BackOffice.

bCentral *See* Microsoft bCentral.

BizTag A tag or indicator that acts as a modifier on data being transmitted using the BizTalk Framework.

BizTalk Framework An XML-based standard that utilizes XML for enhanced electronic commerce performance among and between organizations.

BizTalk Server *See* Microsoft BizTalk Server.

The Business Internet Microsoft's concept that advocates using the Internet and Web technologies for all business transactions both within and beyond an organization's walls.

Boundarylessness The idea that an organization should operate without boundaries and that information should be shared across departments within an organization, as well as beyond the organization's walls to business partners and customers.

Brand management Monitoring, controlling, and shaping the public's perception of an organization's brands, products, and services.

Brick and mortar Refers to organizations that have "real-world" facilities versus just Web sites (though they may have both).

Bridge Hardware that connects two network segments, which may be of similar or dissimilar types

Browser Software that acts as an interface between the user and the Web (both internal and external).

Business components The discrete functions that make up most organizations. Some typical components include human resources, accounting, purchasing, and manufacturing.

Business-to-business (B2B) commerce Tranactions conducted between businesses.

Business-to-consumer (B2C) commerce Transactions conducted between businesses and consumers.

Certified technical education center (CTEC) A training facility or organization that is certified by Microsoft to provide training on Microsoft products.

CheckFree An online bill presentation and payment service of CheckFree Corporation which announced in February 2000 a merger with Microsoft's joint-venture TransPoint e-bill service.

Clickstream The path or collection of Web sites that a person visits.

Client, PC client A computer that uses or receives services from a server computer.

Clustering The combining of processors for power, reliability, and availability. Many processors can be hooked together in a cluster to increase processing power and provide redundancy.

Combinatorial innovation Combining the talents of several organizations to create innovative products and services, with those organizations working together as one to deliver those products and services.

Commerce Department The agency of the U.S. government that is involved in business and other commerce-related areas.

Commerce Server 2000 *See* Microsoft Commerce Server 2000.

Component object model (COM) Microsoft's component software architecture, which defines a structure for building program routines (objects) that can be called and executed.

COM+ COM+ builds on COM's integrated services and features, making it easier for developers to create and use software components in any language, using any tool. COM+ includes Transaction Services and Message Queuing Services for reliable distributed applications.

Corporate identity/awareness The image of an organization, the public's knowledge of the organization's existence, and how the public perceives it.

Critical success factor (CSF) Measurable characteristics, conditions, and variables that, when properly sustained and managed, have an impact on organizational success.

Customer bargaining power The force that customers can exert on the organization because of their ability either to purchase from other organizations that sell the same product or service or to simply go without the product or service.

Customer relationship management (CRM)   The continuous improvement of relations between an organization and its customers.

Cyberbrand   An organization's brand as it exists and is perceived on the Web.

Database server   A computer in a network that performs database storage and retrieval. It contains the database management system (DBMS) and the databases.

Data mining   The process of using information in a data warehouse to identify patterns or relationships between various business factors.

Data warehouse   A large database of historical data, summarized at varying levels of granularity.

Decryption   The unscrambling of characters in a message or transaction. *See also* Encryption.

Defense Department or **Department of Defense (DoD)**   The military branch of the U.S. government. It is under the direction of the Secretary of Defense, the primary defense policy adviser to the President. The Internet originated as a DoD project.

Digest Authentication   An Internet security protocol that is a simple challenge-response mechanism that allows authentication information to be replayed in multiple requests.

Digital certificate   The digital equivalent of an ID card used in conjunction with a public key encryption system.

Digital dashboard   A customized solution for knowledge workers that consolidates personal, team, corporate, and external information with single-click access to analytical and collaborative tools.

Digital nervous system   A combination of hardware and software that allows an organization to share information, process data, and transact business entirely through electronic means. A digital nervous system facilitates, controls, and monitors functions within an organization the same way that a human nervous system performs the same tasks for the human body.

Digital subscriber line (DSL)   A communication technology that allows a computer to share a standard telephone line with regular telephone communication by splitting the line into a high frequency band used by the computer and a low frequency band used by the telephone.

Direct Marketing Association (DMA)   A nonprofit business association for organizations that do direct marketing (through catalogs, direct mail, sweepstakes, and so on).

Direct-to-consumer   A method of selling either via the Web or traditional means in which the goods move directly from seller to consumer. A seller can be a manufacturer, wholesaler, retailer, reseller, or VAR, for example.

Domain Name System (DNS)   An Internet-based system that lets other systems locate computers on the Internet by domain name. The DNS server maintains a database of domain names (host names) and their corresponding IP addresses.

E-commerce or **electronic commerce**   Any commercial activity that takes place directly between a business, its partners, or its customers through a combination of computing and communications technologies.

Electronic Commerce Integration Facility (ECIF)   A National Institute of Standards and Technology (NIST) project to assist in the removal of barriers that are currently preventing the transition from paper-based commerce to electronic commerce.

Electronic currency   A method of online purchasing that uses encrypted data and codes sent to a buyer's bank.

Electronic data interchange (EDI)   An older form of e-commerce, originating in the late 1960s, that enables organizations to exchange information via dial-up lines or dedicated leased lines. Some standard EDI transactions include advance ship notice (ASN) and notice of shipment (NOS).

Electronic funds transfer (EFT)   The electronic transfer of money between financial institutions.

E-mail or **electronic mail**   Mail messages, text, sound, or video sent over an electronic network.

Encryption   The scrambling of data into illegible characters to prevent the use of stolen data if it is intercepted during transmission.

Enterprise Resource Planning (ERP)   A type of software package or set of software functions that automates most or all of an organization's business operations. ERP functionality may include purchasing, invoicing, payroll and other financial applications, manufacturing, inventory control, and others.

Entry barriers   Obstacles that an organization faces when trying to enter an industry or when creating and selling a new product or service.

E-tailer   An online retailer.

E-tailing   Selling online. *See* e-tailer.

Economic value added (EVA)   The spread the operation earns over and above its cost of capital multiplied by the amount of capital invested.

Exchange 2000 Server *See* Microsoft Exchange 2000 Server.

Excel 2000 *See* Microsoft Excel 2000.

Executive information system (EIS) A set of tools designed to organize information into useful formats for senior executives. Information is typically displayed in a graphical format with the ability to examine underlying data.

Exit barriers Obstacles an organization faces when trying to exit an industry or to stop production of a product or service.

Extranet A Web site set up by an organization to communicate with business partners and nonconsumer business customers. Some extranets allow business partners and customers to have direct access to an organization's online transaction processing (OLTP) systems.

FAQ Frequently asked questions. FAQ lists are common on most Web sites and provide information to users who need quick answers to simple questions about the site, its content, or the organization.

Federal Trade Commission (FTC) The government agency that enforces federal antitrust and consumer protection laws.

Financial metrics Measurements that determine the value returned on a total cash investment.

Firewall A security barrier that prevents unauthorized access to a Web server or other organizational hardware. A firewall can be hardware, software, or a combination of both.

Fortezza An authentication system endorsed by the National Security Agency that uses a PC Card as the authentication token. The term means *fortress* in Italian.

FrontPage 2000 *See* Microsoft FrontPage 2000.

FUD factor The element of fear, uncertainty, and doubt that is used against a competitor, or even a customer, to make something happen.

Gateway A link between two networks. Similar to a bridge; can consist of hardware, software, or both.

GB (Gigabyte) One billion (1,000,000,000) bytes or characters as stored by computers.

Groupware Technology that allows people to share information and work collaboratively in a virtual office.

HOLAP Hybrid online analytical processing (OLAP).

Host integration server A Microsoft product that allows legacy systems to be integrated with multitiered client/server and Web-based applications.

Hub   A device in a network that joins computers and network lines in a star configuration.

Hyperlink   A link from one Web page or object (for example, graphic or picture) to another.

HyperText Markup Language (HTML)   The document formatting language used to create the majority of content available on the World Wide Web.

HyperText Transfer Protocol (HTTP)   The communications protocol that connects servers on the Web. Its primary function is to establish a connection with a Web server and transmit HTML pages to the browser

iCalendar   Internet Calendaring and Scheduling Core Object Specification is an interoperability standard, allowing users to send meeting requests to correspondents and publish calendars as Web pages.

Internet Messaging Access Protocol (IMAP)   A standard mail server expected to be widely used on the Internet.

Infomediaries   Organizations or individuals who provide information about products and who locate the best choice or price on the Web.

Infonomics   Information as a large part of the global economy. Some theories hold that information, rather than products and services, will eventually become the value of the economy.

Internet   A group of interconnected networks.

Internet Explorer   *See* Microsoft Internet Explorer.

Internet Information Server (IIS)   *See* Microsoft Internet Information Server (IIS).

IP SECurity (IPSec)   A security protocol that provides authentication and encryption over the Internet.

Internet Service Provider (ISP)   An organization that supplies Internet access to other organizations and individuals.

Interoperability   The ability of technology components to work with each other seamlessly without building significant interfaces and work-arounds.

Intranet   A network that is designed to look and operate like the Internet but that is usually limited and accessible only to those people within an organization.

Internet Protocol (IP)   A set of standards used in communications over a network. Popularized by the Internet and often used in private networks such as intranets.

JScript   Microsoft's implementation of JavaScript.

Java   A cross-platform programming language developed by Sun Microsystems. Used widely for Internet (World Wide Web) and intranet applications.

JavaScript   A popular scripting language created by Netscape. JavaScript is not based on Java, although there are some similarities. The language is widely supported in Web browsers such as Netscape Navigator and Internet Explorer.

Job Object API   Microsoft's job control application programming interface that allows developers to regulate jobs running on a system.

Kerberos   A security system developed at MIT that authenticates users.

Knowledge analyst   An individual who analyzes and defines the knowledge used and/or needed by an organization to achieve a competitive advantage.

Knowledge management   The storage, use, and sharing of knowledge within an organization and across business partners.

Knowledge worker   Term attributed to management consultant Peter Drucker to describe an individual whose primary job involves the collection, processing, management, and application of information, especially when meaningful value is added to purely factual information.

Legacy system   An older computer system (either hardware or software) .

Likert scale   A numerical rating scale used on surveys that may vary in size.

Lightweight Directory Access Protocol (LDAP)   A simple protocol used to access a directory listing, sometimes on the Internet.

LinkExchange   Service offered on the Microsoft bCentral Web site that enables businesses to place banner ads on LinkExchange member networks in exchange for accepting member ads on their own sites.

ListBot   A Web-based program for managing e-mail lists.

Local area network (LAN)   A group of PCs, servers, and other devices connected over a network, usually in a small area such as a department or a single building of a larger company.

Measured marketing   A marketing technique used to target marketing campaigns with precision at a specific audience.

Microsoft Access   Database software that is part of the Microsoft Office software suite.

Microsoft Application Center 2000   A Microsoft software product that enables users to take a Web application built using Windows DNA features and deploy it to PC server farms (also called *Web farms* or *Web clusters*).

Microsoft BackOffice Microsoft's ready-to-use suite of back-office function software tools that can be used as is or combined and customized to meet specific needs of an organization.

Microsoft bCentral Microsoft Web site dedicated to helping small and medium-sized businesses grow online traffic and sales. The site offers various services that are provided both by Microsoft and by vendor partners.

Microsoft BizTalk Server Microsoft's XML-based software tool for the exchange of information among and between organizations.

Microsoft Certified Solution Provider (MCSP) An organization endorsed by Microsoft as a technology solution provider.

Microsoft Commerce Server 2000 Microsoft's Web and electronic commerce server software package.

Microsoft Exchange 2000 Server Microsoft's collaboration, e-mail, and messaging software tool.

Microsoft Excel 2000 Microsoft's spreadsheet software tool.

Microsoft FrontPage 2000 Microsoft's software tool for creating Web content and sites.

Microsoft Internet Explorer Microsoft's Web-browsing software that is integrated into the Windows operating systems.

Microsoft Internet Information Server (IIS) Microsoft's Web server software, providing transaction processing, Web content management, and Web security services.

Microsoft Management Console (MMC) An extensible, common presentation service for system management applications.

Microsoft Message Queuing Services (MSMQ) Microsoft's message queuing technology. Message queuing with MSMQ makes it easy to integrate applications by enabling them to communicate using a standard format and protocol.

The Microsoft Network (MSN) Microsoft's Web portal and Internet service provider.

Microsoft Office Microsoft's suite of productivity applications that includes word processing, database, spreadsheet, presentation, e-mail, and calendar functions.

Microsoft Outlook 2000 Microsoft's e-mail and scheduling application, with integrated calendar, contact, and task-management features.

Microsoft Publisher 2000 A business desktop publishing program that enables users to easily create marketing materials such as brochures.

Microsoft Repository   Component of Microsoft SQL Server 7.0 that, along with the Open Information Model, helps to integrate and store meta data about SQL Server databases, OLAP Services, Data Transformation Services, and English Query.

Microsoft Site Server   An earlier version of Commerce Server 2000.

Microsoft SQL Server 2000   Microsoft's relational database management system.

Microsoft Visual Basic   Microsoft's visual BASIC language tool for creating Windows-based applications.

Microsoft Visual C++   Microsoft's object-oriented programming language for developing visual (for example, Windows) applications.

Microsoft Visual FoxPro   A small database development system for Windows.

Microsoft Visual InterDev   Microsoft's integrated Web application development system for professional programmers. It enables Web teams to design, build, debug, and deploy cross-platform Web applications.

Microsoft Visual J++   Microsoft's Windows-based Java development system used to create Java applications that can run on any platform or to create Windows-specific applications that call ActiveX components or Windows directly. Visual J++ also includes a Java compiler.

Microsoft Visual SourceSafe (VSS)   Microsoft's visual source code version control tool. VSS provides features that manage, control, and catalog program code, Web content, and other application development components.

Microsoft Visual Studio   Microsoft's collection of visual programming tools for creating Windows- and Web-based applications.

Microsoft Windows 2000   Microsoft's next-generation operating system based on the Windows NT kernel. Includes Windows 2000 Professional (client), Windows 2000 Server (intranet server), Windows 2000 Advanced Server (line of business and e-commerce server), and Windows 2000 DataCenter Server (large, critical enterprise server).

Microsoft Windows NetMeeting   Microsoft's online meeting software that allows online meetings to be held in real time.

Microsoft Word 2000   Microsoft's word-processing software included as a part of the Office suite of applications.

MOLAP   Multidimensional online analytical processing (OLAP).

MSNBC   A joint venture between NBC and Microsoft to produce online news, sports, and entertainment content.

Multimaster clustering   Processor clustering with the ability to maintain multiple master copies that are available to all users. Each copy is mirrored and constantly updated to maintain currency.

Multipurpose Internet Mail Extensions (MIME)   A common method for transmitting nontext files via e-mail.

National Institute of Standards and Technology (NIST)   A government agency that assists the private sector with the development of the technical underpinnings for interoperability and works to coordinate and facilitate the standards process.

NetMeeting   *See* Microsoft Windows NetMeeting.

Network interface card (NIC)   Hardware on a single printed circuit board that allows a computer to communicate over a network.

Network load balancing   Technology that allows jobs and resource requirements to be spread across a network of servers.

Network News Transfer Protocol (NNTP)   The protocol used to connect to Usenet and newsgroups on the Internet.

Network operating system (NOS)   System software that runs computer networks.

Newsgroup   A forum on the Internet for discussions on a specified range of subjects.

Notice of Shipment (NOS)   An EDI transaction that tells an organization receiving goods that the goods have been shipped. *See also* Advanced Ship Notice (ASN).

Office   *See* Microsoft Office.

OLE DataBase (OLEDB)   Microsoft's open database programming interface for data access.

OnLine Analytical Processing (OLAP)   Decision support functions or software in which the user analyzes information in various ways.

OLAP Services   Online analytical processing extensions to SQL Server that enable users to perform online analytical processing tasks.

Online transaction processing (OLTP)   Processing operational business transactions as the computer receives them in real time.

Open DataBase Connectivity (ODBC)   Microsoft's database programming interface that provides a common language for Windows applications to access databases.

Operational metrics   Measurements that determine the impact on the organization and its ability to operate day-to-day.

Opportunity cost management   Understanding the impact of not doing something, or doing one thing versus another.

Organization for Economic Cooperation and Development (OECD)   A global agency that assists organizations in economic ventures around the world.

Outlook 2000   *See* Microsoft Outlook 2000

Packet filter   A combination of software and hardware used for security that prevents unauthorized packets of data from getting through to an organization's network.

Personalization services   A Web site feature/function set that customizes the site visit to each individual visitor's preferences.

Physical Address Extension (PAE)   Technology developed by Intel to allow computers to exceed the use of 4 GB RAM memory barrier with the Intel Extended Server Memory Architecture.

Pivot Table   A multidimensional data structure that allows users to switch to different views of the data. Pivot tables are created in Excel.

Point of interaction (POI)   The place (either real or virtual) where the interaction between customer and vendor occurs.

Portal   A Web site that acts as an entry point to the entire Web and provides a variety of services including Web searching, news, white and yellow pages directories, free e-mail, discussion groups, online shopping, and links to other sites.

Porter's Competitive Forces Model   A model developed by author Michael Porter depicting the entry barriers, exit barriers, customer bargaining power, supplier bargaining power, and switching costs involved in a competitive environment.

Post Office Protocol 3 (POP3)   A standard protocol commonly used for retrieving mail from a mail server.

Proxy server   An application that breaks the connection between sender and receiver to check security access authorization.

Public key encryption   A method of encrypting data so that it cannot be intercepted and used by anyone other than the intended recipient. The recipient must have a key (which can be made public, if desired) to unlock the data and make it usable again.

Public Key Infrastructure (PKI)   A security methodology that includes the use of digital certificates and signatures.

Publisher 2000   *See* Microsoft Publisher 2000.

Quantitative knowledge   Numerical data such as financial figures, order quantities, and customer information such as age and income.

Qualitative knowledge   Best practices and non-numerical customer data, such as product comments by customers

RFP   Request for proposal.

ROLAP   Relational online analytical processing (OLAP).

Router   Hardware that forwards data packets from network to another. Based on routing tables and communication protocols, routers read the network address in the transmission and send it based on the address and quickest route.

Sales, general, and administrative (SG&A)   A set of operating expenses incurred by organizations during the normal course of business.

Schema   A description, using some kind of standard language such as XML, of data or information that allows software to use the data for processing and/or analysis.

Service Level Agreement (SLA)   A contract or agreement between a service provider and user that specifies the level of service (for example, system uptime) that is expected.

Self-service [application]   An application or organization function that an employee or customer can use without help from the organization.

Secure Electronic Transaction (SET)   A standard protocol developed by MasterCard and Visa for securing online credit card payments via the Internet.

Secure Sockets Layer (SSL)   A security protocol used on the Internet. A browser sends its public key to a server so that the server can securely send a private key to the browser.

Server Gated Cryptography   A security approach in which a Web server handles the encryption and decryption of messages as a gate.

Simple Mail Transfer Protocol (SMTP)   The standard e-mail protocol on the Internet, which allows e-mail to be transmitted and received using specific standards and communication rules.

Site map   A page containing at least key URLs to a Web site that makes it easy for advanced users to find what they want. A site map should contain at least links to major sections of a Web site.

Site Server   *See* Microsoft Site Server.

Spam   Unwanted promotional e-mail.

Spamming   The term for sending unwanted promotional e-mail.

SQL Server 2000   *See* Microsoft SQL Server 2000.

Streaming media   Transmission over a data network or the Internet of video or audio media. Both the client and server software cooperate for uninterrupted motion and smooth audio.

Structured interviewing   A method of gathering information using specific techniques to elicit objective, measurable responses that can be diagrammed where appropriate.

Style sheet   A master page layout used to create documents in word processing, desktop publishing, and the Web. The style sheet stores margins, tabs, fonts, headers, footers, and other layout settings.

Supplier bargaining power   The force that an organization's suppliers can exert on the organization because of the scarcity of the product or service the supplier sells, the suppliers price, or the logistics involved with getting the product or service to the organization.

Supply chain   A group composed of the parties needed to bring a product or service from inception to end use.

Supply Chain Management (SCM)   Optimizing the activities involved in bringing a product or service from inception to end use.

Switch   A multithreaded hub that forwards data packets between different computers based on some type of lookup table.

Switching costs   The costs that customers or suppliers must incur when changing their business from one organization to another.

Symmetric MultiProcessing (SMP)   A multiprocessing architecture that allows multiple CPUs to share the same memory.

Systems Network Architecture (SNA)   IBM's mainframe network standards that support peer-to-peer communications and distributed computing environments that connect PC and mainframe-based systems.

Three-deep rule   Web design rule that a visitor should never be more than three clicks away from what he or she wants.

Total shareholder return (TSR)   The actual return on a shareholder's dollars.

Transaction server   *See* application server.

TransPoint   *See* CheckFree.

Transport Layer Security (TLS) A security protocol that is a merger of SSL and other protocols. It is expected to become a major security standard on the Internet, eventually superseding SSL.

Two-phase commit A technique for ensuring that a transaction properly updates all records in a distributed database. First, the databases confirm that the transaction has been received. Second, each database is told to commit the transaction and perform the actual update.

UN/EDIFACT United Nations Electronic Data Interchange for Administration, Commerce, and Trade. This is a common denominator for electronic communication standards. This international standard is similar to ANSI's EDI standard.

Unified Modeling Language (UML) An object-oriented design language from the Object Management Group (OMG), a computer industry consortium.

Uniform Resource Locator (URL) An address that defines the path to a file, Web page, or dynamic content on the Web or any other Internet facility.

Usenet One of the forerunners of the Internet. Usenet relies primarily on the exchange of information through the medium of newsgroups.

Value-added network (VAN) A network connection, usually supplied by a third party, that adds value to the hardware setup or transmission.

Value-added provider (VAP) A service provider that adds specific value to hardware, software, or services supplied to organizations.

Value-added tax (VAT) A tax added to each addition of a feature to a product or service.

Value chain A group of organizational staff who facilitates the creation and management of a product or service to consumers. Value-chain members include people involved with marketing, accounting, and other ancillary services in an organization.

vCalendar A standard format for group calendaring and scheduling.

vCard A standard format for an electronic business card that includes fields for photos, sound, and company logos.

Virtual private network (VPN) A secured, private network established over the Internet, using various methods of encryption (data scrambling).

Visitor relationship management (VRM) The art and science of keeping site visitors engaged and interested in a Web site, as well as generating return visits.

Visual Basic *See* Microsoft Visual Basic.

Visual C++   *See* Microsoft Visual C++.

Visual Component Manager   A part of Visual Studio that provides the ability to catalog and share components, specifications, documentation, and other project elements across teams.

Visual FoxPro   *See* Microsoft Visual FoxPro.

Visual InterDev   *See* Microsoft Visual InterDev.

Visual J++   *See* Microsoft Visual J++.

Visual SourceSafe   *See* Microsoft Visual SourceSafe.

Visual Studio   *See* Microsoft Visual Studio.

Visual Studio Modeler (VSM)   An object-oriented modeling tool jointly developed by Microsoft and Rational Software for use with Visual Studio.

Wallet   A browser component (available for both Internet Explorer and Netscape Navigator) that encrypts and stores payment information on the user's computer for later transmission to e-commerce sites.

Web Distributed Authoring and Versioning (WebDAV)   An Internet standard that lets multiple people collaborate on a document using an Internet-based shared file system. It addresses issues such as file access permissions, offline editing, file integrity, and conflict resolution when competing changes are made to a document. WebDAV expands an organization's infrastructure by using the Internet as the central location for storing shared files.

Web farm or Web cluster   A group of Web servers that work together to process requests.

Web hosting provider (WHP)   An organization that hosts Web pages and/or applications for other organizations and individuals.

Web presence   Having a Web site. Being available for contact via the Web.

Web server   A computer that provides Web services on the Internet. The term includes hardware, operating system, Web server software, network communication software, and the Web site content or pages.

Web Store   A Microsoft product that combines the features and functionality of a file system, the Web, and a collaboration server through a single location for storing, accessing, and managing information, as well as building and running applications.

Web workstyle   A new workstyle, facilitated by Internet technologies, which demands more collaboration both within organizations and between organizations and their business partners and customers.

WebTV   An Internet access service owned by Microsoft. WebTV provides access to the Internet via a standard television using a set-top box.

Wide area network (WAN)   A group of local area networks connected over a large geographical area, such as a city or country.

Windows 2000   *See* Microsoft Windows 2000.

Windows Distributed interNet Applications Architecture (Windows DNA)   The new application development model for the Windows platform that enables the Business Internet concept and uses an organization's digital nervous system as its plumbing.

Windows Explorer   A Microsoft product that allows users to view and manage files and directories.

Windows NetMeeting   *See* Microsoft Windows NetMeeting.

Word 2000   *See* Microsoft Word 2000.

World Trade Organization (WTO)   An international organization that deals with the global rules of trade between nations. Its main function is to ensure that trade flows as smoothly, predictably, and freely as possible.

World Wide Web   The graphical portion of the Internet. An Internet service that links documents locally and remotely. The World Wide Web was developed at the European Center for Nuclear Research (CERN) in Geneva from a proposal by Tim Berners-Lee in 1989.

WYSIWYG   "What you See is what you get." The idea of displaying text and graphics on-screen the same way as they look printed.

XML or **extensible markup language**   A standardized scripting and markup language that allows organizations to exchange information.

X.509   A widely-used specification for digital certificates.

Index

Index

CHARLES H. TREPPER

Charles H. Trepper is CEO of The Trepper Group, a Minneapolis-based consulting firm (www.trepper.com) specializing in e-commerce, IT training, knowledge management, and IT process improvement. Mr. Trepper earned his B.S. in Management Information Systems and M.S. in Technology Management at Purdue University and has over 20 years of experience in the information technology field. He is a widely published author and a columnist for *Application Development Trends* magazine. He is also a frequent public speaker and has appeared on television and radio programs in the Minneapolis area as an expert on e-commerce. Mr. Trepper also speaks to business clubs, such as the Minnesota Club Business Forum, about Internet business, and at numerous conferences on Internet trends and Web-based development. Mr. Trepper can be reached at chtrepper@trepper.com.

The manuscript for this book was prepared using Microsoft Word 2000. Pages were composed by ProImage using Adobe PageMaker 6.5, with text in Garamond and display type in Helvetica Black. Composed pages were delivered to the printer as electronic prepress files.

Principal Compositor

ProImage/Jimmie Young

Copy Editor

Susan Christophersen

Technical Editor

Allen L. Wyatt

Indexer

Sherry Massey

For information about Microsoft Press® products, visit our Web site at mspress.microsoft.com